South Asia
Conflicts and Cooperation

South Asia
Conflicts and Cooperation

Col. T.N. Marwah (Retd.)

Gaurav Book Centre Pvt Ltd
Delhi

Publisher
GAURAV BOOK CENTRE PVT LTD
4832/24,Prahlad Lane,S-207 Ansari
Road, Daryaganj, Delhi-110002
Ph.: 43570976, 23278261
Email: gauravbookcentre@gmail.com

Edition: 2015

ISBN: 978-93-83316-16-8

Laser Typesetting
JEE-VEE Graphics, Delhi

Price: 1195/-

Printed
Vikas Computers, Delhi

Preface

Many analysts in India, including this writer, make a distinction between the Indian sub-continent and South Asia. When they talk of the Indian sub-continent, they have in mind India, Pakistan, Bangladesh, Nepal and Bhutan. Of these, India, Pakistan and Bangladesh constituted one political entity before the British left the sub-continent in 1947.

The Sino-Indian border dispute is long running and fairly intractable, despite shows of flexibility in the past. It periodically prompts both sides to rake up decades-old grievances. Yet India and China have taken meaningful steps towards an institutionalised process for its resolution. Since 1988 they have for the most part managed to separate border issues from the overall bilateral relationship. The long-standing relationship between China and Pakistan presents a further obstacle to closer ties between China and India.

Indian analysts, who talk of the Indian sub-continent, wish to keep in mind, in their analyses, the common historical, political, religious and cultural heritage of these three countries. The term sub-continent is used less and less in Pakistan and Bangladesh.

The political leadership and the policy-makers in these two countries do not wish to be reminded of this common heritage. Any highlighting of this common heritage by Indian analysts is viewed by them with suspicion—— as indicating a hidden desire to reverse history and undo the 1947 partition.

As the book addresses this crucial issue quite deftly, it is hoped that it would prove to be a source of great information for the reader.

—Editor

Preface

Contents

1

India and China: Conflict and Cooperation

Not much has changed in the rhetoric of Sino-Indian relations since Mao Zedong, speaking in 1951 in honour of the first anniversary of India's constitution, declared that 'excellent friendship' had existed between the two countries 'for thousands of years'. Yet few of the lofty proclamations made by Indian and Chinese leaders over the years truly reflect the reality of relations between the neighbours. It is surprising that two states with such a rich and sometimes fractious history, including a border conflict in 1962, should have what appears to be a largely reactive relationship.

But neither has developed a grand strategy with regard to the other. An unshakeable and largely unprofitable preoccupation with the past on the Indian side, and an equally intense preoccupation with domestic consolidation on the Chinese side, have left the relationship under-tended. It might best be seen as one of geostrategic competition qualified by growing commercial cooperation. And there is some asymmetry: China is a more fraught subject in Indian national debates than India is for China.

China does not appear to feel threatened in any serious way by India, while India at times displays tremendous insecurity in the face of Chinese economic success and military expansion. To outsiders, India and China show some striking similarities. Both are ancient civilizations reincarnated as modern republics in the mid twentieth century, and are now rising powers. Both have nuclear weapons, burgeoning economies, expanding military budgets and large reservoirs of manpower, and seem to be vying for influence in the Indian Ocean, the Persian Gulf, Africa, Central Asia and East Asia. Yet little attention is paid to the relationship between them. Most scholarship has focused on Beijing's relations with the United States, Japan and East Asia or New Delhi's relations with Pakistan, South Asia and the United States.

Whereas Sino-US ties are often cast as a one-to-one contest for global pre-eminence, moreover, the Sino- Indian relationship is more often seen in terms of the countries' interactions with extraneous actors such as the United States, Pakistan and other South Asian nations. It is also defined by contrasting polities and models of development, with the parties silently competing not just for capital, resources and markets, but also for legitimacy in the arena of great and emerging global powers.

MOVEMENT TO CONFLICT AND FAILURE OF NEGOTIATIONS

In the late 1940s, the advent of new regimes in India and in China brought new border problems and new border policies. The 1947 emergence of the Indian republic led to with- drawal of British power from the Indian subcontinent and the beginnings of a changing power balance in Asia. When the Communist regime emerged strongly in 1949, the balance of power tipped even further; however, border issues would probably have remained, whether China was ruled by the Nationalists or the Communists.

The new Indian republic devoted little time or attention to border conflicts with China in her first two years; rather, India was preoccupied with Pakistan, resolving border conflicts in Kashmir.

In 1947, Muslim disorder grew in Kashmir, and the Maharajah appealed to India for help; Indian troops responded. Pakistan also responded, and bloody fighting continued sporadically until late December, 1948. In January, 1949, a United Nations-supervised ceasefire and international frontier was established; but tensions in Kashmir and Jammu continued for years. In 1954, Kashmir constitutionally became part of India. But tensions between Pakistan and India continued for years; in 1965 and 1971 they would fight again. In 1950, India's attention began to focus back toward China.

Two major Chinese ventures in 1950 would have important impact on the Sino-Indian border problem. In October, the Chinese army advanced on Chamdo, 370 miles east of Lhasa, and Tibetan troops accepted defeat. The Government of India protested what it considered to be a wrongful and unnecessary use of force; yet, Nehru tended to accept Chinese authority over Tibet. By the end of 1950, China was in control of Tibet. In May, 1951, a Chinese-Tibetan treaty was signed; China would set up military and administrative committees in Tibet, the Tibetan army would be integrated into the Chinese army, and all of Tibet's external relations would be handled by China. In 1951, Nehru reacted to events in Tibet by sending an Indian expedition to the Tawang Tract to assert Indian influence up to the McMahon Line.

The second event, also in October, 1950, was China's military support of North Korea in the Korean Conflict. While China's part in Korea would draw upon her military and economic resources, Korea did provide cold weather and mountain warfare skills which China would use in the 1962 Border War.

Relations between China and India were generally good in the early 1950s, and the border issue remained quiet. India exported grain to Chinese troops and civilians working in Tibet. Chinese troops did not enter into NEFA. And India did not challenge occasional Chinese troops in Aksai Chin.

In September, 1951, Chou En-Lai suggested talks to stabilize the Tibetan frontier. While Chou stated that "there was no territorial dispute or controversy between India and China," it seems clear through the early 1950s that China did not accept the McMahon Line as India's northeast boundary. India responded that negotiations would be welcome; yet, no talks began for three years.

In April, 1954, India and China signed an agreement regarding trade, travel and representation between India and the "Tibet region of China." This agreement included a pledge of nonaggression, the "Five Principles of Peaceful Coexistence": mutual respect for the other's territorial integrity/sovereignty, mutual nonaggression, mutual noninterference in each other's affairs, equality and mutual benefit, and peaceful coexistence. The 1954 agreement did not address any major boundary disputes; the agreement simply named six passes in the Middle Sector (between Ladakh and Nepal) as trade passes, without specifying any boundary. In the middle 1950s, Pakistan aligned with the United States, and began receiving U. S. military aid. This disturbed India, and forced Nehru to relax his policy of non-alignment and seek support from Russia. While relations with the Soviets cooled in 1956 following the Russian intervention in Hungary, India did continue to seek Soviet aid, including military aid which would fortify India's position in 1962.

Prime Minister Nehru visited Peking in October, 1954, and raised the question of the border shown on Chinese maps. According to Nehru's account, Chou assured Nehru that the question was of no importance.

Late in 1954, Chinese government pressure in Tibet was stirring up increasing discontent amongst the turbulent Khamba tribesmen in eastern Tibet. Military actions by the Khamba tribesmen jeopardized Chinese lines of communication with Tibet from the east, as early as 1955. The Khamba actions were to have strong implications for the border situation, for it led China into building a new supply route into Tibet.

In March, 1956, the Chinese People's Liberation Army began construction of a military highway between western Sinkiang and western Tibet—directly across the Aksai Chin plateau, an area which the Indians clearly believed to be Indian (south of the Johnson-Ardagh line) and which the Chinese clearly believed to be Tibetan/Chinese (north of the Macartney-MacDonald line). Construction of the 1200 kilometer road, under difficult conditions in Aksai Chin, lasted from March, 1956, until completion in October, 1957.

It has already been noted that Aksai Chin was remote and desolate, and that India had minimal interests in the area; the

Indian government did not even learn of the road's existence until September, 1957! In July, 1958, the existence of the highway was confirmed to India by published Chinese maps which not only showed the new route, but also placed all of Aksai Chin in Chinese territory. In July, the Government of India sent an initial protest to Peking, and sent two patrols to reconnoiter the road. The two patrols were detained by the Chinese, sensitive about the security of her new highway, for one month.

In December, 1958, Nehru wrote a friendly letter to Chou En-Lai about the Chinese maps—but without specifically referring to the military road—showing Aksai Chin as Chinese. Nehru reminded Chou of his statement about "no boundary dispute" between them. Nehru further asserted that these "large parts of India" being "anything but India, and there is no dispute about them." In a polite reply, Chou pointed out that the frontier and boundary had never been officially agreed upon by the two governments. Chou reminded Nehru that no central Chinese government had ever recognized the McMahon Line, which he called "a product of the British policy of aggression." Premier Chou was especially adamant about Aksai Chin, stating that Aksai Chin had "always been Chinese jurisdiction" and that it was regularly patrolled by Chinese border patrols. Chou proposed discussions leading to a mutually agreed survey, and that both sides should maintain their present positions—"maintain the status quo." Chou meant "status quo" to mean the present positions, now, and Nehru read "status quo" to mean the position which had been "until now." This semantic difference would impair future understandings and discussions. Chou's January, 1959 reply also implied that China would be willing to stay behind the McMahon Line in NEFA if China could retain her claim to Aksai Chin. Nehru's March, 1959 reply to Chou was an essentially uncompromising account of the historical basis for the Indian position on the boundary.

In March, 1959, disorder and fighting worsened in Tibet. The Dalai Lama crossed the McMahon Line into India and was granted political asylum. China had long suspected that India was aiding the Tibetan rebels, and the deteriorating situation in Tibet only aggravated Sino-Indian problems. In March, a large number of Khamba tribesmen had escaped into Nepal and India, acquired arms, and then disappeared back into Tibet. China thus felt it necessary to seal off the Indian frontier along the McMahon Line, to prevent Tibetan rebels from crossing into India to acquire arms.

Meanwhile, the diplomatic exchanges continued. But Nehru maintained that there was little to negotiate about the frontiers claimed by India. He was prepared to discuss "minor details" of border delimitation, but only if China would first withdraw from, and renounce her claim to, Aksai Chin. Chou En-Lai consistently refused to accept any of India's claims, and again proposed that negotiations start from the basis of actual position on the ground.

In mid-1959, India became sensitive about China's (anti-Tibetan rebel) activity along the McMahon Line. Indian border police began to establish checkposts along the McMahon Line, and moved border patrols forward toward the frontier of Tibet. This resulted in two clashes in August, 1959. In NEFA, the Indians attempted to occupy the hamlet of Longju, north of the McMahon Line, or at best a disputed border area. The two sides exchanged fire, and the Indian border police soon withdrew to the south.

The second clash occurred at Konga Pass, south of the Karakoram Range in western Tibet. The skirmish at Konga (or Konga La) Pass was a fire fight with losses on both sides—probably nine Indians and several Chinese killed. Author John Rowland gives an empassioned description of how the Indian patrol was captured, mistreated, interrogated, and "brain-washed." There was controversy as to which side fired first, but India publicized the incident as a "brutal massacre of an Indian policy party."

There was uproar in both countries about the Longju, Konga Pass, and other minor clashes in 1959; both sides launched letters of protest. Chou's September, 1959 letter repeated the Chinese position that the border had never been officially delimited; he stated that while China did not recognize the McMahon Line, Chinese troops had not crossed the Line. Chou described the boundary problem as a "complicated question left over by history." He further stated that Chinese troops were on the border solely for the purpose of preventing Tibetan rebels from moving back and forth over the border; he further commented that the Indian responses were provocative and unnecessary. Nehru's September reply to Chou again outlined the history and geography of the frontier question, and again stated that no settlement could be reached until the Chinese withdrew from all territory claimed by India, including Aksai Chin.

Shortly after the Konga pass incident, President Eisenhower announced that he would visit New Delhi. To China, this gave the appearance of India growing closer to both the United States and Russia. This only strengthened China's perception of India becoming more and more anti-Chinese.

In New Delhi, Nehru was receiving some criticisms of his policy of thrusting patrols into the frontier and setting up posts. Several senior Indian Army officers labeled the "forward policy" as militarily unwise, on the grounds that the Indian Army was neither militarily nor logistically prepared to deal with Chinese military strength in the frontiers. His response to this military advice, unfortunately, was to replace the officers with more subservient ones. Not only did Nehru make the mistake of ignoring his senior officers' advice, he also made the simultaneous error of rigidly adhering to three assumptions. He assumed that the Chinese would not stand up against an India backed by both the United States and Russia, that China would not oppose his patrols and outposts, and that Peking would readily withdraw under Indian pressure. All these assumptions were to prove erroneous, especially as Chou had warned Nehru not to pursue such a forward policy.

The diplomatic letters between Chou and Nehru continued through the end of 1959 and into 1960. In November, 1959, Chou proposed that both sides withdraw their troops twenty kilometers behind the McMahon Line, and also twenty kilometers from the line up to which each side exercised actual control in Aksai Chin. This would have removed the Indian army from its positions along the McMahon Line, and would have retained Chinese control, in Aksai Chin, over the Sinkiang-Tibet military highway and a new road which the Chinese built in 1959. While Chou's proposal was, of course, favorable to the Chinese, he was nevertheless proposing talks and a compromise. Nehru's November reply neither totally accepted nor rejected Chou's proposal. Nehru ruled out the idea of withdrawing from the McMahon Line, but proposed instead that each side refrain from sending patrols forward. For Aksai Chin, Nehru proposed that each side withdraw behind the line claimed by the other; this would have necessitated no drawback by the Indians in the west, but would have deprived China of its two Aksai Chin roads. Nehru implied that acceptance of this proposal was a prerequisite for any further talks between himself and Chou. Nehru thus rejected what he must have known to be the best Chinese offer he was likely to get without going to war. Chou's December reply was that, since the Konga Pass incident, China had stopped sending patrols out along the entire frontier. Chou further stated that Nehru's proposal was one-sided, and urged that the two leaders meet in less than ten days. Nehru understandably declined to meet on such short notice, but proposed no alternate date. In late December, China replied with another historical view of her side of the boundary dispute, and again asked for negotiations but without specifying a date. Nehru replied in February, 1960, again giving the Indian historical position and noting that there was little or no common ground on their respective viewpoints. But Nehru did propose further talks, and Chou did come to New Delhi in April, 1960; the talks were a total failure. Like the one-sided diplomatic letters, neither side was willing to change its position; hence, no compromises were presented.

Thus, the early 1960 diplomatic efforts at settlement or even compromise, between India and China, were essentially a total failure. Talks in late 1963 resulted in complete disagreement; each side even published incompatible reports of the discussions.

In 1960, China made a preliminary border settlement with Nepal. By the end of 1960, China had also made a boundary agreement with Burma. The Sino-Burmese border began not at the McMahon Line, but eight miles further south; this placed Diphu Pass—a strategic approach to eastern Assam—in Chinese territory. India was outraged and worried.

But no settlement or compromise occurred in Sino-Indian relationships. China was willing to compromise on NEFA; thus, eastern Ladakh (Aksai Chin) emerged as the major area of dispute. With the continued failure of diplomatic efforts, the uncompromising attitudes of both sides remained unchanged until the outbreak of hostilities in 1962.

By 1961, India had acquired aircraft, helicopters, engineering and other military equipment from the United States and Russia. Thus equipped, the Indian army invaded Portugese Goa in December, 1961. Goa was rapidly constitutionally incorporated into the Indian republic. Although no real protests or opposition occurred as a result of this action, the annexation of Goa reinforced China's view of India as being expansionistic.

This foreign military support also encouraged India to pursue her forward policy in Aksai Chin. In 1961, India had purchased eight Antov transports—complete with 40 Soviet pilots, navigators and mechanics—for use in Aksai Chin. Russian also supplied India with 24 Ilyushin-14 transports and Mil'-4 helicopters, capable of lifting men and supplies to altitudes of 17,000 feet. By mid-1962, India had also agreed to buy two squadrons of Soviet MIG jet fighters. Thus fortified, India pursued a more aggressive foreign policy against China. By the end of 1961, Nehru had sent enough Indian Army troops into Aksai Chin to establish about 43 posts on the Ladakh frontier claimed by China. Many of the Indian outposts were parallel to, but about 100 miles from, the first Chinese military road. However, three of the outposts were near Konga Pass, in the vicinity of the second Chinese highway.

In August, 1961, China began sending a series of angry protests to India. China had one basic argument: that Indian troops had intruded into Chinese territory. Nehru's response to Chou's complaints was that his (Nehru's) purpose was to "vacate the aggression (by the Chinese) by whatever means are feasible to us.... I do not see any kind of peace in the frontier so long as all recognised aggression is not vacated."

The latter half of 1961 brought China and India to increasing confrontations and skirmishes. Exchanges of fire became commonplace. A November confrontation in Chip Chap Valley left several Chinese soldiers dead; this was followed by a Chinese withdrawal. Such "victories" convinced Nehru that the Chinese would not be assertive and that his forward policy of outposts and patrols was the correct course for India. Despite continuing protests from senior Indian Army officers that India should first build up forces and logistic supplies in the frontier before embarking further, Nehru ordered even more aggressive moves into Aksai Chin.

Thus, by early 1962, the Chinese leadership perceived that the Indian government intended to launch a massive attack against Chinese troops; they apparently believed that India had decided to go to war over the issue. China's firm insistence over her territorial rights to Aksai Chin and India's aggressive forward policy of sending troops into the frontier would soon bring further confrontations and eventual armed conflict.

GLOBAL VARIABLES LEADING TO CONFLICT: CHINA

The systemic level variables motivating China towards conflict, like in India, revolved around Chinese national interests, the system's influence on Chinese behaviour through structural constraints, and the role of anarchy in the system. Because of the anarchic structure of the international system, China is no different than India and state security must be its prime end. China's membership in the communist bloc does not grant it any guarantee of protection, and therefore its national interests are calculated in ways of maximizing national security. As such we shall discuss the three main interests affected by the border dispute with India.

As in India's case, the delineation of official borders for the PRC was a prime interest in order to gain legitimacy in the international system. This legitimacy is rooted within the conventions of the Westphalian system, where borders are paramount as they define the extent of sovereignty and political self-determination. The PRC's inheritance of territory which was divided by Western imperialists had a strong legal and pragmatic interest in negotiating legitimate borders with its neighbours. The basis of Chinese territorial definition was on the extent of historical holdings, but the PRC had determined in 1950 to negotiate borders based off the alignments they had inherited. This meant that China would not bog itself down in unreasonable claims in Indochina or other areas of traditional imperial suzerainty. This mentality guided border settlement by peaceful means with Burma, Nepal, Pakistan, Afghanistan, Mongolia, Cambodia, and Laos. Peaceful settlement of the Sino-Indian border however, was not possible due to Indian unwillingness to negotiate based on the perceived legitimacy of the McMahon Line.

A second national interest challenged by the border dispute with India was the Chinese right to non-intervention of foreigners in their domestic affairs. This principle of domestic sanctity from outside interference is also one of the rights of states in the Westphalian system.

Chinese security was undermined by India's role in manipulating domestic events in both Tibet and in Ladakh. The Indian military's establishment of forward posts and patrols of the Ladakh region, beginning in 1960, was direct interference in Chinese domestic areas. While it was true China did not have legal sovereignty over the Ladakh area due to its position south of the McMahon Line, that argument remains moot as international boundaries must be agreed upon at least bilaterally, and the PRC gave it no such recognition. Furthermore, Ladakh, and more importantly the Aksai-Chin plain was a strategically important tract of land connecting Xinjiang and Tibet.

Indian interference in Tibet after the 1959 uprising was also taken as a direct violation of domestic sanctity, and a challenge to Chinese security and interests. The PRC became aware of Indian efforts to covertly aid the Dalai Lama and Tibetan separatists shortly after the PLA moved in to suppress the uprising. In fact, India had gone so far as to allow the CIA bases of operation along the border for a covert campaign in Tibet from 1957 to 1961. Furthermore, a series of four Indian military bases were constructed and manned in Tibet north of the McMahon Line. These actions illustrated India's desire to keep Tibet as a buffer state, and recognize Chinese suzerainty instead of sovereignty in the region, thus directly challenging China's security.

The Chinese interest of maintaining a secure border with India was also threatened by the border dispute. Reinforcement of Tibet after 1959, the Aksai-Chin road way, and Chinese military patrols of the border were an attempt to maintain their territorial integrity. This added military presence created a security dilemma for India, and they began building up and strengthening their own military capacity near contested areas. The adoption of a forward Indian military policy in 1960, coupled with Indian scouting patrols across the border and the construction of military posts around Ladakh and Tibet severely undermined Chinese border security. This led to the PLA "digging in" around contested border areas and effectively militarizing the border.

China's response to the Indian military buildup as well as their covert programs in contested border areas was constrained by the structure of the international environment. A major constraining force on Chinese action was the geostrategic situation in Asia during the late 1950's. Beginning in 1950 with the Korean War, the major battles of the Cold War were fought in Asia in the West's effort to contain the communist bloc. The PRC had to contend with anti-Chinese forces in South Korea, a U.S. backed ROC in Taiwan, a U.S.-fortified Japan, and increasing U.S. involvement in Indochina by 1960. These numerous threats on China's Western front were significant, and severely limited their maneuverability in other areas of concern. Unbeknownst to the West, the PRC was increasingly unable to depend on the support of the communist bloc due to increasing belligerence from the U.S.S.R. on various diplomatic and territorial issues. The Soviets pressured the PRC to acknowledge Indian border claims, and Sino-Soviet relations strained under their own border issues.

Acknowledging the limiting effects of these security threats on Chinese military power, the PRC advocated a policy of peaceful border settlement. China used this policy to its advantage and scored a critical victory in neutralizing a potential Pakistani threat to their security interests by a warming of relations. The geostrategic environment in which the PRC found itself was one of being surrounded by a ring of hostile states. Indian diplomatic intransigence on border issues and known subversion in Tibet added another threat in that ring. Thus, the structure of the international environment drove the PRC to rely on diplomacy to achieve its interests against minor powers in order to preserve its military power for guarding its borders against larger threats. This situation explains a seemingly coincidental rapprochement in relations with Pakistan, India's arch-rival, while Sino-Indian relations simultaneously deteriorated in 1959.

This hostile geostrategic environment ruled out the option of using military force to settle the border dispute with India because of the potential pitfall of starting a two front war. Thus PRC actions along the Indian border were limited by the international structure to defensive posturing, deterrence, and entrenchment. This is illustrated by the numerous Chinese overtures to Indian representatives to keep patrols 20km behind each border. Rapprochement with Pakistan was pragmatic in the freedom of action the PRC gained by not needing to guard the Sino-Pakistani border heavily. Therefore, Chinese policy was constrained by the system to not initiate force against India in order to settle the border dispute, but instead to bolster its defenses. However, the PRC declared that "force would be met with force" on the border issue, and this is evidenced by the PLA counter offensives launched on October 20 and November 16, 1962.

Finally, the anarchy present in the international system played a significant role in the actions of the PRC on the border issue. Unlike their Indian counterparts, China properly assessed the international situation and never lost sight of the fact that only China could assure Chinese security. The emerging Sino-Soviet split was a key element in the PRC's unwillingness to rely on outside support for their interests. Not only did the Soviets urge China to a settlement counter to their interests, but they openly aided India in both the construction of a domestic MIG program and a pledge to help them develop nuclear energy. Simultaneously, Soviet aid to China was severely cut including assistance in developing a nuclear program. Clearly a common Soviet-Sino communist ideology was unimportant to their "allies," as they even ventured to grant India great power status through nuclear development.

In addition to the Soviet military aid was U.S. support of India in the form of agricultural assistance and millions in financial aid packages. Although India pledged neutrality, the PRC clearly believed that they were in the West's bloc. Indian based CIA operations into Tibet and India's role in the Korean War helped bolster this perception. Unable to rely on either superpower for protection or intervention on their behalf, the PRC assessed that any military movements in securing the border would have to be proportional, decisive, and most importantly retaliatory. This assessment was gained from a rational calculation of the potential geostrategic and political consequences of a PLA initiation of force. While neither the PRC nor India possessed nuclear weapons, they feared a PLA offensive into India would be interpreted by the West as communist advance and therefore provoke a nuclear response. In the wake of the Taiwan Straits Crisis, and keeping in mind Sino-Soviet agitation, China was unwilling to risk a potential nuclear strike from the West, especially without full Soviet support. This being the case, China resolved that its armed response to Indian aggression would be purely political. The PRC would paint itself as the victim of aggression, but would then unleash a massive but calculated counterattack to force diplomatic concessions by India on the border issue, thereby resolving the issue once and for all. While the systems level of analysis plainly explains both the motives and limitations of India and China leading to the Sino-Indian War, it is contended that the model overlooks key motivations of either state leading to conflict.

GLOBAL VARIABLES LEADING TO CONFLICT: INDIA

The three main variables motivating Indian behaviour towards conflict with China on the systemic level are: Indian national interests, the system's influence on Indian behaviour through structural constraints, and the relationship between Indian perception of the international structure and reality. To begin a systemic explanation of India's actions we must first identify its national interests, as it is what drives Indian action throughout the international structure. According to neorealist thought the primary end of all states is security. This being the case, not only is security the primary Indian national interest, but any issue relating to national security becomes a primary interest.

Official borders, and their enforcement is a primary interest of each state for obvious reasons. However, in the Indian case this issue takes on greater importance than it otherwise would for other nations. This can be attributed to two factors. The most prevalent factor was that India bordered a nation which not only questioned the legitimacy of the established border, but also violated it. The second factor is the modern international system is formed by the interaction of nation-states, which as defined by the Westphalian system are the only entities capable of legitimately exercising sovereignty.

A key component of nation-state status under the Westphalian system is the existence of demarcated and respected borders. These borders represent the extent of national sovereignty and define where each nation's authority begins and ends. The questioning of India's established border by China undermines both Indian sovereignty and security. Security is undermined first by the direct military and administrative challenge to Indian territory, and second by delegitimizing India's position as a nation-state. If India can neither defend nor define borders respected by other nations, other states may begin to question their position as a nation-state in the system and then their sovereignty. This was a chief concern for India as they regarded the Chinese threat to their border as one compromising their "independence, self-determination, and position as a great power in Asia".

Another issue of national security relating to Indian interests was defense of the McMahon Line. Two key issues aided the creation of security dilemma situation along the McMahon Line. The first was the discovery of the Chinese road connecting Xinjiang and Tibet through the Aksai-Chin area in 1957. The second was the imposition of martial law on Tibet in 1959 by the PLA. China argued that completion of the road southeast of the McMahon Line in Aksai-Chin was simply the reestablishment of a historical commerce route from Xinjiang to Tibet. This road not only represented a blatant Chinese violation of India's McMahon Line border, but it also caused armed tension in the region. Shortly after the roads discovery, PLA frontier guards began patrolling the Aksai-Chin region, but never more than 20km away from the road's location. The issue of the road in Aksai-Chin and the PLA's role in Tibet in 1959 became linked since the majority of Chinese troops entered Tibet via the road from Xinjiang. The surge of PLA soldiers into Tibet aroused suspicions of a forcible border assertion by the PRC. These tensions were heightened by the flight of the Dalai Lama from Lhasa, and the closure of Tibet to commercial and cultural access by India, guaranteed in the 1951 treaty. Defensive maneuvers or not, these activities created a security dilemma along the border as India felt that Tibet was "essential for mastery over South Asia, and the most economical method for guaranteeing India's security". Forced to account for increasing Chinese military power near or past the McMahon Line, India responded by deploying their military in forward positions along the border with China as early as 1960. Accounting for India's national interest with force posturing, they attempted to both affirm the legitimacy of the McMahon Line as a border and to account for the security dilemma created by the hardening of PLA positions in Tibet and Aksai-Chin.

The second way a systemic level analysis accounts for the 1962 war is the manner in which India's policy was defined by the structure of the international system. In looking at the geostrategic positioning of India within the system, it is immediately apparent that they attempted to remain neutral or unaligned in the bipolar structure. India remained a powerful enough state to deter the third world adventurism of either bloc within its territory, but weak enough to be challenged by hostile neighbours. An excellent example of this was the persistent threat of Pakistan on their Northwestern border. The poor relationship of Pakistan and India is rooted in domestic level variables, but a systemic level cause was a disputed claim over the sovereignty of Kashmir. Both sides claim the right to sovereignty over Kashmir, and this has resulted in a heavily armed border. Additionally, appearances of a Sino-Pakistani agreement to hem in India developed with Chinese diplomatic overtures to Pakistan for peaceful border settlement beginning in 1961. This forced India to take a hard-line stance in their border dispute with China out of fear that concessions would show weakness, and endanger their control of Kashmir in a Domino-Theory type logic train.

Another structural element of the international system was the existence of nuclear weapons. Nuclear weapons invalidated traditional calculations of deterrence, and thus the great powers were those whom possessed them. In India's regional calculations neither themselves, nor did any other surrounding nations possess nuclear weapons keeping intact the use of deterrence as a method of securing or defending interests. This being the case, the option of engaging in armed conflict with surrounding nations remained possible as long as in India's force calculations they were superior to their target. A prime example of India's employment of force to further interests was their invasion of Portuguese controlled Goa on December 17, 1961. This use of force to assert sovereignty over perceived territory is an excellent precedent for the October 9, 1962 offensive against the PLA in Ladakh. Force against PLA incursions remained off the table as long as the Indian military believed their strategic position and capabilities to be inferior to the Chinese. Returning from a 1960 diplomatic tour of the U.S., Nehru expressed the idea that due to Soviet and Western military aid, "the military balance had changed in favour of India". Thus in the absence of nuclear weapons, India disregarded the Chinese effort at deterrence and employed the use of force to settle their territorial claims.

Finally, it is necessary to point out how India's perception of the international system, which differed from reality, influenced their decision to employ force against the PRC. India perceived the international system as open to change from a bipolar to a multi-polar structure. This was based in their success of remaining unaligned to either bloc, while still receiving significant military and economic aid from both camps. Given India's strategic geographic position in the system, both superpowers sought to gain the allegiance of India to their side through the use of aid. Understanding this, India played both sides against each other, and assumed that either superpower would be willing to intervene on their behalf in the event of Sino-Indian hostilities for pragmatic and alliance building reasons. Thus, India viewed its use of force as a no lose situation. Either the force would succeed in attaining their national interests, or if Indian power proved to be inadequate, "the superpowers would intervene to prevent any large-scale war between India and China;" therefore, bailing out India from a potential catastrophe. This perception of Indian value to either superpower and the general misperception of the international system would cost them.

Ultimately the Indians failed to acknowledge that while the interests of the superpowers may partially depend on India's well being, the system is ultimately in anarchy and each nation is responsible for assuring their own security. Additionally, India had miscalculated both the willingness and ability of the superpowers to intervene on their behalf. In reality the Soviet Union could not exercise restraint on Chinese actions or compel them to drop the border issue. The Sino-Soviet split had not yet occurred, but its origin is in the late 1950's, and the attempt to restrain PRC actions towards India was a contributing factor in the decline of Soviet influence. Indian belief in U.S. intervention was based on a miscalculation of U.S. interests in Asia, as well as willingness to repel PRC advance based on the Domino Theory. While the U.S. intervened in Korea, Taiwan, and Indochina, India overlooked the essential element common to each. This element was the inability of each nation to resist communist advance on its own. In this case, the projected image of Indian power was a liability. The realities of the international system and its anarchic nature would ensure that their decision to use force would not be consequence free. Now the Chinese causes for war will be evaluated at the systemic level.

ALTERNATIVE EXPLANATIONS OF CONFLICT: DOMESTIC LEVEL ANALYSIS

A valid criticism of a systemic level approach to explaining conflict is that it overlooks key variables and differences between states in the assumption that all states are equal due to constraints that the structure of the international system places upon them. Singer argues that at this level of analysis "actors are characterized and their behaviour predicted in relatively gross and general terms". To account for the generalization of state behaviour inherent in a systemic level analysis a brief domestic level analysis explaining the Sino-Indian war will be attempted. Based on Vertberger's literature review on the subject, my domestic level analysis will be limited to the most influential domestic variable driving China and India to war; ideological and political considerations.

Indian ideological and political causes for war centered on the belief in non-alignment as a viable alternative to the bipolar system. The source of Indian non-aligned thought was that the Cold War was a conflict between the imperialist Western nations, and therefore newly independent former colonies had no reason or interest in siding with their former masters. The Indians by remaining non-aligned, hoped to establish a third pole of power in the international system organized by the nations of the Third World. This third bloc of nations would fight for issues that really mattered to them such as ending colonialism, racial discrimination, and raising living standards in the developing world. Nehru envisioned that this Third World bloc would act as an arbiter in the West's conflict, thereby gaining both moral authority and legitimacy.

In concert with the Bandung Conference in 1955 and the Sino-Indian Panchsheel Agreement, Nehru hoped to expand his concept of non-alignment into a full-blown pan-Asianism movement. This pan-Asianism was based in the common historical experience of colonialism that these nations shared, but Nehru failed to account for historical differences and regional rivalries. Nehru asserted that, "the basic challenge in Southeast Asia is between India and China," but he forgot this reality in supporting an Asian solidarity bloc. Nehru, and India's conception of a non-aligned third world was based on not only its viability, but that India would be both the natural and unchallenged leader of such a group. Traditional Sino-Indian rivalry for influence in Asia challenged Indian thinking as China asserted its right to be the leader of such a group. The need to exert its regional great power status over China led to diplomatic intransigence on the issue of border negotiations. Thus,

India saw Chinese dispute of border areas to be a political challenge to their right to lead Asia, and in turn pushed backed in order to show strength.

Chinese ideological and political causes for war centered on the belief that its Maoist interpretation of communist revolution was not only correct, but purer than the Soviet model. This dispute on the merits of Maoism over Leninism was focused squarely on the Soviet Union's insistence on backing the Indian position in the border dispute through political and military aid. The PRC challenged Soviet actions on three points; that their diplomatic position showed a lack of solidarity with a fellow communist nation, that Soviet support of a bourgeoisie regime in India would not forward the goal of communist revolution, and that India wasn't truly non-aligned but in fact in league with the imperialists. Soviet military aid inflamed the PRC, especially in light of Soviet cuts to Chinese aid, because it appeared as if the Soviets were turning their backs on a Marxist brother. Furthermore, the PRC believed that only through struggle and challenge, not foreign aid, could they achieve the end of global Marxist revolution. Finally, Indian overtures to the West for aid, and their assistance to the West in fomenting problems on China's border led the PRC on a quest to convince the Soviets that they were being used. The PRC concluded that superior PLA military forces and position in the region would force the Indians to rely on Western intervention to bail them out in the event of hostilities. This would both expose the Indians as true imperialists, and score an ideological victory against the Soviet Union in the enlarging diplomatic split.

The domestic level analysis contends that it is domestic differences between states that drive them towards conflict. Examining the most influential domestic factors (according to scholars on the subject) on Chinese and Indian decision making leading to the 1962 war, it seems as if ideology had differing levels of importance for each nation. Indian ideology and their belief in leading a pan-Asian bloc nationalized tensions with China, creating a zero-sum game. If the Indian's backed down they would seem weak, and to avoid this they took a non-compromising stand on border issues. In China, Maoist ideology was more so an issue with hierarchy within the Soviet bloc than with Indian recalcitrance on border issues. The PRC actively believed the Indians not to be non-aligned, but this was not important as ideologically they did not pose a threat to the Chinese communist system. As such, Chinese ideology was not as important in crafting policy, and Zhou Enlai was able to take a pragmatic stand. As Singer points out the overgeneralization of a systemic analysis, he also points out that a domestic analysis suffers from the same weakness but instead an undue focus on state differences. The domestic analysis helps us better understand the importance of the border issue in each nation's context, but in this case it does not adequately explain the actions undertaken by either regime. Furthermore, only with a systemic level analysis can we explore the limitation on action caused by the international structure on each state. Ultimately, Chinese ideology does not explain why they did not take the offensive to oust India as imperialists, or why India decided to change its military policy towards an aggressive forward base strategy. Therefore, a systemic level analysis is more suited to explaining the actions leading to the Sino-Indian War.

While valid alternative theoretical models explaining the causes for war exist, a neorealist systems-level analysis best explains the factors leading India and China to war in 1962. Keeping in mind the historical context of generally cordial Sino-Indian relations prior to 1959 it seems unlikely that solely ideological differences drove the two nations to war. If ideology was such an important motivator behind the militarization of the Sino-Indian border dispute, then it is unlikely conflict would have waited to develop until 1962. Additionally, if Sino-Indian rivalry for dominance in Asia was so virulent why did India recognize PRC sovereignty in Tibet in 1951, and later agree to a mutual treaty of peaceful coexistence in 1954? A domestic level analysis cannot account for these otherwise amicable diplomatic relations.

What a systemic level analysis reveals is certain changes in national interests, geostrategic positions, and the anarchy of the international system brought both nations closer to the precipice of conflict. Various actions and reactions by both nations along the border created a security dilemma for each, and this brought the border dispute to the forefront of Sino-Indian relations. Furthermore, India believed they had the power to reshape the international system from a bipolar to multi-polar world. Their lack of either nuclear capability or significant conventional power exposed their status as simply a minor power of strategic importance in the international system. Thus either superpower was only motivated to preserve their security so long as it was in their interests to do so, and not as an ultimate necessity contrary to Indian belief. The ultimate cause for war in 1962 was India's assertion that it was a major power in world affairs. China's incentive in limiting their defeat of the Indian military was motivated by their interest in de-legitimizing the McMahon Line and consolidating their sovereignty in Tibet. The systems level analysis reveals not only what urged each nation to war, but also explains how the anarchy of the system limited the extent of the fighting.

FROM ENTHUSIASM TO UNCERTAINTY

The modern Sino-Indian relationship has been marked by four distinct phases. Purported friendship and ideological congruence around antiimperialist foreign-policy objectives from 1950 deteriorated into a bitter yet brief border conflict in 1962, followed by a Sino-Indian 'Cold War'. Bilateral normalization efforts after 1976 led to attempts to address differences through dialogue. This was by no means easy, given Indian sensitivities, frequently expressed in the media and in parliament.

In 1998, India pointed to China as the justification for its second round of nuclear tests (the first had occurred in 1974). Although this might have been expected to create significant tensions between the two nations, economic relations have since intensified. Nonetheless, the period from 1998 onward remains one of uncertainty and occasional antagonism, marked by China's full emergence as a global power and the courting of India by other powers, not least the United States, as an important nation not just in its own right but also as a potential counterweight to Chinese power and regional influence. India and China started off on a friendly footing soon after their formation as republics.

This 1950s entente, epitomised by the popular Hindi slogan *Hindi Chini Bhai-Bhai* (Indians and Chinese are brothers), was grounded in the countries' shared sense of having cast off the imperialist yoke through long, albeit completely different, struggles. Both espoused a shared responsibility to lead countries newly emerging from colonization in a quest for peace and prosperity against the treacherous backdrop of US–Soviet rivalry.

As late as 1962, at the height of the India–China border dispute, Chinese Premier Zhou Enlai reminded Indian Prime Minister Jawaharlal Nehru: 'Our two peoples' common interests in their struggle against imperialism outweigh by far all the differences between our two countries. We have a major responsibility for Sino-Indian friendship, Asian–African solidarity and Asian peace.' Despite this common ground, there were marked differences in the ideologies of the two great leaders, Mao and Nehru, who controlled the foreign policies of their respective nations. Mao had led a militant movement that armed and mobilised the Chinese peasantry to win a civil war and establish the People's Republic of China (PRC). Nehru, on the other hand, had, alongside Mahatma Gandhi, led a movement that won an unlikely victory against British colonialism through nonviolent resistance.

Nehru chose a foreign policy of non-alignment while Mao adopted a policy of formal, if intermittent, support for international revolution. India and China, however, could not share the mantle of leading the newly independent colonies of Asia and Africa for long. At the first Afro- Asian Conference at Bandung, Indonesia, in 1955, Nehru took great pride in introducing Zhou to other leaders as if India were, in the words of scholar Manjari Chatterjee Miller, a 'public mentor and introducer of China into the group of developing nations'. Much later, Zhou would comment to a group of journalists that he had 'never met a more arrogant man' than Nehru. At Bandung, China is reported to have reached a 'strategic understanding with Pakistan founded on their convergent interests vis-à-vis India'. This laid the foundation for one of the twentieth century's most enduring alliances, which is still intact. After Bandung, the emerging competition between India and China contributed to an increasingly strained bilateral relationship that was soon put to the test in addressing a serious irritant: the Sino-Indian border. While some have traced the roots of the Indo-Chinese border dispute to a much earlier period, its immediate antecedents lay in the Chinese invasion of Tibet in 1950.

This created significant tensions in India, which had strategic interests in Tibet and 'spiritual bonds' with Tibetan civilization stretching back almost two millennia. Writing at the height of the Sino-Indian border conflict, Indian analyst P.C. Chakravarti expressed India's fears: 'Any strong expansionist power, entrenched in Tibet, holds in its hands a loaded pistol pointed at the heart of India'. Although India officially acquiesced to the Chinese occupation of Tibet, declining to support the Tibetans at the United Nations or to expand the scope of conflict, it did lend limited material support to Tibetan rebels. Controversies soon emerged regarding the Indo-Tibetan border, and the Sino-Indian border in general.

Two areas were of particular concern: the eastern sector (145,000km), which the Indians called the North East Frontier Agency (NEFA) and which the Chinese viewed as South Tibet; and the western sector (34,000km), which included most prominently the Aksai Chin plateau, bordering Kashmir, Xinjiang and Tibet. In 1958, it emerged that the US Central Intelligence Agency and Chiang Kai-shek's agents were financing and training Tibetan rebels in Indian territory. In March of 1959, following an uprising against Chinese rule in Tibet, the Dalai Lama fled to India. In pursuit of Tibetan rebels, Chinese forces came up against and clashed with the Indian Army at Longju. In April 1960, Zhou came to New Delhi for talks with Nehru, which were unsuccessful.

In November 1961, India launched a more overtly confrontational 'forward policy', establishing military posts north of existing Chinese positions in the disputed territories in an attempt to cut off Chinese supply lines and force a withdrawal. This approach was reinforced in April 1962, when China was reeling under the disastrous impact of the Great Leap Forward, facing threats of military invasion from Taiwan and involved in a proxy conflict with the United States in Laos. By July, however, these international challenges were resolved and China focused its energy on countering India's actions.

China attacked Indian positions in both the eastern and western sectors on 20 October 1962, much to New Delhi's surprise. Nehru appealed to the United States for assistance, which President John F. Kennedy was quick to provide. An American aircraft carrier was dispatched to the Bay of Bengal, but was recalled almost immediately when, on 21 November, China unilaterally declared a ceasefire and withdrew to the positions it had held prior to the beginning of the dispute. The war had ended in 31 days with a comprehensive victory for the Chinese. The Sino-Indian war is often cited as a watershed moment in Indian foreign policy, after which Nehruvian idealism began to give way to the pragmatic impulses of subsequent administrations. After the war, India began to align itself more closely with the Soviet Union, which had begun to split from China within the international Communist movement; meanwhile, China and Pakistan developed closer ties.

In 1964, China conducted its first nuclear test, at Lop Nor, which provided impetus for India's own successful 'peaceful' nuclear test at Pokhran ten years later. The 1965 India–Pakistan war was a litmus test of the already established US–Pakistan relationship as well as the new Sino-Pakistani relationship. When the United States declared neutrality and blocked military transfers to both India and Pakistan, Islamabad turned to Beijing for assistance, which it provided in generous quantities. When war broke out, China came down heavily on Pakistan's side and threatened to open a front with India on the Sikkim border. US diplomatic intervention and a United Nations resolution calling for a ceasefire were ultimately necessary to discourage Chinese intervention.

In 1967, as Mao's Cultural Revolution took hold, India and China again exchanged artillery fire in the eastern sector of their disputed border. Chinese forces clashed with Soviet troops in 1969, the same year Beijing began to coordinate with Pakistan to supply arms, training and funding to insurgents in India's northeastern region – activities that China had been engaged in since 1962. As the Cultural Revolution subsided, Washington began cultivating ties with China through Pakistan. During the 1971 unrest in East Pakistan, India faced tremendous pressure from both the United States and China, driving Prime Minister Indira Gandhi to seek a military alliance with the Soviet Union. From that point on, until the thawing of the Cold War, India and China were on opposing sides of a global rivalry.

The US–Chinese rapprochement brought UN membership and a permanent seat on the Security Council for Beijing. India responded to China's new global status with its 1974 nuclear test and the annexation of Sikkim the following year, provoking loud Chinese protests. In 1976, China signed an agreement on nuclear cooperation with Pakistan, though it did not follow through until 1981. Soon after Deng Xiaoping assumed leadership in 1978, the country declared it would no longer support insurgencies in India's northeastern states. This was in keeping with a wider paradigm shift in China's inward and outward orientation.

Deng's foreign policy, based on the principle of *Tao Guang Yang Hui* ('Hide Brightness, Nourish Obscurity') prescribed an internally oriented programme of building up domestic economic strength and disentangling the country from international conflicts. Yet Sino-Indian rapprochement remained uneasy, frequently falling victim to temporary changes in the international and bilateral climate, and to domestic politics.

During the brief interlude of India's Janata government in 1979, then Foreign Minister Atal Bihari Vajpayee paid a historic visit to China. Unfortunately, the visited coincided with the Chinese 'Pedagogical War' with Vietnam and caused Vajpayee much embarrassment. A Sino-Indian border-dialogue process initiated in 1981 quickly turned sour, culminating in a large-scale military stand-off between India and China in the eastern sector at Sumdurong Chu in 1986–87. This impasse was eventually resolved, and Indian Prime Minister Rajiv Gandhi visited China in December 1988, during which he reversed the decades-old Indian stance that resolution of the border dispute was a precondition for the normalization of relations, and admitted that some members of the Tibetan community residing in India were engaged in anti-China activities. The pace of bilateral visits back and forth accelerated, resulting in new agreements to cooperate on the border issue and in other areas.

These agreements established a foundation for greater economic cooperation that withstood the shock of India's May 1998 nuclear tests. Immediately following the tests, Washington leaked a letter from Prime Minister Atal Bihari Vajpayee to President Bill Clinton that justified India's action in terms of the Chinese nuclear threat and its nuclear assistance to Pakistan. Ten days prior to the tests, Indian Defence Minister George Fernandes had declared during an interview that China was 'potential threat number one'. New Delhi's message seemed loud and clear, but after some strident criticisms of the tests and India's justifications, Beijing quickly resumed relations with its neighbour. A critical test of China's new approach was the Kargil conflict between India and Pakistan in 1999, during which Beijing assured Indian Foreign Minister Jaswant Singh of its neutrality.

Indeed, China's statements on the Kashmir issue and other conflicts between India and Pakistan since the 1990s have called for their bilateral resolution, a marked change from China's stance during the India–Pakistan wars of 1965 and 1971. The new millennium saw the resumption of high-level diplomatic exchanges despite intermittent crises in the relationship. In 2000, the seventeenth Karmapa, considered by many Buddhists as the third most senior cleric of their faith, fled from Tibet to India against the wishes of the Chinese government. Nonetheless, high-level visits continued.

In 2005, Chinese Premier Wen Jiabao officially recognised Sikkim as part of India and seemed to acquiesce in India's bid for a permanent seat in the UN Security Council (though China's subsequent refusal to explicitly endorse India's bid at a meeting of the foreign ministers of Brazil, Russia, China and India in mid 2008 belied this understanding). 2006 was declared 'India–China Friendship Year' and celebrated by the exchange of dignitaries and a year-long programme of cultural events. Significantly, the Nathula trading pass on the Sino-Indian border in Sikkim was reopened. Sino-Indian trade was worth almost $38 billion in 2007 (and an estimated $50bn in 2009), up from $117 million in 1987.

In December 2007, India and China hosted their first-ever joint military exercises. In January 2008, Indian Prime Minister Manmohan Singh reaffirmed with Chinese President Hu Jintao and Premier Wen Jiabao that their countries enjoyed a 'shared vision on the 21 century'. In 2009, India–China trade overtook India–US trade in value, making China India's top trading partner.

Irritants continue to plague the relationship, however, particularly where the border is concerned. In 2007 China refused to grant a visa to a government official from the Indian state of Arunachal Pradesh, which constitutes part of China's territorial claim in the eastern sector, on the grounds that he was in fact a Chinese citizen. The official was part of a group of 107 officers scheduled to visit China on a study tour. In retaliation, the Indian government cancelled the entire visit. In 2008, Prime Minister Singh invited Chinese displeasure by visiting Arunachal Pradesh, and President Pratibha Patil's recent visit to the state and to Tawang, a site of confrontation in 1962, aroused similar complaints.

Chinese opposition to the use of an Asian Development Bank loan to India for projects in Arunachal Pradesh revived tension between the two countries in mid 2009 that the new Indian Foreign Minister S.M. Krishna sought to calm by announcing that India would henceforth raise funds for that state internally. The current dynamic Underlying many views of the Sino-Indian relationship is the notion that two rising powers with rapidly growing economies and global ambitions cannot peacefully co-exist at such close quarters. Where spheres of influence overlap there is competition, as in the cases of Nepal and Myanmar.

Standard realist accounts argue China is unwilling to permit the emergence of India as a power beyond South Asia. In the past China has built alliances and partnerships with countries in the Indian periphery, most notably Pakistan, but also Myanmar, Nepal, Sri Lanka, Bangladesh and, more recently, Afghanistan. Combined with the Chinese presence in the Indian Ocean region, this has created some concern among Indian policymakers of strategic encirclement. Still, India has been cautious and, in all but naval strategy, circumspect about countering China's moves. New Delhi continues to follow a one-China policy favouring Beijing, despite growing military exchanges with Taiwan. India's Look East policy, a serious attempt to correct the conceptual drift in India's approach to Asia beyond China, has resulted in substantially growing economic relations with Singapore, Vietnam and Indonesia. Yet India has refrained from seeking out strategic alliances in either East or Southeast Asia.

SECURITY CONCERNS

The Sino-Indian border dispute is long running and fairly intractable, despite shows of flexibility in the past. It periodically prompts both sides to rake up decades-old grievances. Yet India and China have taken meaningful steps towards an institutionalised process for its resolution. Since 1988 they have for the most part managed to separate border issues from the overall bilateral relationship. The long-standing relationship between China and Pakistan presents a further obstacle to closer ties between China and India.

However, China has begun to adopt a more even-handed stance, evident during the Kargil War, the attack on the Indian Parliament in 2001, and the 2008 terrorist attacks in Mumbai. The underlying logic is that Pakistan's growing instability and India's growing power compel China to take a middle path. China's nuclear and missile-technology assistance to Pakistan is of particular concern to India. Future tensions between India and Pakistan could fuel a nuclear arms race on the subcontinent. In light of the Mumbai attacks and setbacks for the Pakistani government's efforts to contain Islamist influence in the country, however, it would be surprising if Beijing were not becoming somewhat wary of Islamabad, given unrest in its own Xinjiang region and the country's persistent fear of terrorism.

Moreover, the prospect of nuclear or military conflict between India and China is diminished by the sizeable gap in capabilities between the two. Tibet is a significant security concern. Indian parliamentarian and author Arun Shourie argues that 'India's security is inextricably intertwined with the existence and survival of Tibet as a buffer state and to the survival and strengthening of Tibetan culture and religion'. For India, the Chinese role in Tibet presents both a threat and a tactical opportunity.

The presence of the Dalai Lama and thousands of Tibetan refugees in India sometimes allows New Delhi to indirectly apply pressure on Beijing, just as China's policies towards Pakistan sometimes do to India. This lever is not often used, however. In 2008, the Indian government took great pains to ensure that Tibetan protestors did not cause any embarrassment to Beijing during the passage of the Olympic Torch through New Delhi. On the other hand, at the height of tensions between the two countries over border issues during autumn 2009, a visit by the Dalai Lama to the Buddhist temple community in the disputed Tawang, nestled in northwestern Arunachal Pradesh, can only have been perceived as provocative by Beijing.

Perhaps the biggest challenge to Sino-Indian rapprochement, and a source of impetus, is the rapidly improving US–Indian relationship. While a much-improved relationship with Washington has helped India counter the traditional pro-Pakistan tilt in US foreign policy, it has also made Sino- Indian rapprochement a greater priority for Beijing. This echoes some of the history of Chinese overtures towards India in the 1970s, which were likely made in part with an eye to diminishing Indo-Soviet cooperation.

As the global contest for influence between the United States and China intensifies, India is likely to become an important factor in this strategic triangle. US approaches to China oscillate between policies of containment and engagement. The former has given birth to a new triangle between the United States, India and China, whereby Washington cultivates closer ties with India, as an established democracy and as a regional bulwark against a potentially aggressive, communist China. On the other hand, the Obama administration's approach to China has reinvigorated engagement enthusiasts in Washington. Indian commentators have observed with some alarm the renewed cooperation between China and the United States in tackling the global economic crisis, as well as increased US–Chinese interdependence resulting from Chinese creditors holding large amounts of US Treasury Bills and US debtors providing the single largest market for Chinese manufactured goods. This has prompted some to question the logic of picking a side in the unpredictable Sino-US relationship.

Ultimately, neither China nor India stands to gain from sparking a regional conflict. Both nations are deeply engaged in the domestic sphere, including generating economic reform, maintaining state legitimacy and juggling ethno-nationalism. Even the ostensible machinations of the United States have done little to hamper the current upswing in Sino-Indian relations. In some key international forums, including those addressing climate change, trade, labour laws, arms control and human rights, China and India have found common ground in countering Western positions, though their tactical alliances have often proved unstable in the heat of negotiation. India's best-case scenario would appear to be an interests-based balancing act between the United States and China.

At worst, India could face conflict with China in the medium term or be left out in the cold as the US and China become closer. In any event, India's hitherto prudent policy of measured engagement with all the major powers is more likely to pay off than bold moves it can ill afford financially at a time when domestic necessities continue to preoccupy its people and politicians.

Economic concerns

China and India are both net importers of crude oil, and both are seeking to diversify their energy supply through natural gas. This has the potential to cast them in direct competition for natural resources from Central Asia and the Persian Gulf. Yet so far both countries have mostly relied on market mechanisms and resisted any temptation to pursue a strategy hinging on exclusive access to supplies. This has allowed them to collaborate in Central Asia and the Persian Gulf, securing sea lanes as delivery channels, and participating in consortiums for exploration and extraction rights in certain areas. In January 2006, India's Oil and Natural Gas Corporation and the China National Petroleum Corporation decided to bid jointly for energy projects in some regions. Both nations also harbour the potential to produce and benefit from non-conventional energy generation. In commodities, China and India account for almost 50 per cent of Africa's exports to Asia, as well as its imports from Asia.

Economic competition in developing-country markets and the struggle for political-economic ties with African governments could conceivably set off a scramble for resources and markets in the region. On the other hand, the major exports from Africa to China and India today (oil and natural gas to China, ores and metals to India) do not overlap. There is some competition among Chinese and Indian producers in export markets for such goods as textiles, garments, leather goods and light machinery. China's accession to the World Trade Organization could potentially have long-term adverse consequences for the growth of Indian exports in these sectors, and China's better and growing integration into global production networks for manufactured goods could have negative implications for India's exports in general.

However, the top 25 exports of China and India in 2004 were almost entirely non-overlapping, and India has excelled mainly at trade in services in the recent past, suggesting that China's trade impact on India will be less pronounced than some have predicted. It is also possible that other Indian export sectors will expand to partially offset declines in India's relative economic welfare. Moreover, growing trade relations between India and China are likely to have a positive effect on bilateral relations. The low politics of trade could foster greater cooperation between the two nations, and not just in the economic realm.

IDENTITY AND PERCEPTIONS

There is a very clear sense in both China and India that their civilizational greatness entitles them to great-power status. In his Budget Speech of 1991, then Indian Finance Minister Manmohan Singh asserted that the emergence of India as a world economic power was 'an idea whose time has come', a remark that is often quoted. China, meanwhile, is often said to retain a Confucian notion of itself as 'the Middle Kingdom' around which international relations ought to be ordered. This perception is compounded by the Chinese nationalist narrative of the 'century of humiliation', a period extending from the First Opium War until the creation of the People's Republic, and featuring serial national humiliations at the hands of foreign imperialist powers, especially Japan.

Some worry that competing conceptions of inherent historical and contemporary greatness among Chinese and Indian policymakers could prove difficult to reconcile in day-to-day relations. It would be easy, however, to overestimate how much China's and India's claims to more international clout could contribute to regional conflict. Although China has essentially achieved great-power status, its foreign policy is notably and pointedly oriented towards maintaining regional stability and creating conditions for China's 'peaceful rise'. Analysts have characterised China's new diplomacy as 'less confrontational, more sophisticated, more confident, and, at times, more constructive' in its approach to regional and international affairs than it has been in the past.

At the domestic level, modern Chinese nationalism has been called 'pragmatic': it is instrumental and reactive, preoccupied with holding the nation together, in part through a strategy of rapidly accelerating growth, rather than with hostility to others. China's leaders are acutely aware of the dangers that await should the patriotism of their citizens become 'virulent ultranationalism'. Contemporary Indian politics and foreign policy evince a similar pragmatic strain, though occasional Indian stridency in multilateral forums stands in contrast to China's more targeted and restrained interventions.

India is not as convinced of its historical uniqueness as it once was, and prefers to cast itself officially as an ordinary if significant nation tending to the imperatives of its economic development rather than a country obsessed by the quest for great-power status. Economic prosperity is seen by most Indians as the key to India's attainment of greater power in the years to come.

This approach has favoured the normalization of traditionally antagonistic relationships with neighbouring countries and a greater commitment to international institutions that might legitimise its emergent status.

Sino-Indian perceptions of each other are somewhat more problematic. A 2006 Pew Global Attitudes Survey found that 43 per cent of Chinese had an unfavourable opinion of India, while 39 per cent of Indians had an unfavourable opinion of China. China's growing military power was, according to 63 per cent of Indians, a 'bad thing' for their country, while 50 per cent said the same about China's growing economic power.

At the same time, 65 per cent of Indians said that China would replace the United States as the dominant power sometime in the next 50 years. Public opinion is one thing; more relevant perhaps is the perception (and potentially a self-fulfilling prophecy) among some members of the Indian foreign-policy establishment of a 'China threat'. Eminent Indian foreign-policy analyst C. Raja Mohan describes India's China policy as standing on three legs: 'say nice things in public about Sino- Indian friendship, Asian unity and anti-Western solidarity; nurse intense grievances in private; and avoid problem solving because that would need a lot of political courage'.

Political debate in India complicates matters further, with pillars of the Right and Left respectively vilifying and eulogising China to the exclusion of more sensible and nuanced assessments of the relationship that naturally do not receive as much airplay. On the border issue, sophisticated, up-to-date analyses of the China–India relationship are often drowned out in Indian public debates by revanchist voices. This increases the likelihood of a China policy driven by misperception and miscalculation.

LOOKING FORWARD

The unconnected nature of China's and India's rise is striking. Bilateral trade, while growing fast, is a small share of overall trade for both countries. Major strategic partnerships have been made with third parties, including Pakistan and the United States. Societal interaction between the two nations is still negligible, though tourism is growing and interpersonal connections related to trade between the two countries are also increasing. Direct flights between India and China, however, only began in 2002, and in 2007, the two nations, with a combined population of over 2 billion, exchanged a paltry 570,000 visitors.

Equally striking has been the remarkably poor understanding until very recently among each country's respective foreign-policy circles of the other's history, society and contemporary policy. In India, many assessments are firmly bounded by the past, with no deep understanding of (or interest in) the drivers of Chinese policy today. In the words of former Indian Army Chief Shankar

Roychowdhury, 'though much water has flowed down the Tsangpo since [the Sino-Indian border war], India's "1962 syndrome" is unaltered'. Only modest academic attention has been paid in India to China, especially compared to Chinese efforts to understand India. As a result, the modern history of Sino-Indian relations has been less about China and India than it has been about extraneous actors such as the United States, the Soviet Union and Pakistan, and multilaterally managed issues such as non-proliferation and climate change.

There has been little effort until very recently to engage in an in-depth, widely gauged Sino- Indian dialogue. Such a dialogue cannot be based on fantasies about purported similarities between China and India (which are sometimes rooted in conceptions of shared Asian characteristics). India and China are probably today more different than they have ever been, both as societies and as economies.

The main coincidence between the two countries is their parallel pursuit of domestic consolidation, with foreign-policy pragmatism underpinning aspirations to great-power status. One important wild card could be domestic sub-nationalism, which afflicts both China and India, but with different characteristics and consequences. India has survived as a nation by cobbling together a sometimes conciliatory and often weak political and security response to various insurgencies and separatist movements.

China, on the other hand, still very much relies on the heavy hand of the state to suppress such uprisings, as seen in Tibet in 2008 and Xinjiang in 2009. Ethnic unrest in China's peripheral territories – Xinjiang, Tibet, Taiwan, Manchuria, Mongolia – has historically been a major vulnerability for the Chinese state, as such episodes could possibly invite foreign involvement. Moreover, the legitimacy of China's leader ship is often questioned at such moments, posing a threat to the future of the ruling Communist Party. Thus, while the prospect is remote, Tibet could conceivably ignite a future Sino-Indian conflict not because of its strategic value but because a well-organised Tibetan revolt might prompt the Chinese leadership to demand unreasonable concessions from

India. Similarly, changes in China's economic fortunes might provoke a nationalistic turn in its foreign policy.

Although Chinese leaders since Deng Xiaoping have exhibited pragmatic tendencies, seminal events such as the Tiananmen Square protests or recent events in Xinjiang could empower nativists, who prefer isolation and domestic purity.

Even modest movement in this direction within China could cause major setbacks in bilateral relations with India, and set the stage for wider confrontation should, for example, a serious border incident occur.

Some also fear that a sustained economic downturn could seriously undermine Sino-Indian relations by threatening the legitimacy of the Chinese state, which could motivate Chinese leaders to attempt to distract the Chinese citizenry from domestic problems by provoking confrontation further afield.

From a Chinese perspective, understanding and respecting Indian sensitivities is also vital. The future of Pakistan remains a key factor in the Sino-Indian relationship, and the future of Kashmir remains critical to the Indo-Pakistani relationship. Therefore any move by China that either intentionally or inadvertently secured gains for Pakistan on the Kashmir issue would invite much concern in India. For example, a recent decision by China to issue separate visas to residents of Indian-administered Kashmir led to a minor diplomatic stand-off. Such moves are, to be sure, contrary to the overall thrust of Chinese policy since the 1990s.

Territorial integrity has occupied the minds of India's leaders ever since the country gained independence in 1947, when more than 500 princely states had to be incorporated into the Indian Union – a considerable task for any post-colonial state. Given this mindset, the Sino-Indian border conflict could prove particularly intractable. Since its formation, the People's Republic has settled its borders with a number of neighbours, often making concessions to the other party. The Indian border, however, remains contentious and a continuing source of ill will between the two nations. Initial formulations by Zhou Enlai in the 1950s had envisaged a quid pro quo settlement whereby India would drop its claims in the western sector in exchange for China's concession of the eastern sector. This proposal was rejected by Nehru at the time, ostensibly under domestic political pressure, and again by New Delhi in the 1980s when Deng Xiaoping revived the plan.

Today, even unverified reports of minor Chinese incursions into disputed areas receive widespread media coverage in India, and elite opinion often responds by amplifying the China threat. Accumulated incidents of this nature might provoke an Indian reaction, driven largely by domestic political actors, that could seriously damage the relationship, though successive Indian governments have guarded against such an outcome. While the legitimacy of the Chinese state hinges on its economic model, that of the Indian state hinges on its political model.

India's ability to manage a multitude of divergent interests and competing claims on state resources within a democratic polity have earned it considerable international political capital. In recent years, India's democratic credentials have allowed it to enjoy disproportionate gains from multilateral regimes, particularly in nuclear technology, relative to its level of socio-economic development. Bolstered by a booming economy, India today stakes a strong claim to being a vibrant and productive (if often chaotic and internally violence-prone) democratic society.

If India's domestic political fortunes were to change, possibly through the rise of more extreme political ideologies, relations with China would likely deteriorate. Similarly, an upsurge in extremist or separatist violence in India's peripheral regions, or of Maoist-style Naxalite violence aimed at the Indian state, might prompt domestic analysts and policymakers to point to Pakistani–Chinese involvement. The greatest threat to the Indo-Chinese relationship arises from widely differing views of the history and ultimate destiny of Tibet.

For China, India's recognition of Tibet as part of China seems grudging and conditional. And its role as host of the Dalai Lama and his 'splittist clique', to use Beijing's colourful phrase, could appear to some Chinese as a threat to their country's cohesion. For India, Chinese repression in Tibet is painful, and many Indians hope it will ultimately prove futile. Careful management by both capitals will be required to prevent developments relating to Tibet from undermining the wider China–India relationship.

India and China find themselves on the cusp of history. China's rise, reinforced by a very difficult decade for the United States, is obvious to all. Beijing has played its cards prudently while carving out a larger role for itself in the management of the global economy. Its military investments and might continue to grow, but appear aimed mainly at overall deterrence and the containment of Taiwan. Its designs in the Indian Ocean, while fuelling Indian anxieties, do not yet seem central to Beijing's wider objectives.

India's own achievements (economic and otherwise), while impressive, in no way match China's. India's overwhelming challenge remains, as Prime Minister Singh never fails to point out, the fight against poverty, but Indian state capacity has been woefully inadequate to the task. Innovative approaches introduced in recent years to boost rural incomes and to short-circuit opportunities for corruption do, however, give reason to hope. The two rising Asian powers are helping shape a new distribution of global power, as demonstrated not just by their growing prominence within the machinery of multilateral economic and security diplomacy (both, for example, are members of the G20) but by the ardour with which they are courted by other international actors.

A new world order seems to be emerging in which China, the United States, a declining or at least static Russia, and India, with Brazil not far behind, all speak internationally with authority on many issues, while EU members struggle to find a common voice. And yet, beyond the recognition of its status as a meaningful global power, India does not yet seem to have much of a project for its global reach, while China, which might well have one, is exercising great prudence in articulating it publicly. In a genuinely multipolar world where the principal powers engage one another constantly across a wide range of issues in many different forums, India and China should be able to manage their parallel rise without generating shocks on their own continent. A more systematic dialogue, going well beyond high-level visits and acknowledging differences instead of emphasising imagined similarities, could lay the foundations for a better understanding of the domestic compulsions that drive the two countries' foreign policies and help both sides manage their nationalist impulses, transform public perceptions and learn to pre-empt situations before they can develop into full-blown confrontation.

THE INDIA-CHINA DIVIDE

The Chinese Communist Party's (CCP) dislike for the 'hardline Hindu nationalist' Bharatiya Janata Party (BJP) is no secret. The shifts in India's China policy since May 1998, as evidenced in the nuclear and missile arena, military spending, and pro-Tibet and pro-Taiwan views expressed by some ministers, are said to have undermined the key assumptions underlying China's India policy. Conversations with officials and strategic analysts reveal that the Chinese are concerned over the rise of BJP as a major political force in Indian politics and its implications for China's strategic objective of supremacy in Asia. Before Pokhran II, China's India-watchers had convinced themselves that there would be 'no significant or fundamental changes' in the BJP-led Government's nuclear policy and that BJP-led India would not take any major strategic initiative (such as overt nuclearisation, strategic alliance with the United States, or support to Tibetan independence).

Although the aspirations for major power status are held by almost all Indian political parties (barring the Communists who fear provoking their Chinese masters), the BJP covets that status most ardently and is the most willing to assert it through military policy. Beijing would prefer a non-BJP weak government like the left-dominated United Front (UF) government before Pokhran II, and the successive Congress governments that preceded it, which had fine-tuned Sino-Indian bilateral relations by playing second fiddle to an assertive China. A policy paper prepared for the Chinese leadership has recommended 'targeting the BJP' as its policies have eroded Beijing's leverage against New Delhi. One analyst compared India with Nazi Germany and Iraq arguing that since the end of the Cold War, India had become too powerful and ambitious (for example, demanding a permanent seat on the UN Security Council) and warned that if India does not wish to suffer the fate of Japan in the 1940s or Iraq in the 1990s, it should give up its ambition for regional hegemony and take concrete steps to improve relations with China.

The main objective of China's Asia policy has always been to prevent the rise of an Asian rival or peer competitor to challenge its status as the Asia-Pacific's sole 'Middle Kingdom'. As an old Chinese saying goes, 'one mountain cannot accommodate two tigers'. That China does not want India to emerge as an equal is evident from its staunch opposition to India's membership of the P-5 (UN Security Council), N-5 (Nuclear Club), ASEM (Asia-Europe Summit), and APEC (Asia-Pacific Economic Cooperation). (India was made the ARF (ASEAN Regional Forum) member in December 1995 despite Beijing's opposition to it.) Speaking at the Munich Security Conference in February 1999, India's National Security Advisor, Brajesh Mishra, hinted at the BJP government's much broader political ambition by predicting that 'in the 21st century a new security order is likely to arise in the Asia-Pacific region in which India should be granted as much respect and deference by the United States and others as is China today.' Beijing's India-watchers believe that only a firm policy based on absolute strength and proactive containment of India will force the BJP-led government to act soberly towards China. Beijing knows that while China's emergence as a great power has been accepted by Western and Asian nations, India's claim to great power is yet to be accepted. So it is in the CCP's interests to keep the BJP out of power. Beijing has been blamed by India's intelligence agencies, media and some politicians for the overthrow of the BJP-led government in April 1999.

Strange as it may seem, the CCP has more in common with its bete noire, BJP, than its counterpart in India, the Communist Party of India-Marxist (CPM). In the BJP, the CCP has met its match, the latter's 'communist' pretensions notwithstanding. Contrary to the popular conception of the CCP and the BJP occupying opposite ends of the political spectrum, the BJP is the CCP's mirror image. Just as the CCP believes in the superiority of the Han race, Han civilisation and the Han culture while displaying patronising and condescending attitude towards minorities such as Tibetans, Mongols and Muslims and downplaying the repeated colonisation of the Han race first by Inner Asian tribes such as Mongols, Manchus and Hsingnus and then by the Europeans, the BJP believes in the superiority of the Hindu race, Hindu civilisation and Hindu culture while downplaying the repeated colonisation of India by Greek, Muslim and European invaders as a result of Hindu disunity and their contributions to Indian culture. What is more, the CCP's goal of a unified 'Greater China' is not much different from the RSS/BJP's dream of 'Akhand Bharat' (United India). Just as the Chinese Communists lay claim to territories annexed by non-Chinese Mongol and Manchu empires (such as Tibet, Eastern Turkestan, Mongolia), the 'Akhand Bharat' concept includes territories (such as Burma and Sri Lanka) brought under control by the British. Much like the CCP, the BJP wants India to be an economic and military superpower in order to 'stand up' to great powers' bullying and coercion. Both have long nurtured the belief that as the two oldest civilisations and once great powers which were subjected to centuries of foreign domination, they must acquire the full spectrum of economic, technological and military (conventional, nuclear and information warfare) capabilities in order to be dominant regionally and influential globally.

Furthermore, the BJP's slogan of 'prosperous and powerful country' bears remarkable resemblance to the CCP's national goal: 'rich country, strong military' (fuguo qiangbing). Interestingly, both are courting the United States to help balance their relationships with each other until they are strong enough to do so on their own. Both want a new international status that is commensurate with their size, strength and potential. Historically and civilisationally, while China was the 'Middle Kingdom' of eastern Asia, India was the 'Middle Kingdom' of southern Asia.

The two parties are thus manifestation of the growing nationalism in India and China. Both also share remarkable similarity in economic outlooks and rhetorical excess. The BJP-led government is as aggressive in the pursuit of national interests as the CCP. Nor is it shy of flexing muscles and warning neighbours with 'serious consequences' if they don't behave-just as the Chinese

Communists have always done! Although both the CCP and BJP have been labelled 'fascist', 'militarist' and 'ultra-natonalist' parties by their critics, the reality is that both are nationalist parties deeply conscious of their countries' history, culture and civilisational heritage to humankind and committed to restoring their countries' great power status. Both China after a century and India after a millenium of decline are keen to assume the great power roles they believe to be their historical and civilisational right.

Both remain suspicious of each other's long-term agenda and intentions, and are attempting to fill any perceived power vacuum or block the other from doing so. At the heart of Sino-Indian antagonism is the familiar Indian suspicion, which has now matured into a certainty, that China is seeking to deny India its proper stakes in the game of international politics. Both see themselves as newly rising great Asian powers whose time has finally come. This means that BJP's resurgent India will face CCP's rising China which will ensure a conflict of interests between the two giants unless their power competition is managed carefully. Their underlying power rivalry and their self-images as natural great powers and centres of civilisation and culture will continue to drive them to support different countries and causes. India versus China, not India versus Pakistan, has always been the main game in Asia. However, post-colonial Asia has not experienced both a strong China and a strong India at the same time. The BJP-CCP clash is borne not out of conflicting, but complementary, visions for their respective countries.

CHINA'S BORDER SPAT WITH INDIA

The recent meeting between India's National Security Adviser MK Narayanan and China's Vice-Foreign Minister Dai Banggio at Coonoor in Tamil Nadu was the continuation of a series of such meetings in the context of the border dispute between the two countries. While this is a good thing to go by, the main point is: what has been the actual progress in the matter? After every meeting, a standard joint communiqué is issued to the effect that the téte-a-téte was fruitful and the dialogue is being maintained in an atmosphere of friendship and mutual cooperation. Diplomatic jargon cannot be limitless; it must end somewhere. Again, from time to time one hears of Chinese intrusion into Arunachal Pradesh, especially in the area of Sumdorong Chu Valley and the northern range of the Mishmi Hills. There is also the occasional media report that China claims this North-eastern state of ours on the grounds of a combination of history as well as geography.

India's drawback is that our foreign policy has always been linked to the vote bank. In fact it was a vote bank issue that created the border dispute with China in the first place way back in the late '50s and early '60s. The origin of this problem is worth discussing as this itself suggests the solution. Soon after China secured Tibet, Beijing sent a delegation to New Delhi under then Prime Minister Zhou en Lai with a proposal on Aksai Chin in northern Kashmir, adjacent to the Siachen Glacier. The delegation submitted to us that movement from Tibet to Sinkiang province was a huge problem because one had to traverse the inhospitable Kunlun Mountains en route. Hence it was suggested both countries could arrive at an understanding by which India could lease out Aksai Chin to China, as this would enable the latter to build an all-weather highway across this stretch of territory.

Thus movement from Tibet to Sinkiang would not then involve negotiating the Kunluns at all and India, too, could use this highway as a bonus. In any case, Aksai Chin was just an ice desert with an average height of 18,000-19,000 feet and nothing grew there, let alone having any human habitation. New Delhi reacted with its usual brash arrogance, thundering words to the effect that 'not an inch of our sacred motherland' would be given, et al. Zhou en Lai was shown the door gracelessly.

The Chinese delegation went back and decided to implement a tenet in Hindi conveying the meaning that if ghee cannot be taken out by a straight finger then a crooked finger would be used! China militarily attacked India and physically captured Aksai Chin by force in late 1962 and built the desired highway through it. China is still very much in occupation of this area, cocking a snook at India now and then! On our part we bemoaned our fate, blamed Beijing for gerrymandering into our territory and generally made a political nuisance of ourselves. Nothing helped, of course.

During its attack on India, China had also deeply transgressed into what was earlier known as the North East Frontier Agency that later became Arunachal Pradesh. However, after delivering a crushing military-cum-political defeat on India, China moved back to its own side of the border in this area. This apart, China disputes an area along the Uttarkhand-Tibet border named Barahoti. China has a strong army garrison in this area at a place called Taklakot that keeps a watching brief over Barahoti. India, therefore, has been well and truly boxed in by China, courtesy New Delhi's folly of riding the high horse with Zhou en Lai's delegation of yore.

Diplomacy has never been a strong point with us and the country has suffered badly as a consequence. The science and art of statecraft continue to be subservient to the omnipotent vote bank as far as our leaders are concerned. New Delhi, for reasons best known to itself, brought out a Lok Sabha resolution in 1994 wherein it was categorically stated that we would retake Aksai Chin by force. Obviously this resolution was nothing but a vote bank gimmick that our näive citizens — including many members of our intelligentsia — swallowed all the way.While firmly occupying Aksai Chin, China periodically needles India over Arunachal Pradesh and Barahoti. Normally, Barahoti remains dormant but Arunachal Pradesh makes news, sometimes with alarm. This has been the state of affairs since 1962. No government at New Delhi since that year has tried to accept the reality and taken any pragmatic steps to reconcile the border situation with China, notwithstanding the fact that currently our relations with China are improving virtually by the day.

The question is, what needs to be done in order to resolve the ongoing impasse? There is only one solution: India must formally accept Zhou en Lai's suggestion of yesteryear but cede Aksai Chin to China. It is doubtful whether China will accept the lease aspect now. The Chinese are a very proud race and will never climb down. In any event, China holds the aces in this matter, never mind the McMahon Line's relevancy to us. Truth to tell, this solution was hinted by China's previous regime under President Jiang Zemin through his then Foreign Minister Tang Jiaxuan during Prime Minister AB Vajpayee's tenure. While the Sikkim issue got reconciled, Aksai Chin could not be followed through due to the change of government in India in 2004.

China is not really interested in Barahoti and Arunachal Pradesh — Beijing uses these two as pressure points on New Delhi to see reason over the border dispute, a dispute that hinges purely on Aksai Chin. The sooner we come to terms with this, the better.

2

Globalization Conflict on Threat Opinion in South Asia

Many analysts in India, including this writer, make a distinction between the Indian sub-continent and South Asia. When they talk of the Indian sub-continent, they have in mind India, Pakistan, Bangladesh, Nepal and Bhutan. Of these, India, Pakistan and Bangladesh constituted one political entity before the British left the sub-continent in 1947. Pakistan was born in 1947 through the partition of the British India and Bangladesh was born in 1971 through the partition of Pakistan after a war of liberation waged by the Bengalis of the then East Pakistan, with Indian assistance.

Indian analysts, who talk of the Indian sub-continent, wish to keep in mind, in their analyses, the common historical, political, religious and cultural heritage of these three countries. The term sub-continent is used less and less in Pakistan and Bangladesh. The political leadership and the policy-makers in these two countries do not wish to be reminded of this common heritage. Any highlighting of this common heritage by Indian analysts is viewed by them with suspicion—— as indicating a hidden desire to reverse history and undo the 1947 partition. They, therefore, talk only of South Asia and have, for all practical purposes, banished any reference to the sub-continent from their strategic discourse. This has to be kept in mind since complexes arising from sub-continental memories tend to influence their mind-set and threat perceptions and have stood in the way of the progress of globalization in this area. They view any Indian enthusiasm for globalization as a concealed attempt towards political and economic re-subcontinentalisation.

THE INDIA FACTOR

The India factor has had an impact on the threat perceptions of all the countries of this region except Afghanistan and the Maldives. This arises due to the following reasons:

- Asymmetry in size, human and material resources and economic and military potential.
- Perceived Indian willingness/tendency to assert its national interests even if they be detrimental to those of the neighbours. Examples: India's role in the creation of Bangladesh, alleged Indian support to the Tamils of Sri Lanka.
- Perceived Indian encouragement of its political favourites in the countries of the region. Examples: India's alleged soft corner for the opposition Awami League in Bangladesh and for the democratic forces in Nepal.
- Continuing differences relating to territory (Kashmir with Pakistan) and utilization of water resources (Pakistan and Bangladesh).

The other countries, except Afghanistan and the Maldives, tend to guard themselves against these factors by avoiding too close economic linkages with India, which comes in the way of the region as a whole benefiting from the fruits of globalization, by developing economic and military linkages with China and by supporting Chinese aspirations for a role in regional organizations such as the SAARC as an observer.

Pakistan and Bangladesh embarked on a policy of liberalization of their economies before India. Despite this, their economic development has not been as satisfactory as they would have like it to be. Amongst the reasons, one could cite the bad internal security situation, which keeps foreign investors away despite a favourable policy framework; political instability due to periodic interventions by the Army in politics; inadequate investment in a modern education system due to the diversion of the limited resources to meet military and strategic needs; and failure to diversify the economy. Pakistan's economy continues to be largely a three-commodity (cotton and cotton textiles, leather goods and sports articles) and one-port (Karachi) economy. Bangladesh's economy continues to be largely textiles, jute and raw materials dependent.

Though India embarked on the liberalization of its economy only from 1991 onwards, its economy has made impressive progress freeing it from its past dependence on traditional goods such as textiles, tea etc. India's rapid diversification and development of its economy have been facilitated by the facts that democracy has taken firm roots in the country; that its internal security problems, though serious, are confined to areas in which the foreign investors are presently not interested; and that its founding fathers had shown foresight in investing heavily on a modern education system, including institutes of excellence in technology, which have significantly contributed to its emergence as a leading Information Technology (IT) power.

Complexes and concerns arising from the India factor continue to come in the way of the normalization of trade relations between Pakistan and India, the improvement in the trade relations between India and Bangladesh and progress towards the integration of the economies of the region through appropriate institutional and policy frameworks. Political factors continue to receive priority over economic and prejudices and fears continue to rule out pragmatism.

However, economic realities ultimately have a way of asserting themselves. One could already see a beginning of it in Pakistan. Its rulers and policy-makers have realized that a favourable policy frame-work and wide-ranging reforms alone will not attract foreign investors. They also need a market and consumers large enough to make their investments adequately profitable. Pakistan does not provide such a market and such a reservoir of consumers. Unless the foreign investors perceive the sub-continent as a whole as a single economic entity and market and are able to sell their products anywhere within this entity, they are reluctant to invest in Pakistan or Bangladesh alone, without guarantees of access to the Indian market.

The realization of this ground reality has already brought about a significant change in Pakistan's policy since Gen. Pervez Musharraf came to power in October, 1999. While continuing to oppose the normalization of economic relations with India till the differences over Jammu & Kashmir (J&K) are settled, he has made an exception in respect of energy supplies.

He is prepared now to allow the foreign investors investing heavily in the construction of oil and gas pipelines to Pakistan from Iran or Turkmenistan to cater to the requirements of the Indian market too in order to make their investments adequately profitable.

Significantly, even the religious fundamentalist parties, who continue to insist on a policy of "Kashmir first and the rest later", have not objected to what Gen. Musharraf describes as the stand-alone exception. If this exception materializes and if the benefits of it are felt by the Pakistani people, this will become more and more a rule than a mere exception.

Such a realization is yet to come about in Bangladesh. The trade relations between India and Bangladesh are not as restricted as those between India and Pakistan. There is a much, much freer flow of trade between the two countries. While encouraging a greater flow of trade with China, Bangladesh continues to prevent pragmatism, profitability and mutual benefits from having a free play to contribute to a rapid expansion of the bilateral economic relations with India.

Four examples could be cited as illustrations of the Bangladesh attitude:

- It refuses to sell its surplus gas to India on the ostensible ground that it wants to conserve it for its future use. At the same time, it has reportedly entered into negotiations with China for selling it through a pipeline to China via Myanmar.
- It refuses to grant transit rights to India to facilitate the movement of Indian goods to India's northeast.

- It has been reluctant to permit a pipeline to bring gas from the Arakan area of Myanmar to India pass through Bangladesh territory.
- During the period from July to December, 2005, the value of Chinese exports to Bangladesh amounted to US $ 1.03 billion and Chinese imports from Bangladesh only US $ 27.9 million. During the same period, the value of Indian exports to Bangladesh amounted to US $ 820 million and imports from Bangladesh to US $ 105 million. India's imports from Bangladesh are still small, but they are four times the value of Chinese imports from Bangladesh. Chinese exports to Bangladesh are nearly 25 per cent more than those of India. And yet, while Bangladesh nurses a grudge against India on the ground that it has allegedly been dumping its goods in Bangladesh and has not been buying enough from there, it does not voice a similar grievance against China.

Feelings of insecurity, an aggressive inferiority complex, and a Me-too syndrome continue to influence policy-making in Pakistan. What India does, it must do too. What India gets, it must get too. One saw an example of this syndrome in action during the recent visit of President George Bush to India and Pakistan, when, during Mr. Bush's talks in Islamabad, Gen. Musharraf reportedly pleaded with him to reach with Pakistan an agreement on co-operation in the development of civilian nuclear energy similar to the agreement offered to India. Mr. Bush had to point out to him that the needs and circumstances of the two countries are different.

These factors——feelings of insecurity, the inferiority complex and the Me-too syndrome—will continue to influence the Pakistani mind-set and policy-making in the short and medium terms. Though there has been progress in the identification and implementation of confidence-building measures and in the promotion of people-to-people contacts, the relationship between the two countries will continue to be fragile and the exploitation of the opportunities for beneficial co-operation provided by globalization will be slow.

While Pakistan's longing for the acquisition of J&K and its painful memories of 1971 could explain its attitude to India, no convincing explanation is possible for the behaviour of Bangladesh. While there are differences between India and Bangladesh over the utilization of river waters, there are no major differences over territory compared to the Kashmir issue with Pakistan and Bangladesh has no negative memories of India's military might in action against it. The anti-Indian reflexes in Bangladesh are largely confined to the present ruling formation headed by Begum Khalida Zia and are not shared by the opposition headed by the Awami League, which was in the forefront of its independence struggle.

India-Bangladesh relations will continue to zigzag—— improving when the Awami League is in power and stagnating, if not declining, when the Bangladesh National Party comes to power. Globalization has not made any significant difference to this zigzag and is unlikely to do so in the short and medium terms.

THE CHINA FACTOR

China is not a South Asian power, but it has acquired a significant South Asian presence, by skilfully exploiting the complexes and reflexes of the countries of the region vis-a-vis India. Amongst the steps it has taken to make its presence felt in this region are:

- The clandestine supply of nuclear and missile technologies to Pakistan, which might one day fall into the hands of Al Qaeda and other jihadi terrorist organizations should the jihadis capture power in Pakistan.
- Strengthening Pakistan's military capability in the Army, the Air Force and the Navy in order to reduce its feeling of insecurity vis-a-vis India.
- Strengthening Pakistan's strategic infrastructure through projects such as the construction of the Gwadar port on the Baloch coast and the Mekran Highway connecting Gwadar with Karachi.

- Strengthening Pakistan's IT capability.
- Strengthening Bangladesh's military capability.
- Helping Bangladesh in the development of its energy resources.
- The reported offer of assistance to Bangladesh for setting up facilities for research into the peaceful uses of nuclear energy.
- Reported military supplies to the royal regime in Nepal at a time when India has cut down its military supplies in view of the suppression of democracy by the King.
- Reported assistance to Sri Lanka for the development of the Hambantota port.

These developments are viewed by many analysts, including this writer, as an attempt to strengthen China's strategic presence and influence in the South Asian region. However, these perceptions, not invalid, have not been allowed to resurrect feelings of animosity between India and China. The border dispute between the two countries continues to remain under negotiations without any visible forward movement. At the same time, there have been significant gestures— —such as the Chinese recognition of Sikkim as a part of India and the bilateral agreement to resume border trade through the Sikkim sector.

The presence of the Dalai Lama and a large number of Tibetan refugees in the Indian territory and their activities— —perceived by Beijing as political behind a religious facade— continue to be a matter of concern to China, but these concerns are no longer articulated in strong language.

China has shown signs of being comfortable with the idea of India emerging as an important power, but it does not seem to be comfortable with the prospect of India emerging as a power on par with China.

This was evident from its strong opposition to India's aspirations of becoming a permanent member of the UN Security Council and its reticence on the question of the Nuclear Suppliers' Group (NSG) relaxing restrictions on the sale of civilian nuclear technology to India, despite India's initiative for separating its civilian nuclear establishments from its military and placing the former under international safeguards. It seems to be opposed to any unilateral concessions to India until such time when such concessions could be made applicable to Pakistan too.

Despite these factors, the trust deficit between India and China has steadily declined. India has been noting with not-openly-articulated concern the steady modernization of the Chinese Armed Forces and the growing Chinese military and economic linkages with the countries of South Asia, but it has not allowed this to come in the way of the steady improvement in the bilateral relations. At the same time, one has also noted the moderating role played by China during the military conflict in 1999 between India and Pakistan following Pakistani military intrusions in the Kargil sector of India's Jammu and Kashmir.

The leaderships of India and China have shown great political maturity in not allowing the continuing differences over the border come in the way of economic and other linkages. Bilateral trade has boomed during the last 10 years—increasing from a total of about US $ two billion to 13 billion. However, it needs to be underlined that this boom has been considerably due to the requirements of raw materials for the rapidly expanding Chinese industries— —particularly its steel industry.

Globalization and the consequent networking and interactions between the policy-makers and the business classes of the two countries have contributed to a remarkable resurgence of interest in each other and to a dilution of the mutual threat perceptions. Nobody in India, any longer, talks —at least openly—of China as a threat. In the past, China was viewed mainly as a worrisome power. Now its image is more positive. The remarkable change for the better in Indian threat perceptions of China is evident from the fact that the Indian intelligence and security establishment no longer opposes, as strongly as it used to do in the past, the presence of Chinese companies even in cities such as Bangalore, India's Silicon Valley, where many of India's sensitive defence and other strategic establishments are located.

The steady forward movement of India and China towards a common shared future of prosperity and mutual confidence can be endangered if the leaderships of the two countries do not skilfully manage the misgivings in China over the implications of the growing strategic partnership between the US and India to its aspired pre-eminence in Asia and the world and the likely tensions in Tibet, when the Dalai Lama ceases to be no more and the Chinese attempt to have their say, as they are bound to, in the selection of his successor. The continuously developing military, nuclear and other strategic linkages between China and Pakistan would remain a source of worry to Indian policy-makers and could stand in the way of the bilateral relations developing to their fullest potential.

THE PAKISTAN FACTOR

A reference has already been made to the Pakistan factor while discussing India-Pakistan relations. Two other aspects, which have not been touched upon earlier, need to be highlighted. The first relates to Pakistan's use of terrorism as a covert weapon to achieve its strategic objective of forcing a change in the status quo in Jammu and Kashmir. The second relates to its long-nourished objective of acquiring a strategic depth vis-a-vis India by bringing Afghanistan under its control and by establishing military and strategic linkages with Iran.

It was these objectives, which led Pakistan to set up a clandestine infrastructure not only in its territory, but also in Afghan territory for training and arming terrorists for use against India. It was from this infrastructure that Al Qaeda, the Taliban and the various terrorist organizations, which are members of the International Islamic Front (IIF) of bin Laden came. This infrastructure continues to function undisturbed creating national security problems not only for India and Afghanistan, but also for other countries.

Pakistan's strategic relationship with Iran, the foundations for which were laid by the late Zulfiquar Ali Bhutto and the Shah of Iran, led to the flow of funds from Iran for Pakistan's military nuclear programme to produce what was described as the world's first Islamic atomic bomb. The recent enquiries by the International Atomic Energy Agency (IAEA) of Vienna into Iran's clandestine nuclear programme have brought out the covert role of Dr. A. Q. Khan, the so-called father of Pakistan's Islamic bomb, in assisting Iran to become the world's second Islamic military nuclear power.

Will the so-called Islamic bomb developed by Pakistan with funds not only from Iran, but also from Saudi Arabia and Libya and any similar bomb developed by Iran with Pakistani complicity fall into the hands of Al Qaeda, the IIF and organizations such as the Lashkar-e-Toiba (LET) and become the world's first jihadi atomic bomb? It is fears caused by the spectre of a jihadi bomb in the hands of the terrorists that should explain India's vote in the IAEA in favour of a continued role by the Agency to pre-empt this danger. Afghanistan, a pre-2001 failed State, is yet to start benefiting from the fruits of globalization. India's efforts to develop trade links with Afghanistan and bring it into the global economic mainstream continue to be thwarted by Pakistan's refusal to grant Indian businessmen transit rights to Afghanistan through Pakistani territory.

The Non-state Actors

The US-orchestrated covert war against the Soviet troops in Afghanistan in the 1980s turned the region into a play ground for non-State actors of various hues, persuasions and motives——— jihadi and sectarian terrorists, trans-national crime mafia groups, narcotics producers and smugglers and money-laundering gangs. These non-State actors turned Afghanistan into a failed State and almost caused the collapse of the Pakistani economy before 2001.

The anti-communist jihadi terrorism of the 1980s gave place to the anti-modernisation terrorism of the 1990s personified by the Taliban, which, in turn, has given way to the revanchist terrorism of the present decade personified by Al Qaeda and the International Islamic Front (IIF). The recently in a keynote addresss to an international conference on terrorism organized the Intelligence Summit of Washington DC from February 18 to 20, 2006, Al Qaeda and the IIF are revanchist in character, medieval in their objectives and frighteningly modern in their methods of operation. Even more than four years after the so-called war on international terrorism was launched on October 7, 2001, the international community is not yet able to get the better of a determined, well-motivated and elusive enemy.

Two of the four epicenters of international jihadi terrorism are located in this area. The first is in the Waziristan area of Pakistan, from where Al Qaeda, the Taliban, the Islamic Movement of Uzbekistan (IMU), the Jundullah (Army of Allah) and the other components of the IIF are making a determined bid to stage a come-back in Afghanistan and Osama bin Laden is planning another 9/11 in US territory. This is also the epicenter from which the continuing use of terrorism against India is fuelled. The second epicenter is located in Bangladesh, which has become an alternate command and control for jihadi terrorists from the Harkat-ul-Jihad-al-Islami (HUJI) and the LET operating in Indian territory. The epicenter in Bangladesh has also serious implications for the future security and stability of Myanmar and Southern Thailand.

Narcotics production in Afghanistan has again increased significantly and the resulting cash flow has nullified any benefits to the war on terrorism from the campaign against terrorism funding mounted after 9/11 under the UN Security Council Resolution No.1373. There is no trust deficit coming in the way of networking and co-operation among the non-State actors. As a result, the non-State actors have benefited more than the State actors of the region from the fruits of networking, freer flow of human beings, the communications revolution and the innovations in science and technology. Al Qaeda and the IIF are making better use of the Internet than the State actors.

Globalization has given rise to two parallel trends towards a radicalization of sections of the youth of South Asia. The first trend is a radicalization of sections of the youth of all communities due to continuing economic and social disparities despite the growing economic prosperity. Uneven distribution of the newly-created wealth and opportunities is a major cause of this trend. There are more haves than in the past, but the number of have-nots is still very high and is more than the total population of many countries of the world. For example, in India, about 260 million people are still below the poverty line.

There has been an aggravation of the divide between the privileged and the under-privileged and of the feelings of relative deprivation among different layers of the society. The result: Ideology, which, according to conventional wisdom, should have become increasingly irrelevant in pragmatism-driven economies, has assumed a new relevance. One sees this in the resurgence and aggravation of ideological terrorism. Example—the Maoists of India and Nepal. The second trend is the growing radicalization of sections of the Muslim youth, more due to religious than economic reasons. Anger against the non-Muslims, who are projected as the enemies of Islam for allegedly committing various wrongs against the Muslims, has given rise to a new kind of terrorism personified by Al Qaeda and the International Islamic Front (IIF). Innovations in science and technology, knowledge of Information Technology and modern means of communication are sought to be used by the revanchist terrorist elements not as forces of creation, but of destruction, not to integrate, but to disintegrate.

The tensions caused by the old divide between the developed and the developing or the under-developed have been reduced, but the attempts by these elements to create a new divide between Islam and the rest have brought in new threats to peace, security and prosperity. As a result of these trends, dealing with threats to internal security has become an over-riding preoccupation of the states of the region, consuming a considerable proportion of their resources, time and attention. Linkages between sources of internal and external threats to security are stronger in the South Asian region than in any other region of Asia. Exploitation of internal tensions by external actors—State as well as non-State—for strategic reasons has come in the way of the region reaping the full benefits of the process of integration and globalization.

The result: Greater progress towards integration with the societies and economies of countries outside the region than of countries in the region. Example: the countries of the region moving closer to those of Southeast Asia, bilaterally as well as multilaterally, than to each other. There has been a positive change in the relations of the countries of the region with countries outside the region such as the US, China, Japan etc., but there has been little change in their relations with each other. Countries outside the region such as the USA, China and Japan are viewed with decreasing suspicion and increasing comfort. There is consequently a greater comfort level in the relations of the countries of this region with such powers outside the region.

However, there are incipient positive trends, which are having an impact on inter as well as intra-regional relationships, despite continuing inter-regional sources of discord. Example: Energy requirements driving India and Pakistan on the one side and India and China on the other towards solutions based on co-operation rather than competition in their energy quest. The likelihood of threats to regional and global trade has been driving the countries of Asia towards a search for co-operative counter-terrorism and maritime security initiatives and mechanisms. However, the persistence of traditional distrustful mindsets in the South Asian region makes the search for such co-operative security mechanisms fractional rather than well-integrated. Example: Pakistan's attempts to keep India out of the co-operative mechanisms in the Gulf area despite India's support for the association of Pakistan with the ASEAN Regional Forum. The trust deficit, which is a defining characteristic of the threat perceptions in the South Asian region, will continue to make the progress towards inter-regional integration slow and halting in the short and medium terms, but it is bound to acquire the needed momentum as the compulsions of economics acquire predominance over traditional sources of mistrust and discord.

SINO-INDIAN CONVERGENCE: BILATERAL AND GLOBAL

Bilateral relations between India and the People's Republic of China (PRC) have indeed come a long way after they touched their nadir in the immediate aftermath of India's nuclear tests in May 1998. China had been singled out as the "number one" security threat for India by India's Defence Minister just before the nuclear tests. After the tests, the Indian Prime Minister wrote to the US President justifying Indian nuclear tests as a response to the threat posed by China. Unsurprisingly, China reacted strongly and diplomatic relations between the two countries plummeted to an all time low.

However, some six years later, the relations between the two countries seem to be on an upswing. The visit of the Indian External Affairs Minister to China in 1999 marked the resumption of high-level dialogue and the two sides declared that they were not threats to each other. A bilateral security dialogue was also initiated that has helped the two countries in openly expressing and sharing their security concerns with each other. India and China also decided to expedite the process of demarcation of the Line of Actual Control (LAC) and the Joint Working Group (JWG) on the boundary question, set up in 1988, has been meeting regularly. As a first step in this direction, the two countries exchanged border maps on the least controversial middle sector of the LAC.

The Indian Prime Minister visited China in June 2003, the first such visit in a decade. The joint declaration signed during the visit stated that China was not a threat to India. The two states appointed special representatives in order to impart momentum to border negotiations that have lasted twenty two years, with the Prime Minister's principal secretary becoming India's political-level negotiator, replacing the India-China JWG. India and China also decided to hold their first joint naval exercise later in the year and discussions on joint air exercise continue. India also acknowledged China's sovereignty over Tibet and pledged not to allow "anti-China" political activities in India. On its part, China has acknowledged India's 1975 annexation of the former monarchy of Sikkim by agreeing to open a trading post along the border with the former kingdom and later rectified official maps to include Sikkim as part of India.

India and China have found substantial convergence of interests at the international level. Both share similar concerns about the growing international dominance of the US, the threat of terrorism disguised as religious and ethnic movements and the need to accord primacy to economic development. India and

China have both expressed concern about the US ' use of military power around the world and publicly opposed the war in Iraq. This was merely a continuation of the desire of both states to oppose the US *hyperpuissance* ever since the end of the Cold War.

Like other major powers in the international system, India and China favour a multi-polar world order where US unipolarity remains constrained by the other "poles" in the system. China and India zealously guard their national sovereignty and have been wary of US attempts to interfere in what they see as domestic affairs of other stares, be it Serbia, Kosovo or Iraq. Both took strong exception to the US air strikes on Iraq in 1998, the US-led air campaign against Yugoslavia in 1999, and more recently the US campaign against Saddam Hussein arguing that these violated the national sovereignty and undermined the authority of the United Nations system.

Both nations also favour more democratic international economic regimes. They have strongly resisted efforts by the US and other developed nations to link global trade to labour and environmental standards, realizing clearly that this would put them at a huge disadvantage vis-a-vis the developed world, thereby hampering their drive towards economic development, a top priority.

Both have committed themselves to crafting joint Sino-Indian positions in the World Trade Organization (WTO) and global trade negotiations in the hope that this might provide them greater negotiating leverage over the developed states. They would like to see further liberalization of agricultural trade in the developed countries, tightening of the rules on anti-dumping measures and ensuring that non-trade related issues such as labour and environment are not allowed to come to the WTO.

In recent years, India and China have attempted to build their bilateral relationship on the basis of their larger worldview of international politics. As they have found a distinct convergence of their interests on world stage, they have used it to strengthen their bilateral relations. They have established and maintained regular reciprocal high-level visits between political leaders. There has been a sincere attempt to improve trade relations and to compartmentalize intractable issues that make it difficult for their bilateral relationship to move forward.

India and China have strengthened their bilateral relationship in areas as distinct as cultural and educational exchanges, military exchanges, and science and technology cooperation. Bilateral trade has recorded rapid growth from a trade volume of US $265 million in 1991 to US $3596 million in 2001.

In 2001, bilateral trade saw an increase of 23.4 percent over 2000. It is expected to rise to $10 billion this year. The two nations are even evaluating the possibility of signing a comprehensive economic cooperation agreement and a free trade agreement by the end of this year, thereby building on strong complementarities between the two. Both states are also taking steps to upgrade their military-related cooperation, leading to greater understanding on the bilateral military front, something that would have been unthinkable just a few years ago.

As a first step in this direction, the Chinese and Indian navies carried out joint search and rescue operations off the Shanghai coast in November 2003. Both states are also seeking to cooperate on the nuclear front with China planning to import heavy water from India to be utilized in the pressurized heavy water reactors near Shanghai.

Many observers have also pointed out a subtle shift in Beijing's stance on Pakistan vis-a-vis India. China's "neutral" position during the Kargil conflict and the intense Indo-Pak crisis following the terrorist attack on the India's Parliament is seen by many as a reflection of China's sincerity in its attempts to improve ties. In keeping with China's attempts to project itself as a responsible regional player, China is seen by some as supporting peace and anti-terrorist efforts in South Asia by cooperating with the US and India. China is also seen as playing a central role in encouraging Pakistan to negotiate with India by using its leverage over Pakistan. After assuming office Prime Minister Manmohan Singh's government made it clear that it favoured closer ties with China and would continue to work towards improving bilateral relations with China. In his first address to the nation, the Prime Minister, Manmohan Singh, also emphasized the carrying forward of the process of further development and diversification of Sino-Indian relations. The late J.N. Dixit, National Security Advisor in the current government, wrote that "the Congress will continue the process of normalizing, strengthening and expanding India's relations with China, which is the most important factor affecting Asian security and stability". One of the first foreign visits of the new Indian foreign minister, Natwar Singh, was to China to attend the Asia Cooperation Dialogue in Qingdao, in East China's Shandong province and apparently had "substantive discussions" with his Chinese counterpart.

All this reflects on India continuing to build its relations with China on the convergence of interests that the two nations have achieved in recent years. Aside from the positive developments, one should not ignore the enormous obstacles that confront this bilateral relationship. There has been a dominant tendency in the Indian foreign policy establishment to focus on the strengths of its bilateral relations with China while pretending that problems confronting the relationship would somehow take care of themselves. The challenges in the Sino-Indian relationship are by no means insignificant nor will China take care of Indian interests. It is for India to recognize them for what they are and evolve a coherent strategy to tackle them.

3

Indo-Pakistan Conflict

HISTORY OF INDO-PAKISTANI WAR

After rumours that the Maharaja supported the annexation of Kashmir by India, militant Muslim revolutionaries from western Kashmir and Pakistani tribesmen made rapid advances into the Baramulla sector. Maharaja Hari Singh of Kashmir asked the government of India to intervene. However, India and Pakistan had signed an agreement of non-intervention. Although tribal fighters from Pakistan had entered Jammu and Kashmir, there was no iron-clad legal evidence to unequivocally prove that Pakistan was officially involved. It would have been illegal for India to unilaterally intervene in an open, official capacity unless Jammu and Kashmir officially joined the Union of India, at which point it would be possible to send in its forces and occupy the remaining parts.

The Maharaja desperately needed military assistance when the Pakistani tribals reached the outskirts of Srinagar. Before their arrival into Srinagar, India argued that the Maharaja must complete negotiations for ceding Jammu and Kashmir to India in exchange for receiving military aid. The agreement which ceded Jammu and Kashmir to India was signed by the Maharaja and Lord Mountbatten of Burma. In Jammu and Kashmir, National Conference volunteers worked with the Indian Army to drive out the Pakistanis.

The resulting war over Kashmir, the First Kashmir War, lasted until 1948, when India moved the issue to the UN Security Council.

Sheikh Abdullah was not in favour of India seeking UN intervention because he was sure the Indian Army could free the entire State of invaders. The UN had previously passed resolutions for setting up monitoring of the conflict in Kashmir. Following the set-up of the United Nations Military Observer Group in India and Pakistan (UNCIP), the UN Security Council passed Resolution 47 on 21 April 1948.

The resolution imposed an immediate cease-fire and called on the Government of Pakistan 'to secure the withdrawal from the state of Jammu and Kashmir of tribesmen and Pakistani nationals not normally resident therein who have entered the state for the purpose of fighting.' It also asked Government of India to reduce its forces to the minimum strength, after which the circumstances for holding a plebiscite should be put into effect 'on the question of Accession of the state to India or Pakistan.' However, both India and Pakistan failed to arrive at a Truce agreement due to differences in interpretation of the procedure for and extent of demilitarisation one of them being whether the Azad Kashmiri army is to be disbanded during the truce stage or the Plebiscite stage.

In November 1948, The Indian and Pakistani governments agreed to hold the plebiscite, but Pakistan did not withdraw its troops from Kashmir, thus violating the conditions for holding the plebiscite. In addition, the Indian Government distanced itself from its commitment to hold a plebiscite. India proposed that Pakistan withdraw all its troops first, calling it a precondition for a plebiscite. Pakistan rejected on the grounds that the Kashmiris may not vote freely given the presence of Indian army and Sheikh Abdullah's friendship with the Indian Prime Minister, Jawaharlal Nehru. However, Pakistan proposed simultaneous withdrawal of all troops followed by a plebiscite under international auspices, which India rejected. Hence Pakistan didn't withdraw its forces unilaterally In addition, the Indian Government distanced itself from its commitment to hold a plebiscite. Over the next several years, the UN Security Council passed four new resolutions, revising the terms of Resolution 47 to include a synchronous withdrawal of both Indian and Pakistani troops from the region, per the recommendations of General Andrew McNaughton. To this end, UN arbitrators put forward 11 different proposals for the demilitarization of the region. All of these were accepted by Pakistan, but rejected by the Indian government. The resolutions were passed by United Nations Security Council under Chapter VI of the United Nations Charter. Resolutions passed under Chapter VI of the UN charter are considered non-binding and have no mandatory enforceability, as opposed to the resolutions.

Sino-Indian War

In 1962, troops from the People's Republic of China and India clashed in territory claimed by both. China won a swift victory in the war, resulting in the Chinese annexation of the region called Aksai Chin, which has continued since then. Another smaller area, the Trans-Karakoram, was demarcated as the Line of Control (LOC) between China and Pakistan, although some of the territory on the Chinese side is claimed by India to be part of Kashmir. The line that separates India from China in this region is known as the "Line of Actual Control".

1965 and 1971 Wars

In 1965 and 1971, heavy fighting broke out again between India and Pakistan. The Indo-Pakistani War of 1971 resulted in the defeat of Pakistan and the Pakistani military's surrender in East Pakistan, leading to the creation of Bangladesh. The Simla Agreement was signed in 1972 between India and Pakistan. By this treaty, both countries agreed to settle all issues by peaceful means using mutual discussion in the framework of the UN Charter.

THE 1971 INDIA-PAKISTAN WAR

On the 3rd of December 1971, the Pakistani Air Force (PAF) struck a number of Indian airfields in northern India. By midnight, India was officially at war with Pakistan. Two weeks later, the war was over. The Indian Army had overrun erstwhile East Pakistan (Bangladesh) and taken 93,000 POWs. It was one of the swiftest military campaigns in recent history.

The Setting

The partition of the Indian Subcontinent in 1947 created two independent countries: India and Pakistan. India, which became independent on 15 August 1947, stood for a secular, equitable polity based on the universally accepted idea that all men are created equal and should be treated as such.

Pakistan, which officially came into existence a day earlier, was based on the premise that Hindus and Muslims of the Subcontinent constitute two different nationalities and cannot co-exist. The Partition created two different countries with most Muslim majority areas of undivided India going to the newly created nation, Pakistan (Land of the Pure).

Pakistan was originally made up of two distinct and geographically unconnected parts termed West and East Pakistan. West Pakistan was made up of a number of races including the Punjabis (the most numerous), Sindhis, Pathans, Balochis, Mohajirs (Muslim refugees from India) and others. East Pakistan, on the other hand, was much more homogeneous and had an overwhelming Bengali-speaking population.

The Roots of Discord

Although the Eastern wing of Pakistan was more populous than than the Western one, political power since independence rested with the Western elite. This caused considerable resentment in East Pakistan and a charismatic Bengali leader called, Sheikh Mujibur Rehman, most forcefully articulated that resentment by forming an opposition political party called the Awami League and demanding more autonomy for East Pakistan within the Pakistani Federation. In the Pakistani general elections held in 1970, the Sheikh's party won the majority of seats, securing a complete majority in East Pakistan. In all fairness, the Sheikh should have been Prime Minister of Pakistan, or at least the ruler of his province. But West Pakistan's ruling elite were so dismayed by the turn of events and by the Sheikh's demands for autonomy that instead of allowing him to rule East Pakistan, they put him in jail.

Origins of the Crisis

The dawn of 1971 saw a great human tragedy unfolding in erstwhile East Pakistan. Entire East Pakistan was in revolt. In the West, General Yahya Khan, who had appointed himself President in 1969, had given the job of pacifying East Pakistan to his junior, General Tikka Khan. The crackdown of 25 March 1971 ordered by Tikka Khan, left thousands of Bengalis dead and Sheikh Mujibur Rehman was arrested the next day. The same day, the Pakistani Army began airlifting two of its divisions plus a brigade strength formation to its Eastern Wing. Attempts to dis-arm Bengali troops were not entirely successful and within weeks of the 25 March massacres, many former Bengali officers and troops of the Pakistani Army had joined Bengali resistance fighters in different parts of East Pakistan.

The Pakistani Army conducted several crackdowns in different parts of Bangladesh, leading to massive loss of civilian life. The details of those horrific massacres, in which defenceless people were trapped and machine-gunned, is part of Bangladeshi history. Survivors compare it to the Nazi extermination of Jews. At the same time, the Pakistani Administration in Dhaka thought it could pacify the Bengali peasantry by appropriating the land of the Hindu population and gifting it to Muslims. While this did not impress the peasantry, it led to the exodus of more than 8 million refugees (more than half of them Hindus) to neighbouring India. West Bengal was the worst affected by the refugee problem and the Indian government was left holding the enormous burden. Repeated appeals by the Indian government failed to elicit any response from the international community and by April 1971, the then Indian Prime Minister, Mrs. Indira Gandhi, decided that the only solution lay in helping Bengali freedom fighters, especially the Mukti Bahini, to liberate East Pakistan, which had already been re-christened Bangladesh by its people.

Pakistan felt it could dissuade India from helping the Mukti Bahini by being provocative. The Pakistan Air Force (PAF) in East Pakistan took to attacking suspected Mukti Bahini camps located inside Indian territory in the state of West Bengal. In the Western and Northern sectors too occasional clashes, some of them quite bloody, took place.

Pakistan was suggesting that should India continue with its plans it should expect total war as in 1965. Only this time, the Pakistanis would concentrate their forces in the West and thereby aim at capturing as much as Indian territory as possible. The Indians, on the other hand, would be fighting a war on two fronts (while at the same time keeping a fearful eye on the Chinese borders). Given this scenario, the Pakistanis felt that India at best would be able to capture some territory in East Pakistan and lose quite a bit in the West. In the end, the Pakistanis knew that the Western powers would intervene to stop the war and what would matter is who had the most of the other's territory.

Confident that another war would be as much of a stalemate as the 1965 Conflict, the Pakistanis got increasingly bold and finally on 3 December 1971 reacted with a massive co-ordinated air strike on several Indian Air Force stations in the West. At midnight, the Indian Prime Minister Mrs. Indira Gandhi in a broadcast to the nation declared that India was at war with Pakistan. As her words came on in million of Indian homes across the Subcontinent, the men at the front were already engaged in bitter combat...

PAF Strikes

For all practical purposes, the war started at about 5:40 pm on 3 December when Pakistan Air Force (PAF) combat aircraft struck nine Indian airfields along the Western borders. The air strikes were followed by a massive attack on the strategic Chhamb sector in the north. In the East, it was the Indian Army which went on the offensive. By late that night, artillery shells were raining down all along the Western and Eastern borders. India and Pakistan were locked in a two-front war.

In the West, the Indian Army had very limited offensive aims and was relegated more to a holding role. The initiative lay with Pakistan. In this theatre, Pakistan had near parity with India in armour and artillery while India had more infantry divisions. Pakistan's most successful thrust was in Chhamb where the 23rd

Pakistani Division (along with two additional infantry brigades, one extra armoured brigade and Corps artillery units) under the able leadership of Major General Iftikhar Khan completely overwhelmed the forward defensive positions of the Indian 10 Division commanded by Major General Jaswant Singh.

Chhamb village was taken and the Pakistanis threatened to advance towards Jammu, the summer capital of the state of Jammu & Kashmir. Heavy fighting continued in this sector for a week until the indecisiveness of the Indian Divisional commander forced the Indian Corps Commander to intervene personally and launch heavy attacks to push the Pakistanis back to a non-threatening position. The Pakistanis surprisingly failed to take advantage of their initial successes in this sector and actually depleted the forces available to their commander, who was killed on 10 December in a helicopter crash. Acting in accordance with its strategy to grab as much territory in the West as possible, Pakistan also launched a major attack on Punch in the state of Jammu & Kashmir. This attack, unlike the one on Chhamb, was completely repulsed, although here the Indian Army was at a locational disadvantage since the Pakistanis controlled the heights around the town. Smaller attacks were launched by Pakistan in Punjab at Fazilka and Hussainiwala. Here the forward Indian defences were breached but the Pakistani Army could not sustain its attacks. A more ambitious armoured thrust in the deserts of Rajasthan was similarly stopped in the famous Battle of Longewal. In all, it appeared that the Pakistani military high command could not make up its mind as to where it should deliver its main punch and kept pulling back until it was too late.

The Indian Army chief, General Sam Maneckshaw, had a completely different set of problems. His strategy had to take into account the Chinese, with whom the Indian Army had fought a full blown war only nine years earlier. The Chinese were now firm Pakistani allies and had been making threatening noises ever since India resolved to intervene in the East Pakistan issue. General Maneckshaw, despite the disappointment of his Corps and divisional commanders, had to hold back his Army in the West, keep a watchful eye on the long and difficult Chinese borders and, at the same time, ensure that his Eastern Army secured its objective of grabbing a good chunk of East Pakistani territory within 2 to 3 weeks. The Indian aim was to install a Bangladeshi interim government in East Pakistani territory before the cessation of hostilities. It was not all clear in the beginning whether things would work out quite the way as planned.

INDIA AND PAKISTAN-NUCLEAR STATES IN CONFLICT

When the British withdrew from the Indian subcontinent after the second world war, it was divided, primarily on religious grounds, into the two states of India and Pakistan. At that time Kashmir was included in India, but the issue of which state it should belong to has been contested ever since, largely because Kashmir's population is predominantly Muslim. In 1947 a United Nations resolution called for a referendum in Kashmir to settle the issue on the basis of what the people wanted. It was, however never carried out and it is generally assumed that the reason for this is because the Indian government feared the popular vote would support unification with Pakistan on religious grounds. Many in Kashmir campaign for independence, a position that neither India nor Pakistan supports.

Around 30,000 people have died in Kashmir in the last 11 years. What happens in Kashmir is at the heart of the continuing tension between India and Pakistan. The possibility of the world's first direct war between two nuclear-armed states occurring is very real. The history of the conflict over Kashmir is well documented with three India/Pakistan wars taking place since 1947. But this time it would be with both sides having access to nuclear weapons. Since the attack on the Indian Parliament building in December 2001, the tension and rhetoric have grown considerably. India accused Pakistan of supporting terrorist groups. Pakistan, in turn, pledges its support for Kashmiri freedom fighters. One state's terrorist is another's freedom fighter. Since the attack in December, Pakistan has arrested around 1500 'militants' and banned five groups, two said to be sectarian, one pro-Taliban and two who have been fighting Indian rule in Kashmir. However, Gen Musharraf has pledged continued support for Kashmir.

Many people living along the border close to Kashmir have fled the area due to the large military presence being built up by both sides. From the end of 2001 there were clashes virtually every night in that border region, with sometimes one or two people being shot. There are claims that large numbers of military silos have been destroyed. In an atmosphere of increased tension and sabre-rattling rhetoric on both sides, this led to the situation in May 2002 where upwards of a million troops were gathered near the border. Any mistake or small incident runs the risk of setting off something far, far worse.

Nuclear Numbers

Estimates on actual warhead numbers vary wildly with reports that India has anywhere between 50-150 warheads and Pakistan 10-100. There is a bit more clarity, however, regarding the missile systems that would deliver them.

India:

Agni (Intermediate Range Ballistic Missile), nuclear capable and tested.

Range: 1,500 miles.

Could reach Karachi in about 14 minutes.

Prithvi (Surface to Surface Missile), nuclear capable and deployed.

Range: 90-220 miles.

Could reach Islamabad or Lahore within three minutes.

Trishul (Surface to Surface Missile), nuclear capable.

Range: 6 miles.

Pakistan:

Ghauri (Intermediate Range Ballistic Missile), nuclear capable in production.

Range: 930 miles

Could reach Bombay in 10 minutes.

One medium-range and one short-range missile, both nuclear capable, were tested in May 2002.

The Current Situation

All this, of course, is fuelled by the continuing rhetoric on both sides. Officials in both countries claimed that they would not use nuclear weapons first, but they seem remarkably keen to use them second. Given the proximity of the two states, it is clear that millions of their own people would die along with millions of their nearest neighbours. India has said that it would not use nuclear weapons first, while Pakistan has clearly stated that it would. Whilst a 'no first use' policy is an important step towards disarmament, it is all too often used as an excuse to build a large 'second use' capacity. Eventually, of course, the 'second use' becomes indistinguishable from the 'first use'. As the tension mounts, the temptation grows to get your retaliation in first. But what are the immediate reasons for the current increasing tension and the risk of war? India appears to be escalating events but its argument is that it is following the lead of the US and the west by zero tolerance of terrorist attacks. It has identified what it sees as terrorists being harboured by another state so it threatens military retaliation.

Both sides have had internal problems as well. In Pakistan, Musharraf has been promising a democratic election ever since the army took control, but there has been only a referendum. Though it was boycotted by many political parties, Musharraf claimed it as a mandate for him to continue. Meanwhile in India, the ruling BJP has lost every state election for over a year, so now uses the well-known tactic of uniting the country against an outside 'threat'. Whatever the reasons for the tensions, the crucial aim is to avoid the devastation of nuclear war.

The British Prime Minister, Tony Blair, visited the region in January 2002 to try to persuade both sides that a war was not a good idea. This took place against the background of the bombing in Afghanistan, in which Britain was an enthusiastic participant. His approach raised concerns about Western hypocrisy, as if war is fine for some countries but not others. The sincerity of Blair's mission was also in question after it transpired that his plea for peace preceded two British trade missions to Delhi in February, both designed to sell weapons to India. Defexpo is an arms fair whose promotional material pushes the weaponry on sale, with everything from small arms to missile systems. India and Pakistan have long been valuable markets for British arms manufacturers. So this arms fair, combined with the resumption of arms sales to Pakistan, as a result of its support for the war in Afghanistan, means that Britain will be arming both sides in any future war. This is, of course, not unique. A similar thing happened during the Iraq-Iran war.

So, what's the answer? The situation in south Asia shows the importance of nuclear disarmament. A war even with conventional weapons would be an appalling waste of life. But this would be turned into a complete disaster on an unimaginable scale if nuclear weapons were used. In the short term there must be more diplomatic language and there must be proper international negotiations at the UN to resolve the problem of Kashmir. Our own politicians could do more to help. How can the British Government's attempts to calm the situation be taken seriously when the Defence Minister, Geoff Hoon, appears on television saying that he would use nuclear weapons against any state if necessary? In the long term, the declared nuclear weapon states (NWS)-US, UK, France, Russia and China-must carry out their obligations under the nuclear Non-Proliferation Treaty (NPT) and get rid of their nuclear weapons. The NPT was drawn up in 1968, giving the definition of a NWS as one that tested nuclear weapons before then. Because India was preparing its nuclear programme at that time, it would not sign. Because India would not sign, neither would Pakistan. Therefore, they cannot sign the NPT as NWS and, since the nuclear testing by both sides in 1998, they cannot sign as non-nuclear weapon states. The NWS made statements at the time of the tests saying how appalled they were at this development. But after 11 September, the US lifted sanctions imposed on both sides, in order to boost its coalition in the 'War on Terrorism'.

If the NWS put the words of the NPT into action, they would be in a position to push India and Pakistan to sign the NPT themselves. After all, part of the excuse given by India and Pakistan for the 1998 nuclear tests was that those nuclear weapon states had done nothing about their NPT commitments, so if nuclear weapons were good enough for them...

Both sides need to be persuaded that nuclear weapons make the world a more dangerous, not a safer, place and to take a step back and realise that peaceful resolutions to conflict are the best way forward. This should happen through the UN. But the UN also needs to look at the continuing nuclear policies of the NWS. There are peace activists in both India and Pakistan working hard to get their views across. Their work has been particularly difficult since the nuclear tests carried out by both countries in 1998. They have the entire might of the government and military propaganda machine ranged against them. We should do all we can to support them.

UNITED STATES' ROLE AND INFLUENCE ON THE INDIA-PAKISTAN CONFLICT

Although the Soviet Union played a critical role in formally ending the second India-Pakistan war in 1965—through the Tashkent Declaration—its close military and security relationships with Delhi during much of the Cold War years decreased its influence over Islamabad, which became increasingly linked to the United States for the supply of arms. China's discreet missile and nuclear linkages with Islamabad, along with memories of the India-China border war of 1962, precluded Beijing's influence over the India-Pakistan dispute. Despite an apparent shift in Beijing's position since 1996 (especially during the Kargil conflict in 1999 when it refrained from publicly supporting Pakistan, and due to its concerns over Islamist extremists in Xinjiang province), elements of future India-China competition make it difficult for Beijing to influence Delhi. While French, European Union or Japanese influence appear limited, a potential British role exists only alongside the United States, with the latter doing much of the 'heavy lifting'. Notwithstanding Washington's unprecedented and simultaneous influence over both Delhi and Islamabad, the nature and extent of its future engagement in the India-Pakistan conflict remains unclear.

Kashmir Dispute

In view of India's asymmetrical relationship with Pakistan—population, size, economic strength and relative military power—Delhi has invariably resisted the role of a third party or the United Nations in its conflict with Pakistan; it is precisely for these reasons that Islamabad has favoured such a role, with the hope that 'internationalization' would provide a favourable resolution of the Kashmir dispute. India's disillusionment with the international community over Kashmir began soon after Independence, when Prime Minister Jawaharlal Nehru took Pakistan's aggression against India in Kashmir to the United Nations on 1 January 1948. Instead of being seen as the aggrieved party, losing Indian territory to an armed attack by Pakistan—following the signing of the Instrument of Accession by the Hindu ruler of the predominantly Muslim province of Jammu and Kashmir on 26 October 1947—India became a party to the dispute. Subsequent UN Security Council resolutions advocating the future of Kashmir on the basis of a UN-mandated plebiscite—after the withdrawal of armed forces by both countries from divided Kashmir—were ignored by Delhi, as was the United Nations force, the UN Military Observer Group in India and Pakistan (UNMOGIP). Since the UN-sponsored ceasefire to the first India-Pakistan war over Kashmir on 1 January 1949, UNMOGIP has been deployed to monitor the ceasefire line—currently, the Line of Control (LoC) (the *de facto* border dividing Indianand Pakistan-administered Kashmir).

For Islamabad, however, the UN Security Council resolutions on Kashmir boosted its position on Kashmir, and justified its stance that it was a territorial dispute between the two sides. This contradicted Delhi's view that Kashmir was 'not a disputed territory', with the only point of contention being Pakistan's 'illegal occupation of a portion of the state', fortified by a Parliamentary resolution to this effect in the early 1990s. Even though it was clear that neither Pakistan nor India were inclined to withdraw forces from divided Kashmir, Islamabad was not averse to using UN Security Council resolutions on a plebiscite in Kashmir for political purposes.

However, Indian and Pakistani positions on a plebiscite and the status of Kashmir appeared to change in December 2003-January 2004. In an interview with Reuters in mid-December 2003, Pakistan's President Musharraf, in a bold move, publicly offered to drop Pakistan's traditional demand for a UN plebiscite in Kashmir, and meet India 'half-way' in a bid to resolve the Kashmir dispute. Musharraf reportedly stated, '... we are for the United Nations Security Council resolutions whatever it stands for. However, now we have left that aside'. Although this was subsequently denied by Pakistani officials, it was clear that this was simply a recognition that a UN plebiscite could never have been implemented, in view of Indian and Pakistani intransigence. Yet, it had been a major irritant to Delhi, which welcomed Musharraf's statement. Subsequently, in the joint press statement of 6 January 2004, following the meeting between Indian Prime Minister Vajpayee and Musharraf, on the sidelines of the twelfth South Asian Association for Regional Cooperation (SAARC) Summit in Islamabad, Delhi implicitly agreed that Kashmir was disputed territory, by explicitly agreeing that Kashmir was to be settled 'to the satisfaction of both sides'.

'Third Party' Involvement in War

Notwithstanding India's aversion to a 'third party' (including UN) role in its dispute over Kashmir, this did not apply to assistance in formally ending wars, or in the 1990s, preventing the outbreak of full-fledged conventional war. The second India-Pakistan war in 1965, for example, ended with a UN Security Council-sponsored ceasefire on 23 September 1965. Three months later, Indian Prime Minister Lal Bahadur Shastri and Pakistani President Mohammed Ayub Khan met in Tashkent and signed an agreement to formalize the end of the war and the withdrawal of their armed forces to positions held prior to 5 August 1965. The erstwhile Soviet-brokered 'Tashkent Agreement' of 10 January 1966 also pledged continued negotiations and the observation of ceasefire terms on the ceasefire line.

During this period, American policy towards South Asia remained fairly ambivalent, although an attempt at engagement on the Kashmir dispute had been made during the Eisenhower Administration in the 1950s. Although the Kennedy Administration was able to initiate direct negotiations between India and Pakistan—in the aftermath of the 1962 India-China war, the talks failed; by the mid-1960s the United States had virtually given up on Kashmir. During the 1971 India-Pakistan war, the United States 'tilt' towards Pakistan—through the deployment of an aircraft carrier task force in the Bay of Bengal in the midst of the war—whatever its intent or purpose—made it difficult for India, among other reasons, to develop a satisfactory 'comfort level' with the United States on security issues. Despite American economic and military sanctions on Pakistan in 1979 in an attempt to stem its covert nuclearweapons programme, Pakistan's role as a front-line state against the Soviet occupation of Afghanistan in the 1980s alleviated this situation. The demise of the former Soviet Union, along with India's economic liberalization in the aftermath of the 1991 economic crisis, began to lead to more favourable Indo-American relations.

In the late 1990s, high publicity American engagement with South Asia took place on nuclear issues, sparked off by multiple Indian and Pakistani nuclear tests in May 1998. On 11 and 13 May 1998, India carried out a series of five underground nuclear tests, twenty-four years after its first 'peaceful nuclear explosion' on 18 May 1974. This was promptly followed by six Pakistani nuclear tests on 28 and 30 May 1998. Although the immediate American reaction was to impose economic and military-related sanctions on both India and Pakistan, their respective importance in United States foreign policy soon generated less coercive measures to counter proliferation. In a significant development, within the Lahore Memorandum of Understanding (MoU), both countries agreed to develop confidence-building measures (CBMs) in the nuclear and conventional fields aimed at the avoidance of conflict within nine months of the nuclear tests. The Lahore documents—signed at the Summit between Vajpayee and Pakistani Prime Minister Nawaz Sharif in Lahore—appeared to provide the momentum towards enhanced and formalized nuclear stability in South Asia.

American facilitation in the Kargil Conflict, 1999

Unfortunately, the Lahore framework remains unimplemented, with the single exception of advanced notification of ballistic missile flight tests on a unilateral basis—in the 'spirit' of the Lahore MoU—although this has generated its own share of controversy over the years. Pakistan's military intrusion across the LoC, allegedly at the time of the Lahore Summit, effectively ended all moves towards regional nuclear stability. Instead, India and Pakistan were involved in an armed conflict with each other for the first time after their nuclear tests; the Kargil conflict of May-July 1999 formally ended with United States facilitation.

In early 1999, Pakistan's regular and irregular forces crossed the LoC and occupied positions in the Kargil sector of Indian-administered Jammu and Kashmir, for reasons that are as yet unclear. When this was detected in early May 1999, Delhi's response was swift and comprehensive, involving the use of land and air forces to evict the intruders from the Indian side of the LoC. After several weeks of increasingly bloody conflict, Indian forces captured the key heights of Tololing (14 June) and Tiger Hill (early morning on 4 July). With Pakistani forces suffering critical defeats, it was expected to be only a matter of time before they were pushed back across the LoC; but, undoubtedly this would have raised Indian casualties further.

Meanwhile, the United States was urging Pakistan to respect the LoC and withdraw its forces across the LoC, while at the same time, urging India to restrain itself from crossing the LoC to open another front in the conflict. Notwithstanding Delhi's public statements on not using force across the LoC, the potential for escalation into a full-scale conventional war raised fears in the international community of the risk of inadvertent nuclear escalation. In early July, the Pakistani Prime Minister flew to Washington, concerned over Pakistan's increasing international isolation. At a hastily organized meeting with President Clinton on 4 July, Sharif requested American intervention to stop the fighting and resolve the Kashmir issue. But Clinton came down heavily on Sharif, and told him that a clear Pakistani withdrawal to the LoC was essential. Clinton also told Sharif that Pakistan was preparing its nuclear arsenal for possible deployment at the instructions of the Army Chief, General Musharraf, which was apparently taking place without Sharif's knowledge. Amidst considerable American pressure, Sharif finally agreed 'to take concrete and immediate steps for the restoration of the LoC', which was accepted by Vajpayee when it was conveyed to him prior to its publicization. In effect, the United States facilitated a formal end to the Kargil conflict, which shortly afterwards saw the withdrawal of all Pakistani forces to its own side of the LoC without many additional Indian casualties. American facilitation on the Kargil conflict—in Delhi's favour— came as quite an unexpected surprise to many in India's Ministries of External Affairs and Defence. This was, in effect, the first time in fifty years that the United States had sided with India against Pakistan 'openly and firmly'. This soon led to a greater 'comfort level' with the United States, followed by Clinton's successful visit to India in March 2000, followed by Vajpayee's visit to the United States in the final days of the Clinton Administration.

American facilitation in the India-Pakistan Border Confrontation, 2001–2002

Even though the United States became involved in resolving the Kargil conflict, it is the Americanled war on terror in South Asia and the subsequent India-Pakistan border confrontation that has brought about a significant change in American engagement in South Asia. Following the American attack against Afghanistan in October 2001—targeting the terrorist Al-Qaeda leadership responsible for the attacks on the United States and their Taliban hosts—Pakistan became a frontline state for American logistics support and intelligence facilities in Afghanistan. A number of American military personnel and equipment also remain deployed in Pakistani military bases in support of the ongoing war on terror in Afghanistan.

However, the attack on the Indian Parliament on 13 December 2001—allegedly by Pakistanbased Jaish-e-Mohammed terrorists—threatened to disrupt the ongoing American-led military campaign in Afghanistan. As part of its 'coercive diplomacy' against Pakistan, Delhi launched 'Operation Parakram' ('valour') on 19 December 2001, which constituted the largest mobilization of the Indian armed forces. This was a deliberate move, taking place amidst the war on terror, to threaten military action against Pakistan if its demands to end alleged Pakistan-sponsored cross-border terrorism were not met.

This included the deployment of India's three strike corps (comprising armoured and mechanized formations) at forward positions on the international border with Pakistan. With Pakistan's countermobilization, nearly one million armed personnel were deployed across the India-Pakistan borders. In view of the nuclear-armed status of both states, there appeared to be considerable risk of nuclear escalation—by misperception or miscalculation—following the break-out of a conventional war. On 20 March 2002, the Director of the Central Intelligence Agency (CIA), George Tenet, warned the United States Senate Armed Services Committee that the chances of a war in the region were the highest since 1971.

Having repeatedly stressed the sanctity of the LoC during the Kargil war, India's prospective actions—threatening the use of force across the LoC—set off alarm bells in Washington and London. Meanwhile, Pakistan appeared equally determined to counter an Indian military attack with conventional and nuclear forces. With the deliberate disruption of normal diplomatic communication, Delhi and Islamabad were communicating with each other on nuclear and conventional matters on a public basis during much of the ten months of the 2001–2002 border confrontation.

These nuclear signals were multiple in nature, carried out at multiple levels, and addressed to multiple constituencies—internal, regional and international. For both India and Pakistan, the most important constituencies were the domestic public, each other and the United States, which had the most influence in the region. For Delhi, the United States could help put pressure on Pakistan to cease cross-border infiltration of militants into Indian-administered Kashmir; for Islamabad, the United States could restrain Delhi from military action.

With tensions heightening following the terrorist attack on an Indian Army residential camp in Kaluchak, Jammu, on 14 May 2002, and Delhi's subsequent nuclear signalling, a flurry of high-level American and British choreographed visits took place to Delhi and Islamabad. The contours of a possible easing of India-Pakistan tensions began to emerge from Jack Straw's visit at the end of May. On 28 May, Straw visited Islamabad, where he urged Musharraf to take action on the ground to counter cross-border 'terrorism' in Indian-administered Kashmir. In Delhi the next day, Straw urged India to exercise restraint and prevent its armed forces from using force across the LoC. He also told Delhi that Musharraf had promised to curb infiltration into India and to close down 'terrorist' camps in Pakistan-administered Kashmir by the time of Armitage's visit to the region in early June. On his return to London on 31 May, Straw publicly expressed his concern over the 'dangerous situation' in the region, 'when you have one million men under arms on either side of the LoC, all in a high state of alert and readiness, both countries have nuclear weapons, and one of them—Pakistan— has said they reserve the right to use them first'. This essentially signalled the issue of travel advisories on 1 June by the Governments of the United States, the United Kingdom, Canada, France, Japan, Australia, New Zealand and others, urging their citizens to leave India and Pakistan immediately, and warned others from travelling to either country. The travel advisories led to an exodus of business visitors, tourists, diplomatic personnel and their dependants, largely from India, as they had already pulled out from Pakistan earlier. Ostensibly ordered for fear of an outbreak of war, this unprecedented step caused much annoyance in Delhi, which perceived it as an attempt to pressure it against launching an attack across the LoC.

On 31 May, United States Secretary of State Colin Powell publicly criticized Pakistan for the 'continuing' infiltration across the LoC, despite Musharraf's assurances that it would be ended. The following day, in an interview with the BBC, Musharraf indicated that 'instructions' had been given by Pakistan to cease such activity. Although it was still too early to say that it had stopped, Powell emphasised that '... when, and if, it does stop, it must also stop permanently'. On 6 June, United States Deputy Secretary of State Richard Armitage arrived in Islamabad to build on Straw's visit, and hammer out a deal between India and Pakistan. After a tough meeting, Musharraf gave Armitage a commitment that he would end cross-border infiltration 'permanently'. This was a considerable improvement on his pledge to Straw a week earlier to curb infiltration into India. While Delhi formally welcomed this development, it expressed caution in terms of implementation. Consequently, Armitage described India-Pakistan tensions as 'a bit down on both sides'. Within days of Armitage's departure from Delhi, the thaw in India-Pakistan tensions was evident. In effect, American facilitation successfully eased India-Pakistan tensions, and ended the ten-month border confrontation—the longest period of military mobilization between the two countries.

India-Pakistan Joint Press Statement, 6 January 2004

In a dramatic development on the sidelines of the twelfth SAARC Summit in Islamabad in January 2004, India and Pakistan agreed to resume an official-level dialogue after a three-year hiatus. The Joint Statement of 6 January 2004 also noted that Delhi agreed to settle Kashmir 'to the satisfaction of both sides', and that Islamabad would not permit 'any territory under Pakistan's control to be used to support terrorism in any manner'.

On 18 February 2004, after three days of official-level 'talks on talks' in Islamabad, India and Pakistan agreed to resume their bilateral 'composite dialogue' in May– June 2004, soon after the Indian general elections. This is to take the form of a 'composite dialogue' on eight issues, including two—on 'peace and security, including CBMs' and 'Jammu and Kashmir'— at the Foreign Secretary-level. The two foreign ministers are to meet in August 2004 to review progress. Both Delhi and Islamabad had strong motivations to reach an accord during the SAARC Summit. For Vajpayee, a personal desire for a stable bilateral relationship with Pakistan—his third and final peace effort—had been initiated with his 'hand of friendship' speech in Srinagar in April 2003, and buttressed by approaching general elections in April 2004; for

Musharraf, two assassination attempts within eleven days in December 2003 had led to a renewed vigour to fight terrorism of all kinds, along with the increasing radicalization of domestic politics.

Vajpayee's rising popularity, seen by the results of the Indian assembly elections in November 2003, also boosted Islamabad's view that it would be advisable to deal with Vajpayee himself. In addition, American pressure on Islamabad to end cross-border infiltration into Indianadministered Kashmir, and to a lesser extent on India—to begin an official-level dialogue with Pakistan— may also have played a part in the success of bilateral diplomacy on the sidelines of the multilateral summit. Even if the United States had facilitated such a dialogue, it would have been advisable to have maintained this in a low-key manner, for fear of undermining the fledgling peace process.

THE KASHMIRI REVOLUTION INTENSIFIES – INDO-PAK CONFLICT

In the midst of the Kashmir Muslim insurgency, tensions between India and Pakistan became so intense that in May 1990, the Pakistani military headed by General Mirza Aslam Beg was willing to use nuclear weapons to "take out New Delhi." It was President Bush's National Security Advisor Robert Gates and Assistant Secretary for Middle Eastern and South Asian Affairs who reportedly helped arrest a deadly encounter between them by visiting India and Pakistan. The two countries, however, increased their exchange of cross-border firing along the LOC. Prime Minister Benazio Bhutto, who was dismissed in the summer of 1990 by Pakistan's President Ghulam Iushaq Khan at the prompting of the military, took a hostile stance toward India to appease the Khan (which she admitted in June 1999) after she was reelected in October 1993. She called India an "imperialistic power and aggressor" in Kashmir. Despite these hostile relations, India and Pakistan held several rounds of talks at foreign secretary levels between 1990 and January 1994, but without any results as they took irreconcilable positions on Kashmir. For example, Pakistan insisted that India stop its counter-insurgency operations, while India insisted that that the talks should focus on Pakistan's cross border aid to the Muslim militants. Following Bhutto second dismissal by President Farooq Leghari, at the orders of the military, Nawaz Sharif took office as Prime Minister in February 1997. Indo-Pak relations temporarily thawed. In March of that year, for example, a dialogue at foreign secretary level was resumed. In April, Pakistani Foreign Minister Gohar Ayub Khan met India's Prime Minister, I.K. Gujral, at the Non-Aligned Movement (NAM) meeting in New Delhi, and in May, the two Prime Ministers met at the South Asian Association of Regional Cooperation (SAARC) summit held at Male, the foreign secretary level but also to form eight joint "working groups" that would look at, for the first time since 1972, the Kashmir issue. Subsequently, by September, foreign secretaries held three meetings despite of artillery exchanges at a number of points along the LOC. In September, the Prime Ministers met again in New York when they attended the UN General Assembly session. This situation, however, changed after the March 1998 parliamentary elections when the BJP-dominated United Front won the election and formed a coalition government that took a hard stand against Pakistan. The Home Minister, L. K. Advani, of the new government threatened to go after the terrorists even into the Pakistan-occupied Kashmir. Indo-Pakistani tensions increased following the nuclear testing in May 1998. This also caused concerns in the international community that the Kashmir conflict would become a catalyst for war that would include the use of nuclear weapons by both countries.

Both countries were severely condemned by the international community and the U.S., Japan, and some European countries imposed sanctions. Following mutual testing, the tempers of both countries were so high that on July 29, when Vajpayee and Sharif met at the tenth summit of the SAARC held in Columbo, Sri Lanka, the encounter failed to break new ground.

Sharif insisted that no progress was possible between the two countries unless the "core issue" of Kashmir was resolved. He characterized the meeting as "zero" and warned that India's "intransigence" was pushing the region to the brink of war. India's foreign secretary, K. Raghunath, responded by terming Pakistan's obsessive focus on the single issue of Kashmir as "neurotic" and that serious dialogue should not be used to "pursue a limited agenda or promote a propagandist exercise."

Intense hostility along the LOC at that same time left contrast, when they met on September 23, for the second time at the UN General Assembly session, in New York, there was a dramatic change in the tenor of their encounter. It was friendly and they agreed to try to resolve the Kashmir issue "peacefully" and to focus on trade and people to people contact. For example, India agreed to buy sugar and powder from Pakistan. After a decade of absence, Pakistan's cricket team visited India in November 1998. In February 1999, Pakistan allowed India to run buses from New Delhi to Lahore and following an invitation by Sharif, Vajpayee visited Lahore. His visit is commonly known as bus diplomacy and at the end of their summit they issued the Lahore Declaration that was backed up by a clearly spelled out Memorandum of Understanding (MOU). In the MOU the leaders agreed to engage in consultations on security matters, to include nuclear doctrines, to initiate confidence-building measures in both nuclear and conventional areas, and to establish appropriate communications mechanisms to help diminish the possibility of nuclear war by accident or misinterpretation. They also agreed to continue their respective moratoriums on further nuclear tests unless their "supreme national interest" was in jeopardy. This declaration, however, was not well received by some elements of the Pakistani military branch including General Musharraf. The Pakistani military provoked a mini war called the Kargil war within the India-occupied Kashmir, during May to July 1999 that undermined the Indo-Pak relations.

THE KARGIL WAR AND ITS COLLISION ON INDO-PAK RELATIONS

The euphoria that followed the February Lahore Declarations by India and Pakistan abruptly dissipated when nearly 1500 Pakistan-backed Muslim militants known miles into the India-held Kargil region of North Kashmir. The militants who were mostly Afghanis together with Pakistani regulars, occupied more than 30 well-fortified positions located atop the most inhospitable frigidly cold ridges, at 16,000 and 18,000 feet above sea level, in the Great Himalayan range facing Dras, Kargil, Batalik, and the Mushko Valley sectors stretching covering over 30 miles. Indian army patrols, between May 8 and 15 detected and came in contact with the militants and on May 26, India launched air attacks known as Operation Vijay (victory) against the bunkers from which the intruders had been firing upon the Indian troops below the ridges. On May 27, two MIG aircrafts were shot down. One pilot was taken prisoner of war (POW) and the other killed. On May 28, a MI-17 helicopter was shot down and the four-man crew killed. As the battle raged on between May 31 and June 11, Indian troops were able to clear up some pockets of resistance and to cut off the supply lines to the intruders by outflanking them. They also launched a major offensive in the Kargil Drass sector accompanied by air strikes on June 6, in order to protect the only highway linking Srinagar to Leh in Ladakh region from Pakistani threat. On June 10, Pakistan returned seven severely mutilated bodies of soldiers to New Delhi outraging India. In the face of India's fury, on June 12, Pakistan's foreign Minister Sartaj Aziz visited New Delhi to talk to Jaswant Singh. But the talks failed. India identified Pakistan as an aggressor that had violated the LOC, while Aziz surprisingly questioned the validity of the line, which was based on the 1972 Simla Agreement signed by both countries. He also called for a joint working group to help settle India's claim of the Kargil, which Singh angrily rejected. Before he visited New Delhi, Aziz had visited China, a Pakistan ally, China, seeking its support, but was coming visit to China was designed to garner. This was especially important to India, since it was the first time Singh visited China after the Pokhram II nuclear tests.

As the battle turned bloodier and more intense, the Clinton administration intervened to help defuse the crisis. In the second week of June, Bruce Reidel, Special Assistant to President Clinton, in a briefing at the Foreign Press Center, asserted the inviolability of the LOC by stating the following: "we think the Line of Control has demarcated the area over the years. The two parties have not previously had significant differences about where the LOC is," and the "forces which have crossed the line should withdraw to where they came from." He noted that the President in his recent letters to both Prime Ministers had stressed that point. On June 15, in separate telephonic conversations, Mr. Clinton told Sharif to withdraw the infiltrators from across the LOC, and Vajpayee that he appreciated his display of restraint in the conflict. To Pakistan's further sense of isolation, the G-8 members, at their annual meeting in Cologne, Germany, June 19-20, came out strongly in support of India's contention that the Kargil crisis was precipitated by mercenaries backed by Pakistani troops. Mr. Brajesh Mishra, the Principal Secretary to Vajpayee, who had taken Vajpayee's letter to Mr. Clinton at the G-8 in Cologne, also took the opportunity to explain the situation to the rest of the G-8 leaders. Following that meeting, a communiqué was issued on June 20 by the G-8, which condemned in unequivocal terms the violation of the LOC and dubbed Pakistan's military action as "irresponsible" in its attempt to change the status quo at the LOC, and called on it to end the intrusion. The communiqué also urged the two countries to resolve the Kashmir dispute with "dialogue". This position was also supported by China. by Gen. Anthony Zinni, Commander-in-Chief of the US Central command. The delegation also included Gibson Lampher, the Deputy Assistant Secretary of State for South Asia, and Karl F. Inderfurth. On behalf of the President Zinni asked Sharif to withdraw the troops from across the LOC and Lampher traveled to New Delhi to brief Brajesh Mishra on the details of their visit to Pakistan. On June 28, a day after Zinni's visit, Sharif rushed to Beijing to seek Chinese diplomatic support of the conflict. The Chinese, however, told him that he could not count on their support, and he cut short his six-day visit and returned home disappointed. Meanwhile, on June 20, Indian troops, after a fierce battle and the loss of 50 lives, recaptured Tololing Rill in the Drass sector, and on July 4, recaptured Tiger Hill, which is considered to be the most strategic point in Drass sector as it overlooks the Srinagar-Leh highway.

As the Indian troops steadily recaptured one hill or ridge after another, and Pakistan's isolation in the world community increased (only Saudi Arabia and the United Emirates supported Pakistan), it desperately sought a face-saving formula to extricate itself from its miscalculated adventure. For instance on June 27, former Foreign Secretary Niaz Naik, a person known to be close to Sharif as well as to the Americans, secretly went to New Delhi, met with Vajpayee and his Principal Secretary Mishra, and slipped back to Pakistan. Although Pakistan's foreign office insisted that it was "Naik's private visit and had nothing to do with Pakistan's foreign policy," it was speculated that he presented a set of "face-saving" proposals to Sharif that would allow Pakistan to escape from the Kargil imbroglio as gracefully as possible. On July 3, Sharif requested a meeting with Clinton on "an urgent basis" and met with him on July 4, in Washington.

The statement indicated that the forces needed to be returned to the Pakistani side. This was followed by the White House statement which stated that the President shared with Sharif the view that the current fighting "contains the seeds of wider conflict" and that "it was vital for the peace of South Asia that the LOC in Kashmir be respected by both parties in accordance with their 1972 Simla accord," and that "bilateral dialogue begun in Lahore in February provides the best approach for resolving all issues dividing India and Pakistan, including Kashmir," and that the President would take a "personal interest in encouraging an expeditious resumption and intensification of those bilateral efforts once the sanctity of the LOC has been fully restored." Mr. Clinton also indicated that he would visit South Asia soon. As the meeting with Sharif progressed, Mr. Clinton frequently called Mr. Vajpayee in order to "keep him fully appraised of the discussion," as the latter had declined the invitation to go to Washington. On July 12, the Congress also turned up the heat on Islamabad when it passed House Resolution 227 "expressing the sense of the Congress in opposition to the Government of Pakistan's support for armed incursion into Jammu and Kashmir, India." Further declaring that Pakistan was culpable in sending armed insurgents into the Indian territory, while stressing that India and Pakistan "resolve all of their differences within the framework of the Simla agreement in order to preserve peace and security in South Asia." It also suggested that the administration block loans to Pakistan from international financial institutions.

Following this agreement, beginning on July 11, the infiltrators began retreating from Kargil as India set July 16 as the deadline for the total withdrawal. On July 12, in Clinton as well as his request to the intruders to withdraw from Indian Territory. He also defended his Kargil policy as something designed to draw the attention of the international community to Kashmir issue. In the war, more than 400 Indian soldiers, 679 intruders, and 30 Pakistani regulars were killed excluding those who were wounded. Sharif's agreement to withdraw intruders upset the military so much that on October 12, he was ousted from power in a bloodless coup. When Musharraf, who is rumored to have been the architect of the Kargil war and who is called Mr. Kargil in India, heard on his return from Sri Lanka that he was being replaced by Sharif's confidant, Lt. General Khowaja Ziauddin, he had his generals remove Sharif on charges of hijacking and treason. Musharraf declared himself the Chief Executive, the Chief of Army, and later as President. Sharif, who was convicted and given a life sentence by a military court, was subsequently exiled to Saudi Arabia in December 1999.

The coup upset India and got Pakistan suspended from the Commonwealth Conference. Tensions between them escalated. Artillery fires across the LOC intensified and on December 24, a New Delhi-bound plane, carrying 178 passengers from Katmandu, Nepal, was hijacked to Kandahar, Afghanistan by the Pakistan-based Harakat ul-Mujahideen terrorists. They demanded a release from jails of 35 Kashmiri militants including the Pakistani cleric, Maulana Masood Azhar, in exchange with the passengers. When India's government refused to concede their demands, they killed a newlywed husband who was on his honeymoon with his wife. Pressured by the passengers' relatives, on December 31, India exchanged the passengers with three hardcore militants including Azhar. This was humiliating to India. India implicated Pakistan in this avail. Unlike his predecessors, Musharraf came out openly in support of terrorists by declaring that "Islam does not recognize political boundaries, and Jihad is a concept of God."

Emboldened by the successful results of their hijacking, the militants escalated their assaults and suicide bombings against innocent bystanders and the security forces. Realizing that negotiations with militants and the APHC leaders were essential to resolve this conflict, in November 2000, on the eve of the beginning of Ramadan (month of Muslim fasting) the Vajpayee government declared a unilateral cease-fire and invited them for talks. It also agreed to talk to Pakistan if the latter ceased supporting cross-border terrorism. The APHC leaders including its chairman Abdul Ghani Bhat at that time welcomed the initiative. They sought visas from the government to visit Pakistan to talk to the militant leaders living there. But they were denied visas because they wanted the Pro-Pakistani leader Syed Ali Shah Geelani of the Jamaat-I-Islami included in the team. The Musharraf government refused to cease supporting cross-border terrorism but agreed to abide by the cease-fire declaration along the LOC.

However, some of the Pakistani-based militant groups such as the Lashkar-e-Toiba, Hizbul-Mujahideen, Jash-e-Mohammed, founded later by cleric Azhas, and Al-Umar-Mujhideen rejected the cease-fire declaration as a sham and vowed to liberate Kashmir with a Jihad directed against pagan India. They escalated terrorism not only in Kashmir, but also in other locations like New Delhi. Their belief being that they will go to Paradise if they die as martyrs fighting pagan India.

Hoping to persuade the APHC leaders to talk to his government, Vajpayee appointed a noted politician and former Congress cabinet minister K. C. Pant as leaders, but also to other politicians from Kashmir who were committed to a peaceful resolution of the conflict. The APHC leaders rejected the invitation on the grounds that Pakistan was not included.

However, on April 30, one of its leaders, Shabir Ahmad Shah, the chairman of the Democratic Freedom Party (DFP), agreed to talk to Pant, even though he had earlier insisted on Pakistan's inclusion in the talks. When it became clear that India's unilateral declaration had only helped the militants to escalate their terrorism, and that the APHC leaders rejected negotiations the Vajpayee government ended the six month cease-fire on May 25, 2001, and invited Musharraf for talks without any pre-established conditions – which he accepted. The talks were held on July 14 – 16, 2001 in Agra, near New Delhi, but they failed because General Musharraf insisted that the Kashmir dispute be the core issue of the talks, which Vajpayee rejected. Although both leaders had agreed to meet again during the November UN General Assembly meetings, it did not take place as India was angered by the suicide bomb attack of the Jammu and Kashmir State Assembly building on October 1, in which forty innocent civilians and the three terrorists who had caused the blast were killed.

The Pakistani Cleric Maulana Masood Azher, leader of the Jaish-e-Mohammed, which is linked to Osama Bin Laden's Al Qaeda, took credit for the bombing. Vajpayee took a tough stance indicating that he would not talk to Musharraf unless he ceased supporting cross border terrorism. Moreover, India's foreign minister, Jaswant Singh, cancelled his scheduled trip to Pakistan to talk to his counterpart. Relations between the two countries again turned tense and resulted in an intense exchange of fire along the LOC. The Bush administration called on India to show restraint as it did not want to jeopardize its Al Qaeda that Pakistan had supported in the past. In January and June 2002 the tensions between India and Pakistan increased along with the threat of another war.

4

Kashmir Conflict and Unrest in South Asia

Regionalization and economic integration are ongoing processes in contemporary world. To many extant, growth of individual countries depends on its approach towards regionalization. Among others, Khan (1998) has underlined the complex and contradictory processes connected with regionalization. According to Khan's analysis, regionalization is a logical outcome of what he calls "fractured or fragmented globalization". The term 'economic integration' nevertheless covers broad areas of socio-political, financial and cultural links with nations of a particular territorial jurisdiction joining together through institutional mechanisms. The Association of South East Asian Nations (ASEAN), European Union (EU), and North American Free Trade Area (NAFTA) are few examples of such integration. The formation of regional integration has been greatly successful in brining historically hostile countries together. Both economic and political factors push regional countries closer and closer (Khan and Larik, 2007).

Economic factors have always prevailed over the political factors ever since the formation of nation states – the classic example is the states in the European Union and the South East Asia where economic dimension have brought long time rivals in the same dais. But the case is much different in South Asia. Here political factors are dominating rather than the economical ones. Among other issues, unsettled Kashmir dispute is seriously hampering the needed bondage between South Asian countries. Pakistan considers Kashmir as its core political dispute with India while India considers it as one of the leading unresolved issue. The Kashmiris have grievances with the Indian government, specifically the Indian military, which has committed severe human rights violations; and with various militant groups that are serious threats to their lives and livelihood. India-Pakistan tensions are worrying for other South Asian counties because these two are main players. And uneasiness between these two countries is dangerous because they bring two nuclear states face to face.

Both governments of India and Pakistan are concerned over Kashmir, for obvious reasons. This forces the Muslims in Kashmir to pay a heavy price for struggling constantly to posses self determination rights. The Kashmiri youths in particular are swinging between destitution and uncertainty since 1947 till date.

Undeniably, youths of any society are inimitably and largely affected by threats, violence and unrests. They are in most cases, main actors of violence, war and unrests. They are also the victims. It is not over-exaggeration when social scientists say that wars and violence are not possible without youths' participation. However, Rodgers (1999) argued that there is the lack of attention to, and thorough documentation of, the positive contributions of youth in society.Nonetheless, participation of youth in unrest, rebellion, violence and war are only a microcosm of the diverse and complicated phenomenon. Huntington (1996) argues that an unusually high proportion of young people in the total population of a society generally lead to increasing insecurity and make such societies prone to conflict. Zakaria (2001) argues that youth bulges (high proportion of young people in the society) combined with small economic and social change provided the fundament for Islamic resurgence in the Arab world. According to Keen (2003), youth violence has resulted from the disaffection of failures in the educational system and a dearth of employment opportunities.

The History that hurts: The purpose of this chapter is not to dig out history. But the arrow always goes back few inches before getting disconnected from the bow and hitting the air. In a nut shell: In August 1947 when the Indian subcontinent became independent from Britain, all the rulers of the 565 princely states, whose lands comprised two-fifths of India and a population 99 million, had to decide which of the two new dominions to join - India or Pakistan. The ruler of Jammu and Kashmir, The Maharaja Hari Singh, whose state was situated between the two new countries, could not decide which country to join but in October 1947, he asked India to deploy its troops to block a militant upraising in the state. Indian government instantly demanded that Kashmir should accede to India first. The ruler signed the treaty, which gave key powers to the Indian government - in return for military aid and a promised referendum. India than sent its forces to Kashmir. As consequences, Kashmir is divided into a Pakistani controlled part and an Indian controlled part. This de facto partition continues to this date with the dividing line being known as the Line of Control.

Who Controls What?

India controls about 43% of the region, including most of Jammu, Kashmir Valley, Ladakh, and Siachen Glacier. India's claim is contested by Pakistan, which controls roughly 37% of Kashmir, namely Azad Kashmir and the northern areas of Gilgit and Baltistan. China controls 20% of Kashmir, including Aksai Chin, which it occupied after 1962's Sino-Indian War, and the Shaksam Valley, which was ceded by Pakistan in 1963 (Kashmir Conflict, Wikipidia).

Core of the dispute: Pakistan says that Kashmir is a disputed territory whose final status must be determined by the people of Kashmir. Pakistan strongly argues that Indian Army soldiers were present in Kashmir before the Instrument of Accession was signed with India, and that therefore Indian soldiers were in Kashmir in violation of the Standstill Agreement, which was designed to maintain the status quo in Kashmir.

India considers Kashmir as an integral part and has sufficient mechanisms and constitutional safeguards to address issues raised by its citizens in any part of the country. Part of India's position is actually driven by the fact that any concession to people of Kashmir may open a floodgate of many other similar movements by other ethnic groups. The current Prime Minister of India, Manmohan Singh however stated after the 2010 Kashmir unrest that his government is willing to grant autonomy within the purview of Indian constitution to Kashmir if there is consensus on this issue.

United Nations Security Council Resolution 122 was adopted on the 24 January 1957 and concerned the dispute between the governments of India and Pakistan over the territories of Jammu and Kashmir. It said that the final disposition of the State of Jammu and Kashmir will be made in accordance with the will of the people expressed through the democratic method of a free and impartial plebiscite conducted under the auspices of the United Nations.

From 2003, Delhi and Islamabad unveiled many confidence-building measures on Kashmir issue. The talks unfortunately got held up following 2008's terrorist attacks in Mumbai. India believes Pakistani based militants carried it out.

Street protests, unrests and insurgency: In 1989, a widespread street protests and armed insurgency started in Kashmir. After the 1987 State legislative assembly election, some of the results were disputed. This resulted in the formation of armed groups and wide spread street protests. The movements were created to voice Kashmir's disputes and grievances with the Indian government, specifically the Indian military. Indian governments always claimed that these armed groups are Islamic terrorist groups from Pakistan-administered Kashmir and Afghanistan, fighting to make Jammu and Kashmir a part of Pakistan. The Pakistani government calls these groups "Kashmiri freedom fighters", and claims that it gives only moral and diplomatic support to these insurgents. Some of these groups demanded independence for the state of Jammu and Kashmir and others union with Pakistan. Pakistan frequently called for the issue to be resolved via an UN-sponsored referendum.

During the mid 1990s, several new militant groups emerged, most of which held radical Islamic views. The ideological emphasis of the movement unfortunately shifted from a nationalistic and secularist one to an Islamic one (The Times of India, 2010).

Suffering of Kashmiri People

The Armed Forces Special Powers Act in India grants the military, wide powers of arrest, the right to shoot to kill, and to occupy or destroy property in counterinsurgency operations. Many human rights organizations such as Amnesty International and the Human Rights Watch have condemned human rights abuses in Kashmir by Indians such as extra-judicial executions, disappearances, and torture. The Indian state police admitted in 2010 that as many as 331 deaths while in custody and 111 enforced disappearances since 1989. An estimated 200 youth have also ex-filtrated into Pakistan occupied Kashmir (PoK) through 2010, for training in handling of arms and ammunition.

Since 1989, more than 68,000 people have died in an armed uprising and subsequent crackdown by Indian forces in Kashmir (The Associated Press, 2011). But According to Save Our Souls' September 2011 quarterly report, there have been 93,682 killings in Kashmir since 1989. The report further said that 107431 children became orphans and 22,760 women became widows since 1989.

A 2005 study conducted by Médecins Sans Frontières found that Kashmiri women are among the worst sufferers of sexual violence in the world, with 11.6% of respondents reporting that they had been victims of sexual abuse.

Points to contemplate: As much for the legitimacy of its own self-image as a democratic citizenry as out of sympathy for the rights of Kashmiris, Indian public opinion needs to ask harder questions to the government about the efficacy of the approach to the Kashmir issue.

Indian citizens in the rest of the country, a large portion of who have never been to Kashmir, understand its problems through the lens of the mainstream national media, and maintain a narrowly nationalist position toward Kashmiri peoples' demands.

Youth cultures are becoming more and more global, but, at the same time, they assume very different forms depending on the local context. But the reins on media are strongly state-dominated and the vocabularies in the news items on Indian media paint an ugly picture of the peaceful protester on the streets of Kashmir. Tags like stone-pelters, mobsters, trouble-makers, anti-national elements and so on. And the peaceful demonstrations are labeled as instigated, orchestrated, militant backed, Pakistan supported and so on.

India continues to garrison half a million soldiers in Kashmir, more the number of U.S. troops in Iraq. And India's half-century-old Armed Forces Special Powers Act, which was extended to Kashmir in 1990, gives troops the legal authority to shoot any person they suspect of being a threat and guarantees them immunity from prosecution. To bring a soldier before a civilian court requires the permission of India's Home Affairs Ministry. There are more than 400 cases still waiting for permission to prosecute troops known to have killed Kashmiri noncombatant civilians. Pakistan's political right and Islamic elements took advantage of troubled India-Pakistan relations, especially the non-resolution of the Kashmir conflict. Many political parties advocates that India, rather than the Taliban, is the major threat to Pakistan. Further, the militant groups based in mainland Pakistan, known for their involvement in Indian-administered Kashmir, use the stalemate on Kashmir to mobilize popular support.

Kashmir dispute distracts Pakistan's security forces from focusing on militants inside the country since a majority of Pakistan's troops remain deployed on the eastern border with India.

Youth sufferings: The violence in the state has also been triggered by the increasing difference in the social opportunities, treatment, systematic biases with limitation in accessing employment and education. Children and youth suffered from the militancy-rife by becoming orphans as well as homeless. It has been estimated that over 15,000 orphans were created due to militancy since 1989 till 2004.

Disturbingly, more and more Kashmiri youth are attempting suicide. This has been a growing phenomenon and recent reports have shown that since January 2011, about 35 young people, both men and women made attempts to commit suicide in Handwara and Kupwara districts of North Kashmir. It is related to the larger social, economic and political dimensions of the region as it lurches from one phase of violence and strife to another. Youth unemployment also has a critical bearing on the ongoing violent conflict in the state. Lack of jobs and opportunities has tended to create frustration, making unemployed youth the prime candidates for recruitment by militant organizations with funds and arms at their disposal. Youth of Kashmir University consistently reported that they continued to have serious psychological and social difficulties as a result of the ongoing violence and deprivation they had experienced during the last few years, such as feelings of hopelessness and profound social alienation. They stated that gaps in family and community support, as well as lack of education, food, clothing, shelter, health care and jobs have dramatically increased their vulnerability to a range of threats. They have also experienced more poverty and lack of education due to ongoing violent conflict. As young people constitute the majority of militia recruits, they suffer disproportionately most from the trauma and psychological effects of ongoing violent conflict.

Kashmiri youth reported that the poor governance and political institutions especially dominancy of one community in governance and administration, weak and hurried political negotiations and transitions, restrictions on social and cultural practices, rigging of elections, widespread and escalating corruption have also been responsible for violent conflict.

Violence undermines Kashmiri youth's right to a sustainable livelihood and to development by disrupting economic production and access to important services. Economic insecurity in turn contributes to their vulnerability to violence and its perpetration. They believed that the ongoing violence had fundamentally been about the marginalization and manipulation of youth.

Some rival groups, terrorist organizations and others use violence as a tool to repress and silence Kashmiri youth's right to be heard. Young people who became orphaned or separated from family have tremendous resourcefulness as they took on major economic and social responsibilities.

The psychosocial impact of ongoing conflict and social upheaval manifested itself in many different ways among young people, who said they often felt unloved, abused and even betrayed by adults and society. Many lived in constant fear of violence and deprivation, and some developed psychological problems that required counseling or other traditional healing rituals to address. Some further broke traditional boundaries by increasingly challenging elder's authority, and demanding more support for their capacities and community roles. Others, however, lacked self-confidence and a sense of self-worth despite the creative skills they had developed to survive during the conflict.

In case of youth whose family members are killed in the ongoing conflict, they lack protection, food, shelter, education and other support and suffer from poverty and unemployment. Those living in migrants camp are particularly concerned about the conditions of displacement, living and civic facilities available.

While many children are killed by weapons, many more die from the catastrophic impact the conflict has on their communities' infrastructure and families' access to food, health care and their ability to maintain their livelihoods (Mazurana & Carlson, 2006).

Regardless of their age or their role in the freedom struggle in Kashmir, young detainees are isolated for days in dark dingy, unhygienic and cramped spaces. Often, youth and children as young as 10 are hunted down, held and then not produced in court.

The persons, who disappeared from the state since the unrest started in 1989, now numbering in the thousands, were all Kashmiri youths. They were picked up by the police or the Indian Army over the last two decades, and never seen again.

Impact on Regional Stability

The European Union (EU) and Association for South East Asian Nations (ASEAN) have not only laid out a solid mechanism for regional economic cooperation but helped resolve the old intrastate conflicts among the member countries. However, it is the drive for economic cooperation that has solidified the regional cooperative mechanisms.

The persistence of conflict both within and between the states is the single most potent factor that has prevented the South Asian region from forging an effective regional cooperative mechanism. It is intertwined in various complex issues and provides a disappointing picture from the political as well as economic perspective. The differences between India and Pakistan over Kashmir, between Sri Lanka and India over the nationality of Tamil people, where Sri Lanka accused India, especially state government of Tamil Nadu for supplying arms and providing trainings to the former LTTE guerrillas in its Southern areas, the problem between India and Nepal on open border, dispute between India and Bangladesh over illegal migration and the demarcation of boundaries involving fertile islands and enclaves and also in sharing the water, are some of the issues that are yet to be resolved (Khan and Larik, 2007). Lack of trust between the two major nations – Pakistan and India over the Kashmir issue is immensely hurting the peace and prosperity of this region along with these other issues.

The first concrete proposal for establishing a framework for regional cooperation in South Asia was made by Bangladesh on May 2, 1980. While the proposal was promptly endorsed by Nepal, Sri Lanka, the Maldives and Bhutan, India and Pakistan were initially skeptical. India's main concern was the proposal's reference to the security matters in South Asia. Indian policy makers also feared that Bangladesh's proposal for a regional organization might provide an opportunity for the small neighbors to regionalize all bilateral issues and to join with each other to gang up against India. Pakistan assumed that it might be an Indian strategy to organize the other South Asian countries against Pakistan and ensure a regional market for Indian products, thereby consolidating and further strengthening India's economic dominance in the region. However, after a series of diplomatic negotiations, the organization was formally lunched in 1985. Since then SAARC has evolved slowly but continuously both in terms of institutions and programs. However, it is true that most of the programs and achievements of SAARC exist on paper.

SAARC has intentionally laid more stress on core issues mentioned above rather than more decisive political issues like the Kashmir dispute and the Sri Lankan civil war that ended in

2009. The most crucial and serious problem that divides South Asian countries is the Indo-Pakistan conflict over Kashmir.

The most powerful argument advanced for the failure of SAARC, is that inter state disputes, Kashmir being the prime factor, can never allow effective regionalization. In contrast, South East Asian countries had also long standing disputes which they were able to resolve through the regional arrangement of ASEAN. Indonesia, Philippines and Malaysia were able to overcome their contending territorial claims in favor of the creation of a trading bloc. In South Asia, unresolved disputes assumed a higher priority than a collective response to internal and external challenges.

Resolution of core issue of Kashmir is the key to good ties, peace and stability of South Asia. As long as the Kashmir issue remains unresolved, this region is likely to remain unstable. A solution of the Kashmir dispute is required as it is only fair to all the people who dwell in this region. To boost regional, economic and cultural cooperation in South Asia, the Kashmir issue has to be resolved in the quickest time. South Asians can not step forward with a wounded leg.

Looking Ahead for a Peaceful and Prosperous South Asia

On a brighter note, Elections held in 2008 had a high voter turnout and were generally regarded as fair by the United Nations High Commissioner for Refugees. Jammu & Kashmir Chief Minister Omar Abdullah met with senior central government officials in mid October 2011 to discuss the removal of the hated Armed Forces Special Powers Act from certain areas of the troubled region. Abdullah announced that AFSPA would be removed from some areas of the state by the end of October (Overdorf, 2011).

To overcome widespread poverty and backwardness, resolve conflicts, benefit from extended regional cooperation and economies of scale, become more competitive and achieve higher growth, South Asian nations need to pursue the goal of regionalization and regional cooperation. But before that, the Kashmir issue has to take a positive turn. Immediate steps should be taken to redress the grievances of the people of Kashmir, specially the youth, with active involvement of the Indian central government. The success or failure of the regional association cannot be measured in numbers. It should be done so with regard to the expectations of the member countries— their national, bilateral and regional agendas.

Despite having diverse ethno-lingual population, the South Asian region has many common cultural values and customs. From classic music to the movies, art and architecture, South Asia presents a common heritage. The clothing, the lifestyle and the food habits are also significantly common. This commonalty of culture provides a very strong platform to integrate the region.

Cultural similarities override the ethnic and linguistic diversities to a great extent. The policy makers need to exploit this common ground for harnessing the other areas of cooperation.

Militant groups need to realize that arms conflict is neither the solution nor it guarantees freedom; Indian military need to understand that brutality does not win hearts; and concerned governments, politicians should bring solutions to the table that promises safety to the Kashmiri people and ensures sustainable peace in the region.

CONFLICT IN KASHMIR

Over 60 years of fighting, little progress has been made in solving the Indian-Pakistani dispute over Kashmir. Every time there appears to be progress, we seem to run up against a setback. These setbacks usually came in the form of aggression from one of the parties, or more recently, terrorist attacks from Pakistani-based terrorists. However, after three major wars, a few major terrorist attacks, and a few nuclear test explosions, the parties are once again poised to discuss peace.

The United Nations and its member states have brokered peace in Kashmir since the beginning, and going forward, they will be called on to do the same. The UN mission on the ground, as well as the diplomats around the world, must continue to walk the tight line of limiting violence and encouraging human rights, while respecting Indian and Pakistani sovereignty. This cautious approach has stopped wars, raised quality of life and most importantly, done no harm in an area considered by many to be the world's most dangerous.

If the UN continues down this path, and receives enough support from western powers, we could see improvements to the Kashmir situation. While a litany of international dynamics make drastic changes unlikely, things such as gradual demilitarization and increased political freedoms are possible. It's just a step in the right direction, but its within reach, and its a step closer to a lasting peace.

The governments of Pakistan, India, and China have fought over the disputed territory of Jammu and Kashmir since August of 1947, when the Indian subcontinent became independent from Britain. Three major wars - not to mention countless minor skirmishes - have been fought over the territory, with most of the conflict coming between India and Pakistan.

India desires to regain the entire territory that was formerly the state of Jammu and Kashmir (now commonly referred to simply as "Kashmir"), including the areas administered by Pakistan and China. Pakistan wants a plebiscite to be held in Kashmir, believing that the Muslim-majority population would vote to join Pakistan.

China would like to keep the territory it has, and for the rest of the region to stay stable enough not to cause them any problems. The international approach to the situation of course varies from country to country, and organization to organization, however most approaches are similar. Most entities, including the UN, take a relatively hands-off approach. The UN urges both sides to pursue a peaceful agreement, and condemns human rights abuses by both sides in Kashmir. However, like most other actors, the UN believes that the Kashmir issue needs to be settled by India and Pakistan themselves. For the foreseeable future it is likely that the UN mission in Kashmir will remain one of observation only.

The current picture, and what events in the recent years (post 9-11) have cooled or warmed relations between Pakistan and India, and how that effects the Kashmir situation. Then, we'll step back and provide some historical context by looking at the major events that have transpired since the conflict started in 1947, and how the situation has changed. Next we'll briefly look at where some of the critical actors stand on the issue of Kashmir, and what role they'll play in an eventual solution. Finally, we'll discuss what the possible outcomes are, how the UN can play a role, and what is most likely to happen.

Current Situation

After more than six decades of dispute, Kashmir remains a fiercely contested territory, with sections administered by India, Pakistan, and China. As will be discussed later, the Chinese claim is not seriously disputed by India or Pakistan, and therefore the issue remains almost exclusively one between India and Pakistan. Currently, there is little to no movement on the Kashmir question. Despite some glimpses of progress, several major events throughout the last decade have stalled negotiations on Kashmir, either by cooling relations between India and Pakistan, or moving other issues to the forefront.

Two events in late 2001 had a dramatic impact on the situation. The terrorist attacks of September launched the American-led Global War on Terror. Washington immediately put pressure on Islamabad to reign in the militancy that thrives in their Northwest Frontier Provinces, in support of the American war in Afghanistan. With Pakistan shifting focus on cross-border issues between itself and Afghanistan, there was less oversight on Pakistani terrorist activities in Kashmir. Simultaneously, the American war in Afghanistan inspired increased militancy amongst ethnic Pashtuns in Pakistan, leading to an increased presence of militant groups in Kashmir.

In December 13, 2001, terrorists attacked the Indian Parliament, killing 9 Indian citizens. While no one knows definitively who was behind the attack, both Indian and American authorities believed that Pakistan-based terrorist groups Lashkar-e-Tayiba (LeT) and Jaish-e-Mohammed (JeM) for the attack. the Indian government claimed that these groups were supported by Pakistan's Inter-Services Intelligence. In the following weeks, both countries mobilized massive amounts of troops along the line of control, leading to fears of a nuclear war. While estimates on troop mobilizations vary, Globalsecurity.org estimated that India had deployed as many as 700,000 troops, with Pakistan mobilizing more than 300,000 along the LoC. These estimates make the 2001 deployment the largest since the 1971 war. The international community urged restraint. Diplomats from the UN, US, and Russia all worked with Pakistan and India to try and negotiate a drawdown, but the efforts appeared to have little effect. Eventually, over a span of several months, both sides backed down and slowly withdrew troops from the border. Despite international mediation efforts, the more likely explanation for the drawdown, was India and Pakistan's keen awareness at the all-out destruction even a non-nuclear war would have. According to government estimates, the troop buildup alone cost each side over $1 billion (USD). Starting in November of 2003, the situation began to warm, as for the first time in 14 years, India and Pakistan signed a comprehensive ceasefire. Not only did both sides drawdown troops from the LoC, but over the following years, both sides took steps to improve relations.. In 2004, air and rail links were re-opened between the countries, a significant step toward increasing economic relations. That same year, the Pakistani and Indian militaries started joint patrols along the line of control. While being limited in scope and frequency, the patrols served as an important symbol of possible future cooperation. In 2005, a bus service was opened between the Pakistani and Indian administered sections of Kashmir, reuniting families that had been separated for decades. In one of the most encouraging displays of cooperation, India and Pakistan worked together after the devastating 2005 earthquake in Kashmir, with both sides contributing money and personnel toward relief efforts.

The peace process appeared to encounter another severe setback in July 2006, when terrorists conducted a coordinated bombing attack on the Indian Railway, killing over 200 people and injuring hundreds more. the attack was claimed by a Pakistan-based terrorist groups with links to LeT. After Indian authorities threatened to once more break off talks between the two countries, Pakistani President Musharraf quickly denounced the attacks as "a despicable act of terrorism" and promised to renew Pakistan's vigilance in combating terrorism within its borders, as well as fully cooperate with India's investigation of the attacks. Indian authorities then quickly backed off of their harsh stance, and in November talks resumed. The next month, President Musharraf put forth a bold proposal, saying that Pakistan would drop its claim on Kashmir in return for phased demilitarization of Kashmir, and a form of independence for Kashmiris that called for joint supervision between Indian, Pakistani, and Kashmiri authorities.

The plan showed the political astuteness of Musharraf. He recognized that due to the growing economic gap between the two countries, Pakistan would continue to fall further and further behind India in terms of military might. He also likely realized the economic benefits of settling the Kashmir issue once and for all, and how that could help him politically against his hard-line Islamist opponents who opposed any substantial compromise on the Kashmir issue. Unfortunately, the plan received only a luke-warm reaction from Indian authorities, and significant criticism from many in Pakistan. In that time period, there were small increases in local self-governance in some Indian-administered regions, but it is unlikely that these moves owed much to Musharraf's proposals.

According to leaked US diplomatic cables, President Musharraf told a US congressional delegation in 2007 that recent diplomatic efforts between himself and Indian Prime Minister Singh had the two sides close to an agreement, saying it would happen "soon - sooner than anyone might think." Although it is like that Mr. Musharraf was painting an overly optimistic for the benefit of the delegation (in the same report he was said to have told the delegation that he does not believe top Taliban leadership had ever been to Pakistan, a statement that is clearly defies overwhelming evidence), this period represented some of the warmest relations ever achieved between the two countries.

Sadly this progress came to a tragic halt with the November 2008 terrorist attacks in Mumbai. More than a dozen attackers from the Pakistani LeT terrorist group conducted coordinated attacks around Mumbai, killing 164 and injuring 308 people.

While Pakistan quickly denounced the attacks and again vowed to fight terrorism in its borders, the Indians still directed a significant amount of their anger at the Pakistanis. In the months following the attacks, Prime Minister Singh openly accused Pakistan of being complicit, saying "There is enough evidence to show that, given the sophistication and military precision of the attack, it must have had the support of some official agencies in Pakistan."

Over the course of the next year, India consistently criticized Pakiștani efforts to prosecute LeT members as insufficient. At a press conference last April, Prime Minister Singh acknowledged that Pakistan took some steps toward prosecuting but said that other "conspirators" were "roaming around freely." specifically citing LeT chief Hafiz Saeed, whom Pakistan refused to prosecute.

Most recently, in February, India and Pakistan agreed to resume talks. Many believe that the move comes on pressure from the US, who is worried about increased Indian-Pakistani tensions complicating their efforts in Afghanistan. The talks have started with very low level contacts, and isn't expected that anything substantial will be discussed until the two sides work up to higher level contacts - which has not happened as of yet. Because of this, it remains unclear if the sides will hold similar stances to those they held at the height of relations in 2007. However, it is unlikely considering both sides' political landscapes have changed, including the replacement of President Musharraf's military led government with the more democratic government of President Zardari. Although Mr. Zadari has initially seemed keen toward warming relations with India, he faces more political pressure to not give up too much ground on the Kashmir issue, since he has to worry about appealing to a wider constituency.

Throughout the events of the last decade, the UN's position on the Kashmir issue has remained fairly constant. At each flare up of hostilities, the UN has urged restraint, sending its own diplomats to act as mediators as well as encouraging important member states to do the same. While there is no evidence to suggest that these UN efforts have had a dramatic effect on moving the two sides toward peace, it would be unfair not to recognize that the UN efforts - and those of the broader international community - have almost certainly played some role in limiting hostilities after peaks in tension, and moving the two sides back to the negotiating table.

In fact, both Pakistani and - even more so - Indian authorities have repeatedly recognized the need for any solutions to be bilateral in nature, and played down the need for outside help. If any solution felt too 'foreign' to Pakistani and Indian citizens, there is no chance the peace would be lasting.

In terms of on-the-ground action, currently the United Nations Military Observer Group in India and Pakistan (UNMOGIP) has 44 military observers who are supported by a staff of 72 local and international civilians. Their mission is to monitor the line of control, while holding both parties to the latest ceasefire agreement. However, with such a small staff, and a budget of just over 16 million USD, they are very limited even in observation capability. Despite these limitations, the group plays an important role in informing the UN's broader diplomatic efforts on Kashmir, and there continued presence in Kashmir sends an important message to both sides that the international community is serious about the peace process. Furthermore, should war breakout again between the two parties, it will be up to the UN to once again broker a ceasefire, just as it has with the first three Kashmir Wars.

History of Issue

In August of 1947, British rule over the Indian subcontinent ended, forming the new states of India and Pakistan. The former princely states of the region were given the option of acceding to either India or Pakistan, or, remaining independent. This decision was to be made by the ruler of the state, not the population. This was critical as some rulers differed from their majority populations ethnically or religiously. This was the case in the State of Jammu and Kashmir, where the Hindu Maharajah, Hari Singh, ruled over a predominantly Muslim population. Initially the Maharajah wished to remain an independent state, acceding to neither of the new dominions. Pakistan was surprised and upset with this decision, having expected that the Muslim majority state would join them. This upset grew worse as word spread of alleged abuse and mistreatment of Muslim citizens in the state.

In October of 1947, Muslim revolutionaries from Pakistan invaded Kashmir, intending to overthrow the Hindu ruler, and have the state accede to Pakistan. The Maharajah was then forced to sign an agreement of accession with India, in order for Indian troops to come in and repel the invaders. It was this pivotal decision that led India to occupy the majority of the princely state, including the region of Jammu and the Kashmir Valley, as it does to this day. Pakistan was able to keep control over the Northern and Western most territories, which it also holds to this day. Since the very beginning, the UN has walked a tightrope of trying to curtail violence and encourage human rights while respecting national sovereignty by leaving the principal matter of final determination to India and Pakistan. To date, the UN Security Council (UNSC) has passed dozens of resolutions on the Kashmir issue. In 1948, Resolution 39 established the United Nations Commission for India and Pakistan (UNCIP) to investigate and mediate during the first Kashmir War. A few months later, the UNSC passed resolution 47, enlarging the mission. A military advisor was appointed, along with a group of military observers. This group became known as the United Nations Military Observer Group in India and Pakistan (UNMOGIP). In 1949, they helped to supervise the ceasefire, which they have continued to do ever since. In 1951, the UNSC passed resolution 91, continuing UNMOGIP's mandate, while calling for the demilitarization. All three of these resolutions also called for, or reaffirmed the need for a free and open plebiscite to determine the future of Kashmir. India, somewhat content over the current line of control, and perhaps frightful that such a referendum would lead to a loss of territory, rejected these calls.

In 1962, China and India went to war over border disputes, including the eastern Jammu Kashmir region of Aksai Chin. The Chinese were victorious, and have controlled the area since. There has not been much dispute in the following decades; Aksai Chin is a largely uninhabited, high altitude, desert. The area is strategically important to China however, as it connects the Chinese autonomous regions of Tibet and Xinjiang. In early 1965 territorial skirmishes in Kashmir between India and Pakistan started to mount. In August, the Pakistanis launched a secret operation, codenamed "Gibraltar," sending thousands of disguised soldiers into Indian held Kashmir to incite an insurgency against Indian rule amongst Muslims.

India soon caught wind of the plan, and launched a massive counter-attack, starting the Second Kashmir War. After weeks of fighting, the sides appeared to be at a stalemate, and losses were heavy on both sides - estimates of 3,000 or more KIA on both sides. There was increasing pressure on both sides from the UNSC - the US, USSR and China in particular - to end the fighting. In September of 1965, the UNSC passed four different resolutions (209,210,211, and 214), all calling for a ceasefire in the second Kashmir War. While initially these pleas fell on deaf ears, UNSC resolution 211, which demanded a ceasefire, was finally accepted by both parties.

In 1971, the two countries went to war again, but this time over Bengali independence in East Pakistan, not Kashmir. In under two weeks, the Indians scored a decisive victory, forcing Pakistan to surrender and give up East Pakistan (forming the new state of Bangladesh). Weary of the USSR's alliance with India, China and the US had tried to use the UNSC to force a ceasefire, but the measure was vetoed by the Soviets. This conflict dealt a major blow to the Pakistani military, and forever damaged their national psyche. The war soured Indo-Pakistani relations for decades. It is also likely that this crushing conventional warfare defeat led to Pakistan's support for guerilla jihadist groups as a policy tool that of course would have significant ramifications in the coming decades, especially on the Kashmir issue.

Although diplomatic relations resumed between the two countries in 1976, it wasn't to last, as relations again went south after the 1979 Soviet invasion of Afghanistan. India was supportive of its ally, the USSR, while Pakistan was strongly supportive of the mujahedeen (as, of course, was the US, China, and UK.) Relations warmed slightly as the Soviet-Afghan war came to a close in 1989, but not by much, and little progress was made during the 1990's. It was in 1989, that the Kashmir insurgency started to develop (mostly in response to discontent over fraudulent elections), with numerous groups emerging, both violent and non-violent, each wanting different outcomes.

On May 11, 1998, things again took a dramatic turn, when India tested a nuclear bomb in an underground facility. Two weeks later, Pakistan tested a nuclear weapon of its own, and the world was brought to the edge of its seat, hoping and praying that the situation would not escalate into a nuclear war. Both sides again massed troops along the LoC in Kashmir. Despite artillery fire back and forth, neither side opted to attack. Both parties faced a critical international response, including sanctions. The UNSC passed resolution 1172, condemning the nuclear tests on both sides, and demanding restraint. Both India and Pakistan criticized the resolution, each claiming that they had acted within their own rights, and that the UN demands were an intrusion on their national sovereignty.

A year later, Pakistan launched a surprise incursion across the LoC in an attempt to capture the strategically important Kargil area. This action led to the Third Kashmir War, with India immediately launching a counter-attack. Again, the Indians appeared to quickly gain the upper hand in the conflict. When Pakistan appealed to longtime ally America for help, the Clinton administration instead criticized the Pakistan infiltration, and demanded they withdraw. Facing similar criticism from the international community, including the United Nations, Pakistan withdrew, and India agreed not to escalate the conflict.

Once more, Pakistan was humiliated in defeat. Prime Minister Sharif's government was ousted in a coup by General Pervez Musharraf, who then became president. Diplomatic relations between India and Pakistan remained broken until the peace agreement of 2003.

Country Positions

India, Pakistan and China are the central players in the Kashmir. Currently, all three countries administer a portion of the territory with India controlling the most, followed by Pakistan then China. While the Chinese claim is disputed by India, it is far less contentious than India or Pakistan's claim. This is partly due to the Chinese's relative strength, but mostly due to the fact that their claim is largely uninhabitable and bears little strategic significance for either Pakistan or India. Therefore, the issue of Kashmir is usually posed as one between India and Pakistan.

While these are the main parties to the conflict, world powers - namely the five permanent members of the UNSC - also play an important role in the conflict. They dictate the International community's collective response to the issue, including the observer force and the bulk of other diplomatic efforts. The United States especially plays a pivotal role, as they give substantial amounts of military and humanitarian aid to both India and Pakistan. The following is a summary of the important actors positions on the Kashmir issue:

India

- The original instrument of accession signed by Maharaja Singh was valid under international law, and therefore all of the territory of Jammu and Kashmir belongs to India.
- Recent UNSC resolutions have more or less accepted the status quo, and have not called for a plebiscite. Previous resolutions calling for a plebiscite are no longer valid because 1) Pakistan has repeatedly violated the terms of the resolutions calling for such a referendum, and 2) The political environment of Kashmir has changes such that a plebiscite no longer makes sense.
- Despite the diversity of Kashmir, it is an important part of India. a degree of disaffection is common in large and diverse nations like India
- All issues between India and Pakistan should be solved through bilateral negotiations
- Pakistan spreads violent propaganda against India, and supports violent terrorist groups in Kashmir
- As documented by the UN and affiliated human rights groups, Pakistan has denied civic liberties to citizens in

their administered territory, and has continually perpetrated human rights abuses against Kashmiri citizens

Pakistan

- The instrument of accession was signed against the will of the Kashmiri people by an oppressive ruler, and is therefore invalid. As a fellow Muslim state, Jammu and Kashmir should have partitioned with Pakistan
- India repeatedly ignored UN calls to hold a democratic plebiscite and let the people of Kashmir decide their own fate
- The popular insurgency in Kashmir shows that the people do not wish to be a part of India, and Pakistan only provides them limited support
- As documented by leaked US diplomatic cables and several NGOs, India carries out widespread human rights abuses in Kashmir, including extrajudicial killings, and mass rapes, and the Kashmiri people have a right to self defense

The United States, The European Union, and the United Nations

- The Kashmir issue is primarily one between India and Pakistan, and any solution must derive from the parties themselves
- Both sides should continue to show maximum restraint, and abide by the terms of the latest ceasefire agreement (2003)
- Both sides should commit fully to stopping human rights abuses, and increase civil liberties for the people of Kashmir
- Pakistan must commit to dismantling domestic terrorist groups, and stop any support for terrorist activities in Kashmir

Additional Points

- Throughout this chapter, there has been little talk of Kashmiri separatist groups, mostly because dozens of groups have formed since the insurgency started in 1989, and they all want different things, and none have a significant amount of political power. Still, each group is important, and there reactions need to be taken into account for any possible solution.

- The US, UK, and their allies in Afghanistan need Pakistan as a strategic ally to stop the influx of terrorists across the Af-Pak border, keep ground supply lines open, and help negotiate reconciliation with the Taliban. While the western powers still hold the most leverage in the form of military and civilian aid, they will tread carefully
- The Western powers, specifically the US and UK, are developing increasingly closer ties with India. They recognize India as a critical regional ally, both from an economic and military standpoint, to help balance out China's influence. This was made abundantly clear when President Obama announced US support for a permanent Indian seat on the UNSC. These strategic ties are the top priority for the US and UK, and therefore they are unlikely to pressure India on the Kashmir issue.
- Russia and China are especially sensitive to issues of national sovereignty (each having significant issues with breakaway regions of their own) and therefore are unlikely to be supportive of any far-reaching UNSC measures

Potential Current Actions

Finding a lasting solution for the Kashmir problem has eluded the world for over 60 years now, and while it doesn't seem likely to happen in the foreseeable future, there are clearly steps that can be taken to move things in the right direction, as well as potential solutions that are becoming more and more impractical. The final solution clearly must have the full support of India and Pakistan, but the UN and its more influential member states must to continue to support the efforts through mediation.

To start with, any solution that involves India giving up territory seems to be off the table for now. India has nothing to gain by giving territory to Pakistan or any independent Kashmiri territory, and the world powers wouldn't pressure India into such a solution. Similarly, it's extremely unlikely that Pakistan would give up any of its territory to India, but it might be more open to some form of Kashmiri independence is it brought the conflict toward a close. A UN sponsored plebiscite also seems unrealistic at this point in time. The political landscape of Kashmir has changed dramatically, and a referendum could not be administered in such a way that would satisfy the Indians, Pakistanis, and Kashmiri separatists.

The most likely scenario is that the status quo will remain the status quo, and with time and UN backed negotiations will start to bring slight changes, such as a gradual demilitarization and increasing self-determination for Kashmiris. To make this happen, the UN needs to continue to facilitate higher level Indian-Pakistani talks following the resumption in February. In the likely event of a future roadblock - such as another terrorist attack or military skirmish - the UN must work to diffuse tensions as quickly as possible, again, just as it always has. Lastly, the UN can help the Kashmir situation with tasks that they have experience in, such as election monitoring or disaster relief, should the need arise.

Until the a solution is brokered between India and Pakistan, the UN also has a responsibility to do its best to fight for the rights or the Kashmiri people. With a limited observation force, and bound by the duty to respect national sovereignty, the UN can't stop human rights abuses by force. All the UN can do is continue to observe, investigate, and 'name and shame' when appropriate, in the hopes that they can curb the abuses. It would probably not be effective to increase the ground forces in Kashmir or ramp up condemnation of either nation; in fact either move could be counter-productive.

Although it seems like little has been accomplished in 60+ years, Kashmir can largely be considered a UN success story. Countless times, they have brokered peace, likely sparing thousands of lives. UN facilitated negotiations have increase economic cooperation between the two countries, making millions of Kashmiri, Pakistani, and Indian lives better. There is no denying that the situation remains a tragedy, and it's very likely that at times the UN could have acted faster or more decisively. However, though their cautious approach, the UN has helped where it can, while not exacerbating one of the most sensitive and complex issues on earth.

THE CHRONOLOGY OF CONFLICT: KASHMIR

Kashmir wasn't always dyed in blood. The people of Kashmir had seen an intellectual renaissance under the rule of Kushans, who ruled Kashmir in 1st century AD, after the fallout of the Asoka dynasty. Kushans loved Kashmir, they often held their court in beautiful springs, and also radicalized the silk route, which got Kashmir commerce and literary reforms. Lalitaditya, the great Hindu king of 8th century AD, has been praised by Kalhana, the first historian of Kashmir, as a just and knowledgeable king, who was highly praised by his subjects. Kaniska institutionalized the Buddhist Council in Kashmir which provided a discourse among Buddhist monks all over the world for decades. The Great philosopher of India, Najarjuna lived and taught peace in Kashmir.

Even though, the struggles of power intensified from 10th century AD, many Hindu and Sanskrit historians have misinterpreted Kashmiri history, as rise of Islam started emerging. Shahab-u-Din, the first Muslim ruler of Kashmir, was married to a Hindu queen, Laxmi and he always internally consolidated all his subjects belonging from different faiths. The valley of Kashmir prospered economically under the reign of his successor, Qutub-ud-Din. Even though the faith of Islam gained popularity, he was tolerant towards Brahmins, and kept Sanskrit as the official language. His rule ended in 1470 AD. His grandson, Sultan Zainul Abideen, popularly known as 'Bud Shah' is perhaps the best remembered Muslim king in Kashmir. His love for Kashmir and his closeness to cultural roots have been ardently recorded. He encouraged poets, historians, artists and intellectuals. He introduced 'paper mache', shawl and carpet weaving traditions which are still in vogue till date. Unfortunately, in the years to come, the fate of native rule came to an end when Mughals invaded Kashmir. This marked an era of weakening sovereignty, a chronology of unfortunate developments, resulting in a blot which hasn't been cleansed till date.

1586: Akbar sees power instability in Kashmir during the reign of Yusuf Shah Chak. He invests in this opportunity and intrudes Kashmir in 1586, ousts out Yusuf, the last Chak ruler and convicts him in far flung Bihar where he dies in misery and isolation. Under the guise of land reforms, nobility and grandeur, Kashmir starts losing its own cultural heritage. People are answerable to alien powers in Delhi. However, Mughal rule in Kashmir slowly sees its decline from 1707.

1751: The Afghan rule comes to Kashmir through Ahmad Shah Durrani. Their rule results in extortion and crude religious fanaticism. They impose heavy taxes, monish handicraft industry. Hindus are subjected to bias, and their role in administrative service drastically declines. Eventually, the Afghan rule ends its 47 year of reign in Kashmir as Sikh dynasty gains prominence.

1819: Maharaja Ranjit Singh of the Sikh dynasty conquers Kashmir and subjects Kashmir to every kind of oppression. Kashmiris live under forcible repression and penury, and earn wages by doing menial jobs. They are heavers of woods and drawers of water. They aren't even exempt from taxations for grave digging and marriage. Cow slaughter is punishable to death. Eventually, Sikh dynasty sees its decline after they lose to the British in the 'Battle of Sobroan' near Sutlej, where feudatory of Jammu, Gulab Singh neglects the battle and plays a significant part in the victory of the British.

1846: Gulab Singh, the Monarch ruler of Jammu, signs 'The Treaty of Amritsar' with the British Empire and purchases Kashmir for Rs. 75 lakhs. The clauses under the treaty integrate Jammu, Ladakh, Baltistan and other hill states including Kashmir under the Dogra reign, as a separate border state. Dogras, under control, treat Kashmir as an occupied state and Jammu as their home state, which neglects the British in any direct intervention, to improve the plight of Kashmiris.

1860: ' The Treaty of Amritsar' is amended due to loyalty displayed by Ranbir Singh, in curbing the first Indian mutiny of

1857. Now, the ruler is allowed to select an heir from his collateral family which results in the succession of Dogras, in an event of present ruler's death.

1889: A British settlement officer, Walter Lawrence surveys Kashmir, and comes to a conclusion that Kashmiris live under such brute oppression which is worse than the Third Estate of the French Revolution.

1929: In Srinagar, an amalgam of graduates from Aligard Muslim University, constitute Reading Room Party with an aim for emancipation of Kashmiris. Ghulam Abbas, an activist from Jammu, reorganizes Anjuman-i-Islam, a Mirwaiz institution, into Young Men's Muslim Association of Jammu for the betterment of Muslims.

1931: The masses of Kashmir gain class consciousness. The revolt against Maharaja Hari Singh gains momentum. It is viciously subjugated by the constabulary of Maharaja. The Muslim majority masses are not allowed to represent in the state administrative apparatus.

The lands belong to rich Hindu 'Jagirdars' who employ Muslims for tilling, and, would give them paddy which would last for petty three months. For rest of the months, Kashmiris would often go to Punjab and other plains to seek industrious labour. They would often die unsung and unwept.

1932: Sheikh Muhammad Abdullah launches 'All Jammu & Kashmir Muslim Conference' against the Maharaja monarchy. It sets out a manifesto to fight for the sovereignty and liberation of the Kashmiri masses. The natives give unconditional support to Sheikh Abdullah. He is widely admired. In the meantime, The Maharaja constitutes 'The Glancy Commission' in an effort to redress the grievances of the masses, by giving recommendations for Muslims in state services.

1934: Maharaja delays the implementation of the recommendations, set out by the commission. This creates chaos and leads to a vehement agitation. Maharaja, under pressure, constitutes a legislative assembly which eventually turns out to be void and powerless.

1939: Leaders among the AJKMC [All Jammu & Kashmir Muslim Conference] get riddled in differences and the party gets a split. Sheikh Abdullah launches his independent party 'Jammu & Kashmir National Conference'.

1946: Sheikh Abdullah harnesses support from the masses. JKNC launches 'Quit Kashmir Movement' against Maharaja Monarchy demanding abrogation of 'The Treaty of Amritsar' and sovereignty for the Kashmiri masses. Sheikh Abdullah is taken into custody.

1947: On 15th of August, 1947, India freed itself from the British Empire. The kings and rulers of the princely states were encouraged to accede into respective Indian and Pakistani dominions based on geographical contiguity, religion and cultural adjacency. In theory, any dominion could have been preferred. In case where a dispute occurred, the collective aspirations and general will of the people formed the basis of consideration. Practically, Kashmir was expected to go with the Dominion of Pakistan based on geographical and religious factors. Since the Hindu Monarch acceded a Muslim majority state to India, a grave dispute arose in case of Kashmir, unlike the case of Junagardh, a mirror image of Kashmir, where India won a plebiscite from the Hindu masses, resulting in the booting out of a Muslim dominated reign.

The Revolt of Poonch: In the spring of 1947, internal unrest begins at Poonch. Muslims rebels stir up public opinion against Maharaja's oppressive and outrageous taxation policy. Several crowds of protestors demanding accession to Pakistan are fired upon. Maharaja dictates the Muslim rebels for surrender under the strengthened Hindu and Sikh garrisons. In late August, the people of Poonch evacuate their kins. The unrest turns into an organized uprising resulting in exodus of 60,000 Muslim refugees to Jammu, till September.

Jammu Muslim Massacre: In September, under the sponsorship of Maharaja's state forces, armed Hindu and Sikh bandits murder thousands of Muslims out in the open. Survivors forcibly flee Jammu. Pakistan sends a telegram to Kashmir demanding probe into savage atrocities committed. An enquiry is promised which eventually never happens. In the meantime, no communal violence is witnessed in Kashmir.

The Kabali Invasion: On 22nd October, the tribesmen from Pakistan, storm into Kashmir, and integrate with Poonch Rebels as an umbrageous reaction against the killings of Muslims in Jammu and Poonch. The Kabali tribe is supported by unofficial people and leaders from Pakistan. However, the tribes also engage in plundering and despoil along the way, resulting in exodus of over 10,000 Muslims. India accuses Pakistan for violating the 'Standstill Agreement'. Pakistan rebuts the allegations. The revolt flares up neighboring Mirpur and Muzaffarabad. 'Azaad Kashmir' comes into existence with an independent government on 24th October, 1947.

Indian Army Aggression: The national army of India invades Kashmir to repel the Kabali invasion, on 27th October. There are also cases where the Indian army is accused of committing atrocities towards common Kashmiris. India launches its first military aggression in Kashmir.

Release of Sheikh Abdullah: In prison, Sheikh Abdullah writes a letter to a friend in Jammu, favouring Kashmir's accession with India. His statement is published at the Congress Press. On September 29th, Sheikh Abdullah is released from the prison, due to increasing pressure from the Indian Government. He would appear in public and would give contradictory speeches of Kashmir's independence before the signing of the accession. On 26th October, he demands the restoration of power to the masses. Then throughout his political life, he would juggle between the accession instrument and the right of self-determination.

Strategical Disputes : Pakistan claims that Maharaja has no right to initiate the 'Instrument of Accession' till 'The Standstill Agreement is in order. Jammu & Kashmir Muslim Conference and the tribal chiefs of Gilgit advice the Maharaja against the accession of Kashmir with India.

The Instrument of Accession: India signs an accession with The Maharaja on 26th October, 1947. The accession is granted provisional approval until the implementation of the plebiscite. It should be noted that there are no legal provisions relating to conditionalties in the 'Instrument of Accession' (IOA). It was the 'White Paper' which was voluntarily designed by the Government of India, thus making a conflict between the legal interpretation and the political promises made to the Kashmiris.

First Indo-Pak War: India demands Pakistan to withdraw its troops for the implementation of plebiscite. On the other hand, Pakistan demands a bilateral demilitarization, with an argument that it would help in the free and fair implementation of plebiscite, considering Sheikh Abdullah's friendliness with Jawaharlal Nehru. India refuses. The first war on Kashmir between India & Pakistan breaks out.

1948: Demanding a resolution of Kashmir, India takes the case of Kashmir, to the United Nations. World over, Kashmir is officially recognized as a disputed territory. UN passes a resolution recommending a third party into consideration: The people of Kashmir.

1949: On 1st January, UN offers a ceasefire between India and Pakistan. Both countries hold up the occupied parts of Kashmir. India regains control of some parts of Kashmir, Ladakh & Jammu, while Pakistan integrates with 'Azaad Kashmir'.

UNCIP Formation: On 5th January. UNCIP (United Nations Commission for India and Pakistan) recommends a bilateral demilitarization, a truce agreement for the future, and an implementation of a free and fair plebiscite. Both countries fail to arrive at any peace resolution.

Indian Constituent Assembly: An ordinance is passed which integrates Article 370 of the Indian Constitution into Kashmir's legal provisions, with foreign affairs, defence, communications and currency under Indian control. Internal autonomy is granted to Kashmir, under the ambit of the Indian constitution.

1951: Indian holds elections and tries to impose its democratic institution in Kashmir. It is opposed by the United Nations. They pass a resolution to declare elections void and stress on plebiscite. India ignores the opposition blatantly. Sheikh Abdullah wins unopposed and rumours of election rigging plague Kashmiri politics.

1952: Sheikh Abdullah signs the Delhi Agreement on July, 1952. It chalks out state-centre sharing of power and gives abidance to Kashmir to have its own flag. Sheikh Abdullah creates Kashmir centric land reforms which create resentment among the people of Jammu and Ladakh. Delhi Agreement provides the first genuine erosion in international resolution of Kashmir.

Nehru's Speech: "On August 1952, Jawahar Lal Nehru gives a negating speech contradicting the settlement provided in the Delhi Agreement: "Ultimately - I say this with all deference to this Parliament - the decision will be made in the hearts and minds of the men and women of Kashmir; neither in this Parliament, nor in the United Nations nor by anybody else"

1953-1954: Sheikh Abdullah takes U turns and procrastinates in conforming the accession of Kashmir to India. Sheikh Abdullah is jailed. In August, Bakhshi Ghulam Muhammad is installed in place of Sheikh Abdullah. He officially ratifies Kashmir's accession with India. On April, 1954, India & Pakistan both agree in appointment of a Plebiscite Administrator.

1956-1957: On 30th October, 1956, J&K Constituent Assembly adopts a fresh constitution, and dissolves the Constituent Assembly, which further defines the relationship of Kashmir with the Indian Dominion. UN strongly condemns the developments and passes a resolution stating such attempts will not result in any final resolution. On 26th January, 1957, the new constitution is made enforceable. Kashmir is now a Republican-Democratic state under Indian Union.

1964: Sheikh Abdullah is released from jail. Jawahar Lal Nehru sends Sheikh Abdullah with a delegation to Pakistan in an effort to find a resolution discourse for Kashmir. In the meantime, masses in Kashmir protest against the implementation of Article 356 & 357, which allows Indian central authority over constituting legislative powers in Kashmir. The special status of Kashmir continues to get eroded.

1965-1971: The nomenclature is changed from 'Sadr-e-Riyasat' to Governor and from Prime Minister to Chief Minister. The Governor is now no longer elected locally, and is installed as per the orders of the President of India. This amendment lightens off Kashmir from its special titles. Free & fair elections in the guise of democracy are championed as just causes, and Indian mainstream parties are allowed to contest in the elections. However, these elections aren't well received by the public. In many cases, international watchdogs accuse India of rigging elections. In 1967, Jammu Autonomy Forum is constituted with the aim of institutionalizing regional autonomy.

1972: Plebiscite Front is banned from constituting elections, and in the meantime, India and Pakistan, both, sign 'The Simla Agreement' which settles a basis for a bilateral solution for Kashmir through talks. The provisions also state that both nations should determine their military policies by respecting the Line of Control (LOC)

1974: Sheikh Abdullah signs an accord with the Government of India, on November, 1974. This agreement retains Kashmir's so called 'Special Status', but its obliged to act under the Indian dominion. Sheikh Abdullah is again made the Head of the state. This time as the Chief Minister of Jammu & Kashmir.

1977-1983: Jammu & Kashmir National Conference wins back to back elections in 1977 and 1983. International watchdogs accuse India of rigging elections again. In 1979, Afghanistan would recommend an Islamic Republic for Kashmir. Sikri Commission is also appointed in the same year in an effort to redress local grievances existent among the masses.

1987-1989: Farooq Abdullah comes into power in the 1987 election. He forms a coalition government with the Indian National Congress. This election, due to the nature of its immense rigging accusations, provides a scope for voicing dissent and it catalyses deep resentment, not only amongst the secessionist political arena of Kashmir, but also suffers huge disfavour from public as well. Armed insurgency also gets on a rise. Due to its catastrophic effects, in the whole year of 1988, world witnesses Kashmiris pouring out on streets, sloganeering anti-India demonstrations, which are deeply resisted by police firing, crackdowns, mass killings and curfew culture. The rigging of 1987 elections provides an offshoot platform for the demand for self-determination. From 1989, the Indian government tries to sabotage the rising secessionist movement through a central rule of authority for seven years.

1990: An ultra-Hindu nationalist leaning regulator, Jagmohan is appointed as the Governor of Kashmir. Farooq Abdullah resigns as the Chief Minister of Kashmir, and all powers are vested in the central rule. In the same year, about 100 protestors are fired upon in Gawkadal area. This event marks as the first brutal mass killing genocide in Kashmir. The people blame this notorious event on the administrators and it becomes the insurgency for the entire population. With violence a catalyst, Kashmir becomes a land of blood dyed subjugation. Over one million people protest on streets and 40 more are slained.

March : A sense of insecurity rises among the Kashmiri Pandit community. Paranoias of pogroms force Pandits for an exodus, as even the Jagmohan's administration discourages any reconciliation between two communities. With the result, more than one lakh Pandits flock off Kashmir.

May: Over two million people attend the funeral march of the slain spiritual leader of Kashmir, Mirwaiz Maulvi Muhammad Farooq; over 100 mourners are fired upon by the police. The grave irresponsibility of Jagmohan's administration forces Government of India for a replacement in Girish Saxena

1993: All Parties Hurriyiat Conference (APHC) is formed on specialist political lines to promote the cause of Kashmiri nationalism. It is aimed to promote a solution based on the UN Charter, its resolutions, and through a tri-partite negotiation between India, Pakistan and Kashmir. The amalgam, since its inception, has received criticism from Indian state actors, and praise from Pakistan and international watchdogs for its political measures and tactics in handling the grave dispute of Kashmir.

1998: Political leaders across the borders sign 'The Lahore Agreement' which includes settlement of all outstanding disputes including Kashmir.

June: Farooq Abdullah designs the RAC [Regional Autonomy Committee] of 8 units comprising of Ladadkh, Jammu and Kashmir without proposing any devolution of political and economic powers.

2000: On March, a notorious event about massacre of Sikhs at Chittisinghpora makes headlines. Kashmiris blame rebel militants recruited by Indian security forces, while India blames foreign militants. No judicial commission has been implemented to enquire about this killing till date. In June, the State Autonomy Report [SAR] puts a discourse on the future political initiative on Kashmir. The central government rejects the recommendation in July. In November, the Indian government announces ceasefire with the armed groups, which gets violated in two weeks after India refuses to acknowledge Pakistan in tri-partite dialogue over the Kashmir dispute.

2001: In July 2001, India & Pakistan under the leadership of PM Vajpayee and President Musharaf fail to arrive at a settlement on the Kashmir issue, despite five long arduous one on one, hours of meetings. Some plans were chalked out on Kashmir including free trade, demilitarization, shared autonomy but they don't get initiated due to failure in reconciling differences due to bilateral complexities.

2002: On May 21, an eminent moderate separatist leader, Abdul Gani Lone is assassinated by unidentified gunmen. This is the same day on which Mirwaiz Moulvi Farooq was killed as well. Kashmir's history is rewritten in blood. Thousands attend his funeral prayers. Several theories of pro-government gunmen or the role of foreign militants has been rumored, but no investigation has been carried out till date.

2008: People are provoked by the state government through a controversial land deal, of 100 acres of land to a local Shrine Board, managing pilgrimages and local Hindu affairs in the valley, near the Amarnath cave, in May. A cave discovered by a Muslim shepherd in the mid- 19th century, is worshipped by Hindus as a deity of destruction. Beginning as a small pilgrimage, it was eventually offset into a mega event by the Hindu nationalist institutions. In June, Muslim masses of Kashmir protest against the land deal, waging a war on streets through wavering of Islamic flags, hurling stones and bricks. On August 11, there is a march towards Jehlum Valley road, which once, connected Kashmir with Pakistan. Similar massive protests followed near the United Nations Observer's Group. Kashmir is locked for months. Over 100 people are killed, over a short span of 2 months, including eminent separatist leader, Sheikh Aziz. It provides a renewed basis for self determination against the Indian state. Many liberal political commentators and intellectuals from India like Vir Sanghvi, Arundhati Roy and Jug Suraiya express their anguish over the turmoil and recommended 'Azaadi' or freedom for Kashmir in open media forums. However, the agitation is eventually crushed by the Indian state through brute army aggression and curfew hegemony.

2010: The last year of the decade in Kashmir provides the most belligerent political atmosphere in waging a war against the Indian state. On June 11, at a protest gathering, Tufail Ahmad Matto, gets killed after receiving a tear gas shell, which blows his brains out. His death provides a charged catalyst in reincarnating the crushed agitation of 2008. Protestors shout anti-India slogans, processions continue even till late nights, people burn government buildings, defy curfew, attack Indian forces in the bunkers, and demand complete demilitarization of Kashmir. Citing human rights abuses, separatist leaders organize protest calendars which last for over 4 months, paralyzing the local life. Over 110 people get killed in the process. Indian Government after witnessing the intensity of upheaval recommends autonomy proposals, job generation promises and compensation to victims. These developments, however, are all are blatantly refused by both leaders and masses of Kashmir. The Indian government also announces the role of three eminent interlocutors in mediating the Kashmir dispute which till now has resulted as a futile and ineffective exercise.

THE CONFLICT IN KASHMIR: THE TERRITORY AND COMMUNITY OF KASHMIR

The region of Kashmir has been a disputed region between India and Pakistan since1947. Kashmir is a beautiful region nestled between Pakistan, India, and China. The majority of the region's 13 million people live between the Himalayan Mountains and the Pir Panjal Mountains in the Kashmir Valley. Kashmir has two important water supplies that flow through it, the headwaters of the Indus River and the Jhelum, which flows through the Kashmir Valley. The climate of Kashmir is considered mild, which allows for moist soil year-round. The people of Kashmir are 70% Muslim with the remaining 30% primarily Hindu. Kashmir is largely a farming region that produces rich supplies of corn, wheat, rice, fruits and vegetables.

The region of Kashmir has changed drastically over the last fifty years, largely due to human actions and the redrawing of its political borders. In 1947 Maharajah Hari Singh, who controlled the area, signed an "Instrument of Accession" to India, which would give control of Kashmir to India in exchange for India's military assistance. The reason Maharajah was seeking military assistance was that Pakistan had invaded the land to unite all land that contained Muslims.

Background History

The government of India promised the people of Kashmir that they would be able to vote for their future sovereignty. This never happened. Since 1947 the countries of Pakistan and India have fought three official wars with the United Nations stepping in and setting a "Cease Fire Line" each time. The conflict has never been settled and in 1998 both India and Pakistan detonated nuclear weapons during tests, which escalated the severity of the conflict.

Both Pakistan and India have laid claim to the region of Kashmir over the past fifty years. Both nations claim to have vested interests in the region. Pakistan has two major concerns/ interests to the region. The first major concern is that the headwaters of the Indus River begin in the Kashmir region. This is of huge importance to Pakistan because this river serves as a major resource to Pakistan. If the headwaters of this important river are in another country, especially a country with whom they have been in conflict since 1947, then, ultimately, the control of the river does not lie in Pakistan. Pakistan also claims that the majority of the population of Kashmir is Muslim and has taken a vow to unite all Muslim people in the region.

Three Main Reasons for the Conflict

Three main facts get to the root of the Kashmir conflict. First is geography, the beginning of the Indus River is found here. The importance of this river to Pakistan has already been discussed and is a major factor in the conflict. Secondly, the fact that over 70% of the Kashmir population is Muslim. With Pakistan being a Muslim state and India being a Hindu state (which controls the majority of Kashmir) the cultural factor of religion plays a huge factor in this conflict. The third fact is India's historic claim to the region and the fact that, for over 50 years, they have not been willing to budge on this issue.

On the other side of the dispute lies India. India currently controls most of the territory of Kashmir, including the Valley of Kashmir and Indus and Jhelum rivers. India claims that Kashmir is an integral part of their territory and will not relinquish its control of the region. This claim is rooted in India's original control of Kashmir in 1947 and is fueled by its rivalry with Pakistan. India currently has over 500,000 troops in the region and Pakistan has "hired" Muslim mercenaries from neighboring regions to join in the fight. Added to the already tense situation, both of these countries are new members of the Nuclear Club, with neither nation agreeing to pass the United Nations decisions and cease-fires.

AN DOMESTIC CONFLICT AMONG INDIA AND INDIA-CONTROLLED J&K

The Kashmir conflict is a duo-conflict; it is both an internal conflict between India and India-controlled Jammu and Kashmir (IJK) and an external conflict between India and Pakistan. The external dimension of the Kashmir conflict has been the focus of much study. In view of the recent developments in the India-Pakistan bilateral relationship, it is timely to re-focus on the internal dimension of the conflict. This proposal seeks to address that and purports that there can and should be fruitful problem-solving between the central Indian government and the Srinagar-based state government of IJK. This proposal recommends that the "Autonomy Model" be pursued as the solution to the conflict.

The Kashmir conflict is a duo-conflict; it is both an internal conflict between India and India-controlled Jammu and Kashmir (IJK) and an external conflict between India and Pakistan. The external dimension of the Kashmir conflict has lasted more than five decades and many solutions have focused on that dimension. These solutions essentially require the joint decision-making and implementation of India and Pakistan, which poses two problems.

Firstly, the solutions generally require two estranged and unwilling neighbours to work towards either giving up a slice of the pie they have paid high costs for keeping or to work through layers of administrative details to reach a workable condominium. In the latter, there is the possibility of fresh cause for future discord between the two countries; joined India-Pakistan administration presents a potential for friction, no matter how slight. The situation may be analogous to insisting two enemies become in-laws. Overall, these solutions, by concentrating on the New Delhi-Islamabad axis, relegate the Kashmiris to the sidelines, and deny them decision-making power.

Secondly, the latest warmed-up relationship between India-Pakistan requires an updated approach and solution responsive to the changes. Given the good chance that India and Pakistan will unlikely fight another war soon over Kashmir – although that does not translate into immediate resolution of the conflict itself – it is timely to focus on the internal dimension of the conflict, especially since Kashmir has not yet been included in the peace talks between India and Pakistan. In particular, Pakistan is under real pressure from the US, its patron country, to stop support for Kashmiri insurgent terror activities. With funding and backing for Kashmiri separatist activities collapsing, it serves Kashmir well to re-strategize and re-examine the available options and with Pakistan "taken off its back" for the moment, India is more likely poised to consider Kashmiri requests more openly than before. In short, this period of cease-fire interregnum is pregnant with opportunity for peace-making between India and IJK.

Focus of Proposal

This proposal seeks to address the home-ground problem between India and Kashmir directly; there can and should be direct problem-solving between the New Delhi central government and Srinagar-based state government of IJK, and it should be recognized that taking Pakistan out of the equation can be liberating and can move the problem-solving process faster.

Decision-Making Criteria

The best solution-model will have to meet the following criteria:

- High in benefits.
- Low in costs.
- Close match with each party's interest.
- High feasibility.

Interests

The positions of India and IJK really mask certain key interests. The principal interests of India may be summed up as the following:

- To uphold the political integrity of India.
- To benefit from the resources of Kashmir.

Kashmir is symbolic of the cornerstone of India's nationhood: a secular India able to embrace all different religious affiliations, which sets it apart from Pakistan's two-nation concept that believes Muslims and Hindus cannot coexist, and which led to the partition of India into India and Pakistan. As the "centerpiece of India's bouquet of democratic diversity," Kashmir represents more than territory; former Prime Minister Vajpayee stated during the Independence Day address in 2002 that "Jammu and Kashmir is an integral part of India...For us, Kashmir is not a piece of land; it is a test case of a secular nation. Jammu and Kashmir is a living example of this."

As evident in the past fifty years of Kashmir conflict, India will pay almost any price to defend that ideology, whether the enemy be Pakistan or Kashmir itself. Allowing the cornerstone of Kashmir to be removed – or voluntarily giving up that cornerstone – renders the entire political foundation on which India rests severe structural damage and can lead to the collapse of the house. Although Kashmir's secession may not necessarily motivate other states to secede, that threat seems real in the minds of Indian politicians.

Kashmiri interests are not as easily defined as those of India. This is due to the different political aspirations of the Kashmiris. The Kashmiri "public" is really several small ethno-linguistic groups and three large distinct religious groups: Muslims, Hindus and Buddhists, who can be crudely delineated along geographical lines, with the Muslims in the Kashmir Valley, Hindus in Jammu and Buddhists in Ladakh.

According to the 1981 census, the Kashmir Valley has a population of 3.1 million, or about 50 percent of the population of the whole IJK state. This area has a 95 percent Muslim majority who are mostly pro-*Azaadi* or pro-Pakistan; Jammu and Ladakh constitute the remaining 50 percent of the population and are largely pro-India.

This scenario is complicated by the different political leanings – pro-Pakistan, pro-independence (*azaadi*) or pro-maximum autonomy – of the Kashmiri insurgent groups as largely represented by All Parties Hurriyat Conference (APHC) and Jammu Kashmir Liberation Front (JKLF). However, since separatist sentiments are evidently mostly contained in the Kashmir Valley – where 50 percent of Kashmir's population is – and not all of the 50 percent are extremist or maximalist in separatist claims, it may be fair to suggest that more than 50 percent is moderate in claims or are open to negotiation so long as the outcome comes closer to the Kashmiri desire for an improved state of affairs. This nebulous "improved state of affairs" can be understood as having:

- Peace restored, so that normalcy can return.
- A revived economy and jobs.
- *Azaadi*, which means freedom, but that can also mean self-determination.

Up till the present, the disruption of daily life by Kashmiri insurgents and militants infiltrating across the Line of Control (LoC) between IJK and Pakistan controlled Kashmir and the presence of armed soldiers on the lookout for militant elements have driven the numbers seeking psychiatric help up and brought suicide rates from about one to two per day about fifteen years ago – before the turmoil started – to five a day presently. A return to normalcy will necessitate a gradual demilitarization of the zone and is so crucial in bringing back the tourists; IJK's – and particularly Kashmir Valley's – economy is so dependent on tourism.

The last interest is somewhat less straight-forward, since for the maximalists, *azaadi* can only mean independence from India. Assuming all of Kashmir Valley's Muslim population want to break free from India, whether to form an independent Kashmir or to merge with Pakistan, it will mean that about a near maximum of 50 percent of Kashmir wants to secede. The remaining 50 percent of the population, being largely pro-Indian, is likely to request greater autonomy and devolution of more power from the central government to its state government.

DETERMINATION THE CONFLICT DOUBTFUL REGION OF J&K

We will present various solutions that we have considered that could bring peace to the disputed area of Jammu and Kashmir. The precise contours of solutions to the conflict in Kashmir are, of course, uncertain. There are many proposed resolutions from which to choose; new ones could still be devised, but it is important to consider the present status of the Line of Control while devising a plan for the future. All the feasible options can only be long lasting if the actions are undertaken while keeping the aspirations of Kashmiris living on both sides of the LOC in mind. While resolving the problems in Kashmir is an integral aspect of the peace process, it is equally important to remember to keep the wishes of Kashmiri people in mind. A solution without the participation, wishes and aspirations of Kashmir people would not last. Past solutions that have been suggested include recognition of the Line of control as it is. Currently a boundary - the Line of Actual Control - divides the region in two, with one part administered by India and one by Pakistan. India would like to formalize this status quo and make it the accepted international boundary. But Pakistan and Kashmiri activists reject this plan because they both want greater control over the region. Pakistan has consistently favored the idea that Kashmir should join Pakistan. In view of the state's majority Muslim population, it believes that it would vote to become part of Pakistan. However a simple majority (plebiscite) held in a region which comprises peoples that are culturally, religiously and ethnically diverse, would create large, disaffected minorities. The Hindus and Sikhs of the Kashmir Valley, the Hindu majority of Jammu, and the Buddhist majority of Ladakh have never shown any desire to join Pakistan and would protest such an outcome.

In the same spirit of the argument, India, of course, believes that the entire state of Kashmir should be a part of India. Such a solution would be unlikely to bring stability to the region, as the Muslim inhabitants of Pakistani-administered Jammu and Kashmir, including the Northern Areas, have never shown any desire to become part of India.

In addition to making decisions about the whole region, there have also been proposal of a smaller independent Kashmir. An independent Kashmir could be created from the Kashmir Valley - currently under Indian administration - and the narrow strip of land that Pakistan calls Azad Jammu and Kashmir. This would leave the strategically important regions of the Northern Areas and Ladakh, bordering China, under the control of Pakistan and India respectively. However both India and Pakistan would be unlikely to enter into discussions that would have this scenario as a possible outcome.

Some have considered the possibility of having an independent Kashmir Valley as an option. This possibility is supposed to address the grievances of those who have been fighting against the Indian Government since the insurgency began in 1989. But critics say that, without external assistance, the region would not be economically viable. The rest of the paper considers the possibility of an Independent Economic Zone of Kashmir and some of the policies that need to be implemented for this option to be a viable one. We argue that Kashmir can become an independent entity that is economically sustainable if proper resources and policies are filtered into the region by the State as well as the Central Government.

Independent Economic Zone

One creative proposal is to turn the entire area into an Independent Economic Zone where both India and Pakistan can engage in free Trade. This would require both armies to withdraw under conditions of honour and dignity; it would not prejudice their positions on Kashmir as a whole; it would stop further degradation of a magnificent mountain area; it would save thousands of lives and billions of rupees that are spent on special military forces by the government; and more importantly, try to heal a running sore among Kashmiri hearts.

Any agreement to withdraw forces would, of course, have to be backed by assurances. An independent entity such as the United Nations can be involved as an "enforcer" in such scenarios. There have been examples in the past where such actions have been undertaken. Ground-based and air surveillance, such as is used along the Mexico–US border, or was used in 1973 to monitor the Sinai Desert Cease Fire, could ensure this. The mountain terrain would present special difficulties, but from reports of recent discussions, it may be assumed that these can be overcome.

This scenarios requires detailed knowledge of the situation on the ground with a deep understanding of political considerations. Both sides need to recognize each other's claims, agree not to change the status quo by force, and agree not to introduce irregulars. This would be followed by 3 steps:

1 End the fighting without disengaging or redeployment.

2 Introduce technical means of monitoring and surveillance, permitting meaningful reductions of forces to be negotiated.

3 Work out a complete demilitarization.

At present, with possibly up to a million armed men facing each other across the Kashmir border, talk of ending the fighting and of bringing peace to the region seems remote. But the dawn always comes after the darkest period: perhaps there will also be a dawn for the state of Jammu and Kashmir.

It is also crucial to look at the feasibility of the option. Kashmir has a sizable population and enough land and infrastructure to support itself. However, it requires a lot more resources to continue building the necessary framework to be a successful entity, in the purely economic as well as social sense. Both the Government of India and Pakistan needs to be actively involved in the development process of the region to build the necessary infrastructure of the well beings of its residents as well as foster good educational institutions and aid the tourism industry for long term growth.

In retrospect, India and Pakistan have spent a lot of resources, both in terms of monetary contribution as well as human capital, in trying to resolve or perpetuate the problem. Thus, the proposed solution is much cheaper in comparison to the past willingness to pay in both countries. The costs of the Kashmir conflict are said to be increasingly unbearable for all involved. Over 40,000 lives have been lost since the insurgency began in 1989. The governments have spent tens of billions of rupees on feeding and fighting the conflict rather than on alleviating poverty and improving literacy and health programs for the staggering number of poor in all of India and Pakistan.

5

Nepal: Post-conflict Governance

The present world conditions reveal that the world is neither a fair nor a friendly place for mankind. More than half of the world's population lives in misery and hunger while rest in comfort and luxury. Insurrections, tribal hostility and war between nations have been common throughout history. Some estimates that higher than 70 million people lost their lives during the II World War in which 12 million civilians were killed as a direct result of military action mainly bombing. After the end of the II World War, the United Nation was formally established on October 24, 1945 for the purpose of peace and security worldwide. But United States and Britain, on one side and Soviet Union on the other remain for a new power struggle maintaining blocs of allies on the basis of mistrust, suspicion and hostility. This cold war continued for more than 45 years in international politics. With the division of Soviet Union that ended the cold war period in 1989-90. Since then, US and its allies are playing hegemonial role in international arena in the name of international peace and security.

In the post cold war period (1989-1999) more than 100 armed conflicts occurred, out of them 95 percent were within intra-states (40 percent against government, 55 percent territory related) and remaining 5 percent were inter-states. It had resulted death of millions of people including physically and mentally wounded, 20 million refugees and 27 million people internally displaced

(IDPs). Similarly, at the beginning of 21st century on Tuesday, September 11, 2001, terrorists hijacked 4 planes and had three of them crashed into "Twin Towers" of the World Trade Centre, America. This led coalition war against terrorism in Afghanistan later in Iraq on various allegations that resulted replacement of both Taliban and Saddam Hussein Regime respectively. But till now there is no sign of peace and development in those countries.

In the global situation, Third World refers to the economically under-developed countries of Asia, Africa, Oceania, and Latin America, with common characteristics, such as poverty, high birthrates, and economic dependence on the advance countries. The situation of third World has the lowest standard in living, economic growth, education, life expectancy and highest population growth and infant mortality rates. Therefore, millions of inhabitants are dreadfully improvised, malnourished, disease-ridden, and unable to live productively with honor and dignity. Among them, many are into foreign debts; unable to pay, threatening the political stability which led more vulnerable in the context of foreign intervention and failed state. Similarly, many conflicts together with disasters affect people live in areas outside of government control.

An acute example of a situation illustrating the characteristics of both compound and complex emergencies is the Horn of Africa. For the past several years the situation in the Horn of Africa has been characterized by internal conflicts in Ethiopia, Sudan, and Somalia. These conflicts have been exacerbated by recurrent droughts and have resulted in famines on a massive scale and the flight of large numbers of people across national borders. During the last half of 1991, the situation in many parts of the Horn remained highly volatile and fragile, largely due to conflict and a breakdown of law and order. This resulted in further population displacement and in intense misery for millions of people. There are often persons who are most in need and they are often the most difficult to reach with aid and support.

Similarly, South-Asia is the place of more than one fifth of world's population. In the last few decades, it has been one of the most conflict prone regions in the world. States located in this region have taken longer than expected in overcoming their mutual suspicion and relating to one another as an enemy. For example; On Wednesday Nov. 26, 2008, armed group attacked Heritage Taj Mahal Palace and Tower Hotel in India's financial capital, Mumbai. In response, joint counter operation took almost 60 hours where around 195 people were killed including 20 security persons and 22 foreigners with 327 injured? This resulted in war like situation between India and Pakistan. Thus, interstate hostility and intrastate conflict has lingered in the South Asia region.

Nepal's Situation

Nepal a birthplace of Lord Buddha and the land of Sagarmatha (Mount Everest) has an area of approximately 147,181 Square Km., length 885 Km. (East to West) and Width 193 Km (North to South). A Land-locked country is surrounded by India in the East, West and South and the autonomous region of Tibet of the People's Republic of China in the North.

Nepal as a modern state came into existence in 1769 AD when Prithvi Narayan Shah, the King of Gorkha, united several principalities scattered in the southern rim of Asia. Since decades, Nepal is facing external influences and internal turmoil situation leading it into a nearly failed state like Africa (. Having its open border with India has both positive and negative implications. In one way, it provides free access to the people of both the countries whereas in other hand has promoted transnational organized crimes (terrorism, hijacking Indian Airlines flight IC 814 Kathmandu to Delhi, trafficking of human, drugs, illegal arms and ammunitions, kidnapping, extortion, contract killing, etc.). Bhutanese and Tibetan refugees are another problematic aspect of Nepal. After 1990 the successive governments could not fulfill the aspirations of common people. State mechanisms have indulged in rampant corruption and bad governance, as well as political instability and emergence of organized criminal groups. At the same time, Nepal Communist Party (Maoist) insurgency movement started in 1996 from Rolpa, Rukum and spread all over the country ultimately in 2006 King Gyanendra had to shift executive power to the 8 political parties. After the constitution assembly election, Nepal has been declared republican country on May 28, 2008. Though then rebellion Maoist Party leader Puspa Kamal Dahal heading the coalition government, the situation of the country has remain as it is. In addition, the number of other armed groups has started militancy starting from Terai (Madhesh) to other parts of the country demanding various type of autonomy. After more than a decade long conflict and now in the transitional phase Nepal is experiencing tremendous increment of conventional, modern and political related crimes. Among the committed crimes many are unreported if reported; the cases are not properly investigated.

This has led to a humanitarian tragedy and an obstacle to reconstruction and rehabilitation.. Other costs and impacts include the destruction of physical, human, and social capital. It has further led to lower investment in physical and human capital; the disruption of markets and other forms of economic and social order; the diversion of human resources and public expenditure from productive or productivity-enhancing activities; the migration and transfer of financial assets abroad.

It has also created unemployment, poverty, illiteracy, inflation, hoarding, price hikes and rampant corruption.

These are the seen impacts but we tend to forget the indirect/ unseen impact that an individual, family, community, a country and a world has to pay a price in every second which could be coded as hidden cost. For example; in the economic dimension then Vice Chairperson of the National Planning Commission, Dr. Shanker Sharma revealed that an estimated Rs. 40 billion (approximately 500 million US Dollars) was lost in the fiscal year 2001-2002 alone due to destructive activities. So what could be the hidden cost a person (financial crises due to unemployment/ disable/displaced, family conflict, unable to treat when ill etc.) undergoes within this situation is high time to talk about.

Therefore, present scenario of law and order situation, peace, security and development in Nepal is still in a fragile state hence it is pity that it is unable to focus on issues like peace, social justice and development. In contemporary situation of Nepal it seems that power is lying in the hands of non state actors such as criminals, warlords, armed gangs having the characteristics of failed state.

Understanding Post Conflict

Usually, period of post conflict starts after the peace agreement among the actors of the conflicting parties to solve the major issues. In several situations, UN and other international organizations monitor the implementation of peace agreements that applies in both Intrastate and interstate conflict resolution. Through the agreement, the phase of conflict settlement starts which consists of usually content oriented and restricted to the Track I level (high level political and military leaders, etc.)

In several occasions, diplomatic and military measures are taken to stop a violent conflict and/or enforce a peace agreement. This is usually carried out by a third party military force to bring an end to armed hostilities in a conflict situation. The concept of peace enforcement has become one of the new 'instruments' for international organizations.

It means that wars are brought to a halt through direct military intervention under the multilateral organs. Similarly, peacekeeping is the third party military forces usually organized by UN to separate the armed process of conflicting parties and to reduce violence, normally at the request of the parties as part of a ceasefire agreement. It plays a role of civil tasks such as monitoring, policing and supporting humanitarian intervention. It can occur preventively before the outbreak as well as after the cessation of open conflict.

This peacekeeping concept was developed for the first time as UN Emergency Force (TJNEFI) in 1956 Another important task during the post conflict is conflict or crisis prevention so as to prevent existing tensions from escalating into violence and to remove sources of danger before violence results.. In the context of Nepal, after handing power by the King Gyanendra to the parties in 2006, United Nation, Mission to Nepal (UNMIN) involved as.a third party along with the civilian, humanitarian and other expert components at the request of then Prime Minister and Maoist Chairperson that is continuing even after the Constitution Assembly Election.

The tasks ahead in the post conflict management in Nepal are; to mitigate and contain open conflict in community among various actors. Control and handle a conflict in order to limit its negative effects and bring it to an end and to prevent and vertical (i.e. intensification of violence) or horizontal (territorial spread) escalation of existing violent conflict with applying actions on all levels and Tracks. A comprehensive conflict transformation involves negative destructive conflict into positive constructive conflict and deals with structural, behavioral, and attitudinal aspects of conflict. In this process participation of the rural population, strengthening the civil society is also important aspect of transformation. Similarly, institutional reform (Constitutional drafting, integration of minorities (ethnic and religion) through power-sharing, territorial divisions of power, federalism, accountability through decentralization, protection of minorities, rule of law etc.) and security sector reform are other important areas of post conflict management.

THE COLLISION OF CONFLICT ON SOCIAL CIVILIZATION NEPAL

To know the complex and multiple roles of civil society in peace building, it is very essential to examine their strengths and weaknesses and their relationship with the state and market institutions. Protracted conflict erodes the monopoly of state's power and undermines its basic functions—preservation of human rights, law and order, voice, visibility, justice, education and health. It also transforms social capital of pluralistic, multiethnic and multi-cultural societies and undermines the capacity of communities to engage in peace building. Opposing pressures of conflict actors alter the basic functions of civil society and community and sometimes tear apart their critical support base. The state, which defines the legal framework of civil society functions, may become strict in disciplining and controlling the organs of civil society, such as the media, NGOs, trade unions, human rights groups and professional associations thereby changing the institutional framework and reducing their freedom of action to address the multi-dimensionality of violence and their vicious tendencies. State authorities often cast doubt over civil society's ability to transcend urban, partisan, paternalistic and class bias and believe that they are competing with existing structures of political power backed by the financial resource of the international aid community and demanding the restructuring, federalizing, democratizing and decentralizing of the state.

The lack of monopoly of state power and inability to create autonomous structures of civil society for designing peace-building give reason to fear that the massive aid package will produce unintended negative effects for conflict resolution. As a result, peace building under the leadership of civil society carries the danger of political instability. "A democracy can only release the potential for political integration following successful political stabilization and institutional consolidation".

The relationship of the civil society with market institutions also undergoes substantial change with the growth of illegal proliferation of arms trade, economy of violence, money laundering, growth of the black economy, breakdown of agriculture, capital flight, extortion, theft, fraud, corruption, human and drug trafficking and providers of information to armed groups rather than providers of basic public goods and services.

Violent conflict divides citizens along the faultlines of the polity especially between the forces of change and beneficiaries of the status quo, between demands for a power equation and structural transformation, between unfair control of the economy and social justice, and between the absolutization of identity based on religion, ethnicity, class, regional and religious groupings and an identity based on citizenship.

Conflicts along these faultlines weaken their social cohesion and harmony thus stripping the citizens of power, access to resources, status and identity. Conflict polarizes civil society sometimes making them uncivil, partisan and spoilers of peace, divides communities and destroys development infrastructures thus leaving the poor, women, disabled and children vulnerable to a deepening humanitarian crisis. As state protection becomes fragile, powerful actors rely on force to achieve their political goals and armed actors seek societal control through kidnapping the citizens of rival groups, killings, threats, coercion, rape and violence.

Sometimes vigilante groups spontaneously emerge with a sense of revenge and act at their own will. Theft, deception, graft and dacoit have become endemic to gain opportunities to plunder and loot. The victims of "violence and theft lose not only what is taken from them but also the incentive to produce any goods that would be taken by others. There is accordingly little or no production in the absence of a peaceful order" (Olson, 2001: 119-120). Criminal groupings in rural areas have become government-free, enriched themselves and became susceptible to increasing lawlessness. Very often, victims have to depend on informal local and family-based institutions, religious organizations and traditional groups in securing individual survival, security and livelihood and seeking conflict transformation into peace.

Human rights groups document communication of school teachers, community organizations and local citizens where rival groups are demanding that they abandon their posts under threat of death.

Such action evacuates the democratic and development space. Deadly conflicts transform the nature, role and capacity of civil society, thus increasing individual mistrust of one another. But, it also opens up new forms of social capital and internal coping mechanisms that provide relief, welfare and social protection. New associations of conflict-victims— widows, children, disabled, youth, orphans, mutual aid groups, charity-based institutions, etc.— in the form of civil society establish networks with local, regional and international organizations seeking critical support for their causes. Deadly conflicts also trigger peace movements, such as civil rights, human rights, women's rights and environmental rights and empower civil society, mobilize public opinion and create alternative structures strong enough to make actors of conflict listen to their concern, voice and action.

In a conflict zone, there is no conflict monitoring and specific law enforcement office that can handle the investigation, protection and sanctioning of human rights violations within the community.

Many conflict related cases go uninvestigated unless there is a legal request demanding further research. Leaving hate crimes and intolerance largely undocumented and uninvestigated undermines the justice system in the future. Due to a combination of societal pressures, however, many women and children victims of conflict and violence hesitate to file an official complaint that would expose them to public scrutiny.

As a result of funding gaps, the state system is unable to meet the accelerating demand for relief, education, social protection and rehabilitation so needed by conflict affected citizens. Their only hope lies in non-state, civil society and humanitarian organizations as they are expected to allow the citizens to participate in the society according to their abilities. Victims' pressure for conflict transformation into a peace process is genuine and they learn to act as part of the global civil society.

Protracted conflict has also forced citizens to invent new coping mechanisms at formal and informal institutions levels. In the case of Nepal, National Human Rights Commission of Nepal (NHRC), UN Office of High Commissioner for Human Rights (OHCHR)-Nepal, other human rights groups and peace groups and the media have a special responsibility to minimize the violation of human rights, ensuring protection for staff and civil society activists, maintaining communication along conflict lines and contributing to peace building.

Members of a civil society require vigorous protection by state institutions as well as monitoring by non-governmental and international organizations to ensure the preservation of their social, political, economic and social rights even as they appeal to the state and its rivals to respect humanitarian laws and Basic Operating Guidelines (BOG) for humanitarian supplies in times of complex emergency. Strengthening the community against violence requires development of the connectors of society, bonding with local authority figures and mobilizing their interpersonal trust, communication and cooperation for conflict mediation. In Nepal, media persons have identified their own role in reporting objectively, facilitating communication among local groups, offering solution-orientated news, discouraging anti-women news and articulating a collective voice of victim for social transformation, reconciliation and social justice. Armed forces employ discriminatory methods to secure their own strongholds. Through these actions, they violate the freedom from arbitrary interference in an individual's private life, as protected in both the Universal Declaration of Human Rights and Constitutional law. Reporting from conflict zone is especially difficult and journalists often face threat from rival groups.

NEPAL: QUEST FOR ELUSIVE PEACE

Amidst the continuously expanding sphere of Maoist influence, political uncertainties and growing international interest, Nepal continues to remain one of the most volatile countries in South Asia. Recent developments have, once again, reconfirmed that while the Maoists have been successful in gradually pushing their agenda through violence and intimidation, the four-party coalition government led by Sher Bahadur Deuba is increasingly finding it difficult to evolve a coherent strategy to counter it. In fact, ever since his reinstatement on June 2, 2004, Deuba has been trying to work out a framework to deal with the eight-year old insurgency, which has claimed approximately 10,000 lives. However, the limited success of counter-insurgency operations, the government's inability to forge consensus on the peace process, the continued opposition by the Nepali Congress-led political front, the emerging differences within the government, the withdrawal/collapse of state institutions and a sustained Maoist offensive have made the government increasingly vulnerable and catapulted the Maoists into the political centrestage. In this context, Deuba's visit to India from September 8-12, 2004, was an attempt to strengthen his regime both politically and militarily.

According to the joint statement issued on September 12, 2004, both the countries viewed the Maoist insurgency as a common threat and agreed to further intensify cooperation in curbing their activities. India reassured more assistance to Nepal's security forces in addition to existing support in terms of arms, ammunition, helicopters, intelligence sharing and training. At the same time, India also reportedly pointed out that there is no military solution to the Maoist problem and the government should initiate a meaningful dialogue process. However, Deuba's success on this front will be determined, to a great extent, by his ability to retain the legitimacy of his regime and strike a balance between the key players in Nepal's politics-the King, the political parties and the Maoists. The Maoists' predominance in Nepali politics has been facilitated by the inability of successive governments in addressing the basic problems such as poverty, underdevelopment and discriminatory social order.

A fractured polity, the absence of an elected government and continuous power struggle between the King and the major political parties have provided the Maoists with an opportunity to control approximately half of the territory. Besides, the near collapse of development work and civil governance in violence-affected areas, breakdown of the rule of law, and lack of democratisation at the grassroots level sustain the Maoist activities. Consequently, the Maoists have not only set up parallel structures of governance in many parts of the country including their own visa and taxation system but have also been able to exert considerable influence in urban centres for example, the week-long blockade of the Kathmandu Valley imposed on August 18, 2004. Though the visible impact of the blockade was not significant because the Maoists 'suspended it for one month' on August 24, 2004, they were, nonetheless, able to gain significant psychological advantage particularly the capability to cut off links to the capital city at will. The deteriorating situation was further aggravated when the Maoist-affiliated All Nepal Trade Union Federation (ANTUF) enforced indefinite closure of 47 industrial establishments, hotels and transport services to press for their demands, which include among others, making public the whereabouts of its workers and leaders who have allegedly disappeared from government custody, compensation to the families of those killed by the state, removal of the terrorist tag slapped on them and increased wages and facilities to workers. Though the ANTUF agreed to withdraw its call on September 15, 2004, after the government agreed to release two of its detained leaders and make available information on the whereabouts of people 'disappeared' from custody within one month beginning September 22, 2004, it is unlikely to restore the confidence of the business community due to continued threat of extortion and the government's inability to provide protection to industries. Simultaneously, the Maoists continued with their violent campaign, attacking district headquarters, government infrastructure, security forces and civilian population. On September 10, 2004, the Maoists were reported to have exploded two bombs at the American Information Centre at Gyaneshwar in Kathmandu. No one was injured in the incident after which the US government decided to suspend all Peace Corps activities.

The absence of a comprehensive counter-insurgency doctrine has enabled the Maoists to grow from strength to strength. The main thrust of counter-insurgency operations has been the excessive use of force and towards that end the government has worked on a policy of strengthening the Royal Nepal Army (RNA) with sophisticated weapons from India, the US, the UK, Belgium and other countries. It is estimated that approximately 25 per cent of the total national budget is now allocated to security. However, despite considerable augmentation of the strength of the RNA, the situation on the ground remains alarming. Though the security forces have achieved some success in counter-insurgency operations, the task is becoming difficult due to lack of adequate state presence in the violence-affected areas. As a result, the government has not been able to supplement the success of counter-insurgency in one area with strengthening/restoration of civil governance, institutions of law enforcement and democratic process. The experience of the counter-insurgency operation has, therefore, necessitated an assessment of the broad direction of government policy and implications of continuous strengthening of the RNA. There is an apprehension that while the continuation of this approach may not be able to contain the Maoists militarily, it might catapult the RNA into an important player in Nepali politics with its own stake. It might further strengthen the King and weaken the democratic government and its ability to pursue a meaningful peace process.

The impetus to the peace process is being reinforced by the realisation that there cannot be a purely military solution to the problem. The Maoists are in a stronger position as is evident from their tough stand on talks. Reports in the first week of September 2004 said, the Maoists have ruled out the possibility of dialogue with the Deuba government favouring instead direct negotiations with King Gyanendra and have reiterated their demand for a Constituent Assembly election under the aegis of the UN. It is clear that the present Maoist demand will further strengthen the King and reinforce the perception that the government is not in a position to play a decisive role.

Consequently, the role of the monarchy becomes important. When King Gyanendra appointed Deuba in June 2004, he had spelt out three tasks before him: to take on board all major political parties on important national issues, find ways to deal with the Maoist insurgency and prepare the nation for elections. If Deuba fails to deliver on these counts, the King might be compelled to remove him from office. Given the fact that an extreme Right Wing opinion within the political spectrum wants the King to play a more active role, the success of the present government will depend largely on the King whose inflexible approach has thus far only complicated the problem.

The differences within the mainstream political formations have only added to the complications. While Deuba has been able to form a coalition government with the help of the Communist Party of Nepal-United Marxist-Leninist (CPNUML), he has failed to evolve a consensus even within the ruling coalition on issues such as ceasefire, external mediation and elections to the Constituent Assembly.

The UML reportedly favours unilateral ceasefire by the government as a prelude to the resumption of negotiations while Deuba insists that unless the Maoists show any sincere commitment towards a result oriented peace process; declaration of a unilateral ceasefire would be meaningless. On the question of the Constituent Assembly, the UML has hinted that the issue is not closed and could be addressed during the peace talks. In January 2004, the UML presented a nine-point roadmap favouring either amendments to the new Constitution or the preparation by the House of Representative. On the question of external mediation involving the UN, Deuba has rejected the idea on the ground that the issue was an internal one; the UML, on the other hand, incorporated a possible UN role in its nine-point roadmap. However, it has yet to expand on the type of role it envisages for the UN in the conflict.

Outside the government, the four-party alliance led by the Nepali Congress has refused to participate in the peace process and has announced fresh agitation against what they call 'regression'. Members of this alliance have been pressing for the restoration of parliament and a consensus government that should initiate dialogue with the rebels. They argue that the new government will command more credibility and legitimacy, and certainly strengthen the government at the time of the talks with the Maoists. Nepali Congress Chief G.P. Koirala has refused to participate or nominate a representative for the high-level peace committee formed on August 12, 2004, under the leadership of the Prime Minister. The objective of the committee is to coordinate the peace process and finalise the political agendas for negotiations. Reports suggest that he is holding a parallel dialogue with the Maoists in order to bring them to the political mainstream.

While there appears to be a broad consensus on negotiating with the Maoists, it, however, cannot be achieved until the political parties bridge their own political differences and evolve an effective negotiating strategy. In the light of this, a pertinent question emerges: does Nepal need external mediation to break the deadlock. Those who favour external mediation argue that despite two rounds of ceasefire and negotiations in 2001 and 2003, the government and the Maoists failed to reach a minimum consensus, hence an impartial body like the UN could play a vital role in facilitating the peace talks. The UN system has, on a number of occasions, expressed its desire facilitate peace talks and has sent special emissaries to explore the possibilities of securing a role. But the government has shown little inclination for any external mediation.

Does India have a role to play in breaking the deadlock? India's concerns at the stalemate between the Nepalese government and the Maoist insurgents are growing. The geo-strategic position of Nepal, open borders and a history of good relations makes Nepal important in India's strategic calculations. Internal instability in Nepal will have serious security implications for India.

The exploitation of open India-Nepal borders by the Maoists, their deepening linkages with Indian leftwing extremist groups such as the Communist Party of India Marxist-Leninist (People's War), the Maoist Communist Centre of India (MCCI) and the Northeast insurgent groups and the unbridled use of India-Nepal open border for shelter, training, supplies and arms smuggling pose serious security threat to India.

Further, there is apprehension that Pakistan's Inter Services Intelligence (ISI), active in border areas, could forge links with the Maoists to de-estabilise the region. Therefore, India needs to ensure that its core interests are not hurt in the confrontation between the Deuba government and the Maoists. India has been providing military assistance to Nepal based on assessments that the RNA was the only force capable of keeping the Maoists at bay. India has also taken a number of steps to contain Maoist activities on its soil and strengthen coordinated security strategies on both sides of the border.

Conceding that it may not be possible to defeat the Maoists militarily, it is in India's interest to ensure that the Maoists should not be able to exploit a divided polity. While supporting the Constitutional monarchy and multiparty democracy in Nepal, India has repeatedly emphasised that only the monarchy and Nepal's democratically elected parties can solve the Maoist problem, provided they work in unison. Towards this end, it is in India's interest to facilitate a peace process with an aim to restore and strengthen a viable and sustainable democratic government in Nepal.

NEPAL'S SPECIAL SECURITY PLAN: POLITICAL STUNT?

Nepal is a one of the most leading domicile of many ethno-political insurgents. Since longtime, the country has lost its normalcy of law and order, good governance, civil supremacy, and democratic practices due to fast growing ratio of institutional and private criminal and their rebellion activities. Sadly, the country is terrorized and under control of ochlocracy. Neighbouring countries both India and China are fed up, they consider Nepal as a transit hub of ethno-pharisaic terrorist and regressive elements who want their disintegration, and has nabbed the peace and prosperity of their nations. India accuses that Nepal is a center for anti-Indian terrorist and insurgents who use Nepal as it's' rehearsal center. Similarly, the China also believes that Nepal has become a nucleus for the anti-China forces, whose aims is to disintegrate China and separate the Tibet from China. Besides, Bhutan also accused Nepal, as a principle sources that generate Bhutan centric insurgents who have spread revolutions for massive sociopolitical change.

Sadly, a recently released index from Foreign Policy depicted Nepal as 25th most likely nation to become a failed state, out of the sixty most vulnerable countries. The group found that conditions in Nepal are more disturbing than in Lebanon, Burkina Faso and Colombia. Nepal has got bed image internationally and internally due to poor security management system, so the M. K. Nepal headed government wants to repair the security sector and willing to achieve its normalcy. People and international community too are keeping continuous pressure to the government to secure duly public lives, liberty, and properties. People want to live in peace, prosperity and harmonious environment. They are unable to see more violence, criminalities and abuses of human rights. They do not want to be again a victim of warfare and have no more stamina to suffer with crude humanitarian crisis. The public want full assurances of physical and psychological security from government in entire part of the nation; people seek to see quick improvement in existing securitymechanism and asking government to come with effective special security plan and strategy. In this context, the UML led cabinet has recently designed and enforced a government-claimed strategic security plan called Special Security Plan (SSP) which is highly criticized by regional and ethnic political forces. However, the productivity of the SSP is yet to examine.

The government claims that special security plan aimed to improving the deteriorated law and order situation across country. It is said that the main objective of the plan is to control anarchy, promote human rights and end impunity. Basically, the Home Minister describes, the SSP focuses in five areas including controlling the road blockades besides curbing organized and serious types of crime. It will take up special security measures for Kathmandu Valley, tangible improvement in the security situation of the Tarai especially in the eastern and mid-western regions where scores of armed groups have posed a threat to law and order in the southern plains bordering India.

It proposes to effectively mobilize the three security agencies - Nepal Police, Armed Police Force and National Investigation Department- under a unified command. Moreover, ensuring essential service and nabbing criminals are the core tasks. The plan aims to strictly prohibit the closing of public offices and educational institutions.

The plan claims that the government will deploy well-equipped security personnel with adequate arms and coordinate with security staff deployed in various areas of the border. The plan aims to provide security for those targeted by criminals. To take special care of the crime-prone and to massively mobilize security personnel are also strategies under the plan. To increase the productiveness of the plan, the security agencies will manage security forces with weapons to patrol on motorbikes, security picketing twenty four hours, no closure of offices, blockade of roads and traffic, emergency frisking and searches, cordon and search in suspect areas. The special security squad comprises at least twenty Nepal Police and thirty Armed Police Force personnel. The special security team has been given the authority to carry out raids in suspicious places, security checks in different parts of the district with the help of local police and can also hold suspicious persons in their custody for investigation purposes. The team would also arrange security for high-level government officials and political party leaders.

The above described plan is reader friendly and written in systematic order as also experienced during the regime of previous government. However, people do not see any new invention in recently introduced special security plan. There is nothing new. All the exaggerated provisions are made continuous in law since years, so it is not more than *"Old wine in new Bottle"*. The plan also sounds like the same provision which was introduced during the Gyanendra's autocratic regime, where the King Gyanendra had imposed the special security plan to control the Maoist activities and democratic movement against his direct executive rule. Moreover, the experts illustrate that it is just a political stunt rather than a no-hit plan that provides an effective and efficient security system as developed security culture has. The plan is lacking the major characters that are supposed to be deal with the post-conflict situation and even during the ongoing insurgency.

Indeed, the country is passing through the fragile situation, law and order is limited in constabulary only. The criminalities and mutiny have reached at climax, though all governmental efforts of improvement have been found zilch. Since early years, all the government used their political stunt to win the heart and mind of people that, though it is poignant that public are being more victimized and situation is worsening more and more. People do not see any tangible improvement or positive changes, except the mounting news and speeches in Medias. The drawing and design of SSP is faulty and being enforced without needy homework. The SSP suffers with eleventh hour syndrome which is most unfortunate, so how can people expect a successful implementation of SSP. Actually, the plan has clearly shown that government has not yet understands the true nature of security needs. The Government should understand that security is not only a physical presence and beefed up activities of security personnel, rather it requires true self-build physical and psychological security assurances that people should feel secured in stress-free manner by their hearts and minds.

The security plan cannot be enforced effectively and efficiently till it gets broader public support, legitimacy and peoples' participation. Further, most important part is enough research based "implementable technical preparation". It demands essential reform and reengineering in legal, personnel, operational, organizational, physical, functional, resources and administrative areas are also essential before to enforce such plan, however the SSP lacks all these things except the verbal stunt and well written story. There are not yet any substantial changes and essential step found in restructuring in laws, resources, and technological enhancement related to local administration, police and security, Intelligence, public service delivery and other related approach of Insurgency management, crime control, market regulation, high way management, drug abuse control, smuggling and boarder security control, kidnapping and robbery control etc.

The Chief Districts Officers led district security committees are the principal mechanism at ground level to enforce the SSP, though the CDOs are popularized like a most superior powerful local authority, without having expertise, resources and controlling power. They are similar like a hand bended *"Army Fighting in War without Arm and Weapons"*. Also the existing defined security professional of unified command are incapable to deliver the SSP, if they are not empowered and updated properly accordance with the need of the national and strategy of the SSP. The huge lapses in coordination among the security agencies are found a major dearth of SSP. The SSP has assigned crucial role and responsibilities of Regional Administrators and CDOs, but most of the positions are either vacant or operated by juniors that create the issues of poor coordination, order disobeying, seniority complex, inter-intra organizational conflicts, responsibility shifting, and many more problems during implementation of pre to post phase of operation and management of the SSP.

Furthermore, the SSP has no any technical foundation. It has absence of the proper involvement of security management experts. Most of security related planners and professional are untrained, generalist and suffering with traditional mentalities. The performances of such officials are really questionable. There is no any special mechanism and indicators that could figure out the capabilities of their doings. The existing introduced pathetic ruling cultural concept is like "Our People is good People" not "Good People is Our People", whether whatever the consequences comes, it does not matter for our policy makers and politicians. Thus the pre to post operations e.g. appointment, transfer and promotion of security related officers are being on the basis of chakri-chaplusi, and bhan-sun, that how government can expects a good productivity from the SSP without hammering the vicious problem of exiting security system.

Most of the security agencies are in crisis of resources, physical facilities and technological access. However the so-called SSP didn't address the issue in practical matter. Furthermore, the provisions of career development, morale and motivation enhancement of security personnel's are too low. Grievances, frustration and unwanted pressures, interferences and disturbances are too high in field, but the SSP has not analysed the issue during the preparation of its concept, which has become now a blunder and felt as limit of the SSP into paper and verbal speech. Writing honestly, people do not feel any changes and improvement in ground level. The liveliest proofs are that even the president, prime minister, senior political leaders and ministers are not being able to walk freely or to attend any public program in free and fair manner. Most of them are getting often disturbed and has to face rebellion reaction, even after the enforcement of the SSP. The plan is not being implemented in Tarai as well as in many ethnic dominated regions including Madhes, Limbuban, Tharuban etc. because it has no any public legitimacy. The program does not govern any schemes for public participation, so it will become totally failure in the ethnic and communal regions. Minor and disadvantages ethnic people have accused that the SSP enforced by elite-ethnic dominated government just because to encounter and suppress to the minor-ethnic activists who are fighting for their ethnic rights, freedoms and inclusive representations against the continuous hegemony.

The free and independent movement and operation of national highway is also a part of the target which seems bit successful because the road blockage, robbery and dacoit's influence in public transpiration seen somehow controlled after implementation of the SSP, it is because the arm police forces are deployed throughout the highway and also making individual patrolling guard inside the each public transportation, but the way seems not sustainable since the cost of such stagey is huge which cannot be continuous affordable by our nation. In addition, the market regulation is also a major target of the plan but black marketing, irregular price hiking, and artificial shortage of public goods and services, qualities degrading activities are observed continuous and has seen no any upbeat affect of SSP. One of the weakest points is coordination among intra and inter-agencies; the SSP does not offer any specific approaches, tools and techniques that help authorities to build intra organizational coordination for synergy effort.

A study found that Nepalese security system cannot be improved without restructuring and democratizing the security mechanism in professional way. Basically, the district level security system is ineffective because they do not have even minimum access and facilities for minimum resources, technologies, trained and skilled personnel's and strong enough approaches for horizontal and vertical coordination that requires for any well organized security management functions. Besides, public trust over the government and local security mechanism is a most essential phenomenon which can be developed through civic engagement and justifiable inclusive participation approaches. The success of any security related special plan requires at least minimum common consensus in central as well as in local level among the all stake holders, before to enforce into practice since a nominal dissatisfaction or frustration by a stake holder may cause to failure or infectivity of plan. Particularly, in the SSP case, Regional Administrator and CDO requires more justifiable role, authority and resources and controlling power over the entire related agencies accordance with the spirit of civil supremacy. The effective management and mutual cooperation of track 1 (governmental agencies), track 2(NGOs CBOs, Civil Society etc) and track 3 actors (respective people, society, ethnic groups, community people) requires to administer properly the SSP.

The government also needs to work in identifying the special justifiable indicators that can clearly distinct between the political and criminal activities. The local security systems are in saver confusion to know political activities and criminal activities. It is because most of the Nepalese political leaders define the criminal and political activities in their own way. The funny thing is if "A" group or party halt highways and burn few vehicles that means for the party or group as democratic practices but if the "B" group or party does the same thing than others including government meant it as terrorist or a part of criminal activities. So, there is clear distinction required by laws & legitimate consensus to identify that how the security forces need to deal with such activity. The dual standard needs to be end instantly.

The market regulation has become a huge headache for nation, so the government requires immediate action to constitute a powerful joint supervisory mechanism in local, regional and central level that should be handled and operated by a constitutional commission, otherwise the issues of market regulation may limit in political stunt and people will have to victimize continuously.

Additionally, the passiveness, silence and infectivity of central level authorities including the Cabinet, Ministry of Home Affairs, Foreign Affairs, Finance Ministry, and Ministry of Local Administration etc are also added extra burden to defeat the SSP, because they are not serious and sincere even to consider the urgent and sensitive reports and requests that comes day by day through the channel of district security committees. Therefore, the National Security Council or a constitutional committee should play a crucial role to evaluate, monitor and correct the passiveness, silences, ignorance, and ineffectiveness of the respective central agencies.

The national as well as local level authorities are suffering with serious "Responsibility Shifting Syndrome". In Nepalese scenario *"Responsibility Shifting"* a long-rooted amusement found continues in the central level authority who often accused to the local level and vice-versa for any wrong things and doings in security affairs. It is pity to mention that there is no culture of candid accountability bearing in entire governmental agencies and authorities of Nepal. One agency accused to other for deteriorating security situation. All concerned agencies are equally responsible but it is never accepted by any responsible authorities. Therefore, the honest and practical commitment along with well managed timely strategic action in ground level required for successful implementation of the SSP, otherwise it will be proved similar pirates version of the SSP that was also previously experienced during the past regimes.

THE CHINESE DEGENERATE WORKERS' STATE

By Spring 1949, the PLA had reconquered China North of the Yangzi river. After the collapse of the KMT armies in Manchuria in late 1948, most KMT-held territory and towns were surrendered without any fighting. Fu Tso-yi, for example, surrendered Peking in January 1949 as soon as the PLA advanced towards the city, indeed, he joined them in the march South.

In April 1949, after the expiry of a last deadline for Nationalist surrender, the PLA crossed the Yangzi and entered South China. They met little resistance and disarmed some two million KMT troops in a period of six months. In September, the Political Consultative Conference met in Peking and established a central government headed by Mao Zedong, leader of the CCP, Zhu De, a principal commander of the PLA, Soong Ching-ling (the widow of Sun Yat-sen and sister in law of Chiang Kai-shek), Li Jishen, leader of the Revolutionary Committee of the KMT (and the butcher of the Canton Commune in 1927) and Zhang Lan, President of the Democratic League.

The CCP had achieved its aim of establishing a popular front coalition government. Mao Zedong had outlined the policy that such a government would follow in 1945: "The task of our New Democratic system is to promote the free development of a private capitalist economy that benefits instead of controlling the peoples' livelihood, and to protect all honestly acquired private property."

This was the policy which was followed between 1949 and 1952, which meant both defending capitalism and containing and if necessary repressing the demands of the workers and peasants. When in 1952 the CCP decisively struck out at the bourgeoisie, expropriating their property, it was a moment not of the CCP's choosin. It was a vital defensive measure forced on the Stalinists by the onslaught of US imperialism. As Mao was to declare in 1957 "socialism": "came to our country too suddenly."

The economic life of China at the time of the accession to power of this government was only one step away from complete paralysis. The collapse of the central administration, soaring inflation and the displacement of millions of people from the areas of military operations were accompanied by floods and droughts that affected 20 million acres and threatened 40 million people with starvation. Coal production stood at 50 per cent of its previous highest point, iron and steel were down by 80 per cent, cotton goods down by 25 per cent, grain 25 per cent, raw cotton 48 per cent and livestock 16 per cent.

To make matters yet worse the railway network was out of operation with 50 per cent of the track destroyed and most of the maritime fleet was in Hong Kong, Taiwan or Singapore. The first priority of the People's Government was expressed in the Common Programme of October 1949: "A policy that is concerned with private and public interests, that benefits the bosses and the workers, that encourages mutual aid between our country and foreign countries in order to develop production and bring prosperity to the economy."

In other words, the existing framework of capitalist property relations was to be maintained. The policy of tolerance and encouragement extended to the "national" capitalists was not extended to the "bureaucratic" capitalists. Their possessions were immediately nationalised, giving the state control of nearly one-third of all industrial production.

While the state had majority holdings in heavy industry (70 per cent of coal, 90 per cent of steel and 78 per cent of electricity) heavy industry was historically chronically underdeveloped in relation to light industry, much of which was often dependent on imported materials. It was in light industry that the "national" capitalists now dominated along with the distribution and transport networks. This group owned two-thirds of all industrial capital in 1949.

The modern sector of the economy was, however, a small percentage of the economy as a whole. In 1945 it had been calculated at between 10 and 15 per cent. Largely because of its years of control in the "liberated zones" the CCP/PLA already had within it a relative experienced administrative cadre. However, with the partial exception of those who had been in Manchuria this cadre lacked experience of urban and industrial administration. This lack was partly made up by the entry into the CCP of ex-officials of the KMT regime and educated elements of the middle classes in the cities. At the time of liberation, a sample of 6,000 cadres had the following composition: 2,500 middle class, 1,150 ex-KMT officials, 400 liberal professionals, 150 members of the privileged classes, 140 from the working class. Workers made up a mere 2 per cent of party members in 1949.27 With a membership of this sort it was possible for the CCP-dominated government to take state capitalist economic measures such as nationalisation and statification, primarily aimed at the universally hated "bureaucratic" capitalists, so long as this remained within the general framework of capitalist property relations.

In March 1949, the state formed six major trading corporations for the distribution and procurement of Food, Textiles, Salt, Coal, Construction materials and "miscellaneous" goods. In addition, a network of state owned retail outlets was established. These two measures, coupled with the introduction of a new currency, a sliding-scale of wages linked to the monetary value of essential foods, an enforced loan at 5 per cent interest from capitalists and the state distribution of goods that had been hoarded by the KMT and its supporters, allowed a rapid improvement in the living conditions of the masses and brought inflation under control. By mid-1951 it was down to 20 per cent and prices were essentially stable in 1952.

That, despite this statification of essentials, the popular front government was anxious not to scare the "national" bourgeoisie into fleeing, can be seen from the assurances given them by Chen Yun the Chairman of the Financial and Economic Commission, in August 1950, "... industrial investments undertaken for a long time by the national capitalists, if they remain progressive in character, will be useful to the state and the people." The Agrarian Reform of June 1950 shows the same clear intention of maintaining friendly relations with the capitalists in order to maintain production. Article 4, dealing with whose lands could or could not be expropriated, said:

"Industry and commerce shall be protected from infringement, industrial and commercial enterprises operated by landlords, and the land and other properties used by the landlords directly for the operation of industrial and commercial enterprises, shall not be confiscated."

The new land reform was only applicable in the south where, as we have noted, the ties between landlords and the urban bourgeoisie were stronger than in the north. In addition to the strictures on landlords' lands, it was also expressly forbidden to confiscate all the "surplus" lands of the wealthiest peasants and that of the "richer middle peasants" was to be left alone entirely.

Mao explained why at the third session of the Central Committee, 6 June 1950: "... our policy towards the rich peasants ought to be changed. Their excess land must no longer be confiscated, but their life must be preserved to speed up the restoration of production in rural areas."

Despite these limitations imposed by the state, the land reform did involve a massive transfer of land in South China, some 7 million acres out of a Chinese total of 17 million. On average all individuals over sixteen held one-third of an acre after the reform. As in the country generally, so in the cities the chief priority of the new government was to re-establish order Far from utilising the entry of the Liberation Army to ensure a proletarian takeover of the towns and industrial plant, Un Biao, commander of the Fourth Army, issued the following proclamation in January 1949:

"The people are asked to maintain order and to continue their present occupations. KMT officials or police personnel of provincial, city, county or other level of governmental unit district, town, village, or Bao Jia personnel are enjoined to stay at their posts". In addition, whilst granting statutory rights to workers' organisations the People's Government showed in its Labour Law of 1950 that its interest lay solely in regularising the labour-capital relationship, not in abolishing it. With regard to disputes, for example, it laid down the following procedures: "the first step in procedure for settling labour disputes shall be consultation between the parties the second step shall be mediation between the parties by the Labour Bureau [a state department-Eds] and the third step shall be arbitration by the arbitration committee established by the Labour Bureau."

The nature of the unions set up by the government, and modelled on those of the Soviet Union, can be judged from the fact that one of the Vice Chairmen of the All China Federation of Trade Unions was Chu Xuefan, previously the head of the yellow unions of the KMT, the Association of Labour. In addition, the Minister of Labour, U Lisan was simultaneously vice- president of the ACFTU. The Chairman of this body made perfectly clear what the priorities of the government were: "The immediate and sectional interests of the working class must be subordinated to the long term and over all interests of the state led by the working class."

That "subordination" was to be taken absolutely literally was shown by Un Biao when he sent his troops against the workers of the Sun Sun Textile plant in Shanghai who had occupied their plant to prevent its removal to Manchuria, under the government's policy of thinning out industry. Ten workers were killed or wounded in the clash. While capitalist representatives shared the government with the CCP, between 1949 and 1951 and the policy of that government was clearly to defend capitalism, the repressive apparatus of the state-the police, army, secret police etc., remained firmly in the hands of the Stalinists.

This special form of dual power already witnessed in Eastern Europe and Yugoslavia, continued to exist until it was resolved decisively against the capitalists. The popular front period played an important role for the Chinese Stalinists in demobilising the aroused workers and peasants. At the time when capitalism was at its weakest and the mobilisations of the workers and peasants at their strongest, the CCP acted to limit those mobilisations and to restrain them within the limits of capitalist property relations.

The dangers of this policy of maintaining and strengthening the capitalists swiftly became apparent. The utopian goal of the Stalinists a stable New Democracy where capitalists and Stalinists worked in harmony was never a possibility. The onslaught of American imperialism in the Korean war produced a growing threat of capitalist counter-revolution inside China amongst sections of the remaining bourgeoisie. America and Chiang Kai Shek were ready to act as their heavily armed allies.

This forced the CCP towards the close of 1951 to move swiftly to resolve the situation of dual power in its favour through a bureaucratic, anti-capitalist workers' government. As in the other Stalinist social overturns this necessitated striking out at both the capitalists and suppressing the last remnants of the independent workers' movement.

The immediate cause of the change of policy and, eventually, the nature, of the government, was the outbreak of the Korean war in June 1950. As American armies (supposedly UN) advanced towards the Yalu River (the border between Manchuria and Korea) under the rabid anti-communist, MacArthur, the People's Government was forced to change its policy both internationally and domestically.

The initial victories of the PLA under Peng Dehuai, which forced the US back beyond the 38th parallel, were met by Washington with the rearmament of Chiang Kai-shek and the delivery of considerable economic aid to Taiwan. The US Seventh Fleet took up station between Taiwan and the mainland, thereby forcing the Chinese to divert troops from Korea to the coastal province of Fujian. In addition a total economic blockade of China was instituted. The New York Times, 5 April 1951, reported that, "MacArthur favours a Nationalist second front on the Chinese mainland and is convinced that the fate of Europe will be decided in the war against communism in Asia." Now, under both economic and military pressure from imperialism and fully aware of the potential alliance between foreign, Taiwan based and domestic capital, the CCP took steps to mobilise the masses against the "national" capitalists. In the countryside, the Agrarian Reform was accompanied by the building of the People's Tribunals, organised by the Party cadres with the purpose of applying a degree of terror and intimidation to the landlords. Although the campaign was limited to the terms of the Agrarian Reform, the wave of executions, fines and expropriations both broke the class power of the landlords and served to bind the peasantry yet closer to the regime.

At the same time the control of the CCP ensured that this did not go beyond its own predetermined limitations. Indeed, so bureaucratic was the procedure for ratifying redistribution of land that, in Canton province it still had not been completed by December 1952. A parallel movement was set in train in the cities for similar purposes.

The so called "three anti's" campaign, introduced alongside the "five anti's" campaign at the end of 1951, was aimed at CCP and government functionaries. The masses of members who had been recruited to the CCP on the basis of its popular front programme, were now considered unreliable a massive purge took place in the party, involving the expulsion of over one million members (a fifth of the party) between 1951 and 1952. It was also in this period that the Stalinists struck out against the left.

Chinese Trotskyists, many members of the 'nternationalist Workers Party had been active leading strikes in Canton and Shanghai. They had suffered repression before 1952 at the hands of the CCP, but at the end of that year a nation wide raid by the secret police completely decimated the Chinese Trotskyists two or three hundred were thrown into gaol. Leading members Cheng Ch'ao-Un and eleven others were only released 27 years later in June 1979. The "Five anti's" campaign which ran parallel with the "three" was aimed at weakening and intimidating the bourgeoisie. Mass meetings were held throughout the country to whip up feelings against the capitalists. Businesses were investigated for fraud and corruption. In the first six months of 1952 nearly half a million businesses were inspected and over three quarters found guilty of infractions.

Many were heavily fined, contributing $850m to state coffers. Those who could not pay were nationalised instead. By these bureaucratic methods, albeit backed up by mass mobilisations and denunciation sessions, the CCP-led government, a bureaucratic anti- capitalist workers' government came to control 64 per cent of wholesale trade and 42 per cent of retail trade by mid 1952. Initially, this led to a fall in production as the bourgeoisie retaliated by closing down plants. Between January and February 1952, at the height of the campaign, production fell by 34 per cent and the state was obliged to slow down the campaign.

Once again Chen Yun offered reassurance: "Private factories will, according to concrete conditions, be guaranteed a profit of around 10, 20 or up to 30 per cent on their capital." Once again private capital survived in China, but it was now severely curtailed in its freedom, state control of orders placed with private industry, for example, was a powerful weapon for ensuring that the capitalists did not step out of line. This respite was short lived however and in 1953 at a government convened National Congress of Industry and Commerce the remaining capitalists were told that the first aim of the government was to have a fully socialist economy in which private industry would have no place.

After 1951 primarily under pressure from imperialism, the popular front government was transformed into a bureaucratic, anti-capitalist workers' government which removed the foundations of the class rule of the capitalists, "not by decree but by relentless, high-pressure gradualism". In this way it ensured that its prime enemy, the independently organised revolutionary working class, remained firmly excluded from political power within China. Because the fundamental bastion of the bourgeois state its bodies of armed men had already been smashed, the CCP was able to carry out the military-bureaucratic overthrow of the Chinese bourgeoisie relatively peacefully.

It was against a background of economic blockade by the West, majority state control of heavy industry and effective control of trade in the modern sector that the government of the People's Republic moved against the essential foundations of capitalism with the introduction of planning in 1953. At first this took the form of annual plans for 1953 and 1954, these were then incorporated into, and used as a basis for, the First Five Year Plan 1953-57. This was not published until late 1955.

The introduction of planning in 1953 on the clear basis of subordinating the operation of the law of value, marks the establishment of a degenerate workers' state in China. The plan was modelled on the Five Year Plans of the Soviet Union. Planners exhorted plant managers to take careful heed of the "advanced experience" of the Soviet system. The ability of the plan to even begin the industrialisation of China was, in a large measure, due to the aid provided by the USSR. Since 1950 China had been in receipt of an annual $300m loan from the Soviet Union. In March 1953 this was added to by a commercial agreement with the USSR, supplying China with many of the materials necessary for industrial expansion.

The plan revealed the dynamic lodged within the post capitalist property forms, and, at the same time, the way in which the bureaucracy acts as a fetter on the full realisation of this dynamic. The bureaucracy claimed that 1953 saw a 13 per cent increase in industrial output over the 1952 level, while in 1954 output rose a further 17 per cent higher than the total for 1953.

However, the exclusion of the masses from political control of the plan meant that these advances were undermined by the bureaucracy's tendency to plan blind. In 1955, when the collection of statistical data took place on a national scale, the figures often disguised the problems of the plan. In 1956 these surfaced. On March 18th 1956 the People's Daily was forced to admit that only just over 50 per cent of the capital construction programme had been fulfilled. Shortages, particularly in construction materials, began to block the fulfilment of targets. Inflationary pressures mounted and the bureaucracy was forced to reduce its targets in heavy industry.

As usual with bureaucratic plans the fulfilment of targets did not mean that the goods produced were of a high quality. The tyranny of the "target" in fact meant that workers often took little care with their products, and ended up producing shoddy goods, but at a faster rate! These features of bureaucratic planning have been apparent in the Chinese economy since 1953. They are an inevitable product of a regime under which the working class is excluded from political power. In China the economic power of the bourgeoisie was destroyed, bureaucratically, through induced bankruptcies and, after 1955, by state purchases of majority shareholdings. In 1956 the modern sector of the Chinese economy was virtually 100 per cent nationalised, and the bourgeoisie as a class was eliminated. But perched at the top of this workers' state was a Stalinist bureaucracy, ruling over the working class.

The independent base of the CCP, built up over years of war, provided the Chinese Stalinists with the means to pursue their own policy, independently of Stalin, at certain decisive moments. This did not mean that the CCP was not Stalinist. It merely confirmed the ability of certain indigenous Stalinist parties to prosecute Stalinist polices in spite of the wishes of the Kremlin. The initial hostility of Stalin to Mao's seizure of power was in reality a hostility to an independent Stalinist force, similar to Tito's YCP. The Sino-Soviet split in 1963 brought these hostilities once more to the surface. It illustrated the tendency of Stalinism to fracture along national social patriotic lines. In no way was it a sign of the CCP's transformation into a non-Stalinist party.

MAOIST INSURGENCY IN NEPAL: INTERNAL DIMENSIONS

It is no secret that Nepal, a country sandwiched between two Asian giants – India and China, is suffering from the worst political crisis in its history. A constitutional democracy that was established following the 1990 People's Movement appears to be on the verge of collapse due to continued success of Maoist guerrilla insurgency or "People's War" that was launched in February of 1996 by the Communist Party of Nepal-Maoist (CPN-Maoist). The Maoist People's War has become a direct threat and a death-knell to the government of Nepal.

The CPN-Maoist first fired its salvo of "People's War" on February 12, 1996 seeking to destroy constitutional monarchy and aiming to establish a Maoist people's democracy. By the end of December of 2000, the insurgency has taken the life of an estimated 1600 persons (unofficially the figure goes as high as 4,000 dead.) There are four categories of people killed in the process: Maoist guerrillas, police, alleged informers of police, and innocent civilians. Independent observers say that police has killed more innocent civilians in fake "encounters" than the Maoist guerrillas. The police administration is also accused of extra-judicial killings in captivity and disappearance of persons under custody.

Geopolitics of Insurgency and Government Policy: The insurgency that began from 3 mid-western mountain districts of Rolpa, Rukum, and Jajarkot, western district of Gorkha and an eastern district of Sindhuli has now spread to 68 of Nepal's 75 districts. According to government's own admission 32 districts are believed to be the hardest hit where guerrillas roam freely and organize open mass meetings. By mid-January 2001, the Maoists have declared the formation of a provisional revolutionary district governments in Rukum, Jajarkot, Sallyan and Rolpa districts.

A close study of insurgent activities in the country show that the most affected area is contiguous and concentrated in the mid-western region. This is one of the most backward and least accessible districts of Nepal. The affected areas are all too close to Kathmandu. Many of the affected areas are spread out along Terai districts close to India. Nepal government officials have reportedly filed a complaint with New Delhi that the Maoists are seeking shelter in India. The most disturbing situation for the counter-insurgency planners is that many of the Maoist affected areas are inhabited by a large number of well trained retired Indian and British Army Gurkha soldiers. Authorities suspect that some of these retirees are providing training to Maoist guerrillas.

The Maoist insurgency-hit areas cover 165 of the 205 parliamentary electoral constituencies of Nepal. The insurgency has directly affected the lives of roughly two-thirds of the 24 million people of Nepal. The state is on the verge of defeat. The police operations have failed to control guerrillas. There is a widespread realization that if the guerrillas continue to expand their zone of influence at the current speed, they will be able to beat the Nepali State within a short span of time. Such realization is reflected in the government's recent activation of the National Security Council and its decision to create a para-military force comprising 15,000 men (to be increased to 25,000-men gradually) with modern sophisticated weapons. Although the royal army has not been officially ordered against the guerrillas, the government has decided to establish six new military bases at battalion level around insurgency hit districts. Twenty-five district headquarters are now under Royal Nepali Army (RNA) protection. Another twenty-five district administrators have reportedly sought RNA protection.

Since the start of insurgency in 1996, different governments of Nepal have treated the Maoist war as a 'law and order' problem. The government has sought to contain Maoists by means of police operations code named "Operation Romeo," "Kilo Shera Two," "Jungle Search Operation," and "Search and Destroy." The state has justified authoritarian policies in the name of suppressing the insurgency, but without addressing the basic inequalities that plague Nepali society. These police operations have applied the policy of "encircle and kill", a policy similar to China's Chiang Kai-shek's "extermination" of communists campaign in 1930s. In the process of this "encircle and kill" policy the police operation has in many places actually killed more innocent civilians than the guerrillas, a fact noted by several human rights organizations including the Amnesty International.

Insurgents' Strength: Despite the killings of hundreds of Maoists, real or imagined, under the policy of "search and destroy," Maoist insurgency does not appear to be dying. The insurgency, in fact, has appeared in districts which otherwise had been considered an area of influence of constitutional ruling parties. While no one knows exactly how many guerrillas are there in the jungles of Nepal, yet some experts believe that number of full-time guerrillas under arms is around 2000 and another 10,000 irregulars or militias armed with homemade guns. In almost all battles between the police and the Maoist guerrillas, the insurgents have proved their military superiority. These incidents have shaken the whole country and has established the fact that Maoist insurgency is a living reality and that the Communist Party of Nepal (Maoist) is an undeniable political force.

In view of the present day political uncertainties characterized by competition for office between and among parties of all shades and sizes, continuing split between and among parliamentary royal communists, and Nepali Congress's undeclared divorce with socialism, the chances for Maoist politics to reign Nepal appears pretty high. If history is any guide, Nepali communists, no matter how much divided they may be, have never been totally rejected by the electorate. In 1994, Unified Marxist & Leninist (UML) got an opportunity to form the government. The inexperience in ruling the country, on the one hand, and greed for power, on the other led to not only the exit from the government but also the vertical division of the UML party. The vertical split of UML has brought about qualitative as well as quantitative changes in the political balance of the country. The split has also helped in raising the centrality of Maoist movement. In fact, the communist movement has now polarized into Maoist and non-Maoist blocs. This process of polarization is a good source of power to Maoists. The failure of other left groups in forming and maintaining unity has certainly helped Maoists.

Popular Support

The successive failures of government's police operations in Maoist insurgency clearly shows that the insurgency is taking momentum with substantial popular support. This is no longer simply a law and order problem. Why are the people in rebel areas providing sanctuaries to insurgents? Why are insurgents finding sanctuaries in areas, which in the past had been strongholds of constitutional parties? Independent observers argue that the government suffers from political instability and rampant corruption. The money allocated for development of interior areas never reaches there. A large number of villages are totally ignored by economic planners. There are no schools, no roads, no electricity, and no medical facilities. At the national level, the educated unemployment is increasing at geometrical proportions. Close to 100,000 rural youths failing high school examination every year have neither a job nor a school to go where they could be kept busy. These unemployed youths, 15 to 18 years in age, are joining the ranks of armed guerrillas. The Maoists, however, have problems of providing arms to these willing recruits.

Background of Communist Movement: Maoist insurgency must be viewed in the light of Nepal's history of communist movement. The communist movement in Nepal that first appeared in 1949 after the formation of Communist Party of Nepal under the leadership of late Pushpa Lal Shrestha emerged as an intellectual opposition to Nepali Congress's policy of compromise. Even during the days of king's absolutism Communist movement was unclear in its goals. A few communist leaders then argued that their main enemy was domestic feudalism led by the king while others insisted that Nepali Congress with its support from expansionist India and imperialist America was the main enemy. As a result, Nepal saw at one moment as many as 19 communist parties!

The Maoist movement has emerged in the background of this history of Nepal's communist movement. The Naxallite movement of Jhapa in early 1970s, too, had the same background. The Jhapa movement evaporated in a few years due mainly to the suppression of Naxaliites in India, youthful inexperience of leaders expressed in term of middle class extremism, decline of Maoism in China after Mao's death in 1976, and lack of Jhapa-type militancy in other districts of Nepal. The leaders of Jhapa movement gradually took to the constitutional path and even participated in Panchayat elections as "pro-people Panchas."

New Realities: The present day Maoist movement, however, must not be viewed in light of Naxaliite movement of the early 1970s for several reasons: first, Maoists unlike Jhapali Naxaliites do not have the advantage of geographical continuity from India. Second, Maoists do not enjoy the ideological support from Radio Beijing. So the charges of foreign inspiration is a moot point here. Third, Maoists have learnt many lessons from the mistakes of Jhapa uprising. Fourth, the communists of all shades and sizes are now available in every village of Nepal. Many of them are disillusioned with the inability of their leaders who have participated in parliamentary system telling the cadres that there is an alternative to armed revolution.

That the Maoist insurgency has survived five-year period and continues to enter into news phases is in itself a clear indication that the movement is no longer a temporary phenomenon without social bases. The official approach of viewing Maoist movement as an activity of individual killing and pure terrorism has not helped to solve the problem. While it is true that there is middle-class extremism inside the Maoist movement but it is not the extremism directed by indiscriminate terrorism. The terrorist acts perpetuated by insurgents are carefully selective and are limited to the killings of alleged police spies and informers who are also notorious in the villages. In the past such extremism used to evaporate within a short span of time but there is no indication of such evaporation this time around anywhere near the sight. In fact, it is on the march towards new stages with each day passing.

New Characteristics: Broadly speaking, communist movement in Nepal in the past has been left-intellectual movement. The participating intellectuals in this movement had comprised of upper caste (Brahmin-Chhetri-Newar-BCN). In other words, past movements were basically the movements against BCN ruling elite by the BCN non-ruling elite. That scenario, however, has changed now in view of the broader participation of persons from other castes particularly the untouchable castes such as Kami, Sarki, Damai, etc. In the past when non-ruling BCNs were fighting the ruling BCNs there was always scope for mediation and compromise due to the network of family relations. No such network of family relations exists now between BCN elite and guerrillas coming from untouchable lower castes, which narrows the chances of mediation and compromise.

Another notable characteristic of Maoist movement is the degree of women's participation in guerrilla ranks. Women's political participation in the past had been limited to electoral areas, especially, in voting and occasional candidacy in elections. It is a big surprise that Nepali women now have joined guerrilla organization under arms. More than a dozen women have already given their lives while fighting the police operations. According to an estimate about 30% of Maoist guerrillas comprise of women. This is totally a new phenomenon in Nepal, which must not be taken lightly.

Furthermore, more and more persons from Janajati people (Rai, Limbu, Gurung, Magar, Tamang, etc.) are joining the ranks of Maoist insurgency in the hope that they will be "emancipated" from the "clutches" of BCN. Although it is not quite clear whether these Janajatis will remain loyal to Maoist cause in the aftermath of the success of Maoist people's war, suffice it to say here that a peaceful settlement of the problem is no where near the sight.

Summary and Conclusion: Fighting a guerrilla war is an expensive proposition for any state. Guerrilla war has no front lines. Guerrillas operate in the midst of, and often hidden or protected by, civilian populations. The purpose of guerrilla war is not to engage an enemy army in direct confrontation, but rather to harass and punish it so as to gradually limit its operation and effectively liberate territory from its control. Efforts to combat such a guerrilla army- counterinsurgency- often include programs to "win the hearts and minds" of rural populations so that they stop sheltering the guerrillas. In guerrilla war, there is much territory that neither side controls; both sides exert military leverage over the same place at the same time. This makes guerrilla wars extremely painful for civilian population because the government armed forces fighting against guerrillas often do not distinguish them from civilians, and so strike both together.

Nepali strategic planners have failed to find a way in which people would stop giving sanctuaries to guerrillas. This could have been done by means of massive economic development package to people in the early period of insurgency. The relief package that the government has allocated after so much of killings has become irrelevant. Counter-insurgency measures require civil-military coordination in which clean civil administrators are expected to disburse economic development package. Here lies the problem. Nepal's problem is not the Maoist war but an entrenched coalition of corrupt politicians and bureaucrats that profits from Maoist war. It is very much likely that the economic relief package announced to combat insurgency could be yet another opportunity to corrupt civilian as well as military authorities for embezzlement. Counter-insurgency measure, if applied and executed by clean hands, will help minimize the distribution crisis, which in turn, will help to neutralize popular support to guerrillas. Otherwise, it remains a protracted problem and there is no way to obstruct Maoist revolution. The government forces, under the present policies, could win couple of battles here and there but will never win the war. The best they could expect is a negotiation for the safe passage with the victorious Maoist People's Guerrilla Army in years to come.

MAO'S LEGACY AND THE FUTURE OF MAOISM

It's time then to talk of Mao's legacy. As we have seen, Maoism has a definite view about how to get to socialism, and about what needs to be done to meet the basic needs of everyone in a poor country. Development is to be on an egalitarian basis — we are all in it together and everyone rises together. What then of Mao's legacy, Maoism? Surely, this is open to all who share his Weltanshuuang, his method of analysis — materialist dialectics — his values, his vision, and choose to embark together on the long march to socialism, knowing before hand, that the journey is fraught with considerable peril. What then of Maoism in India, one might ask? Maoist China did its best to feed, clothe and house everyone, keep them healthy, educate most of them. Contrast this with the deplorable conditions in India at the end of the 1960s and even today — the tragedy of India ruled by her own big bourgeoisie — and one gets wind as to why there are some in India who look to the Maoist model of development as the way to a richer and fuller life for all. Anu — whom we started this article with — was one of them.

However, while one may have deep respect for such people, one needs to ask the question: Are the basic path and strategy of revolution that were necessary in China in the 1930s and 1940s right for India in the 21st century? Well, India differs very significantly from the China of those times, more so in its history, geography, class and social structure, traditions, and in the nature of its "semi-feudalism"/backward capitalism, the accommodation of the big bourgeoisie with imperialism, the strength of the repressive apparatus of the state, the nationalities question, and so on. And, importantly, while Chinese history is replete with periodic widespread peasant uprisings, Indian history, in a comparative sense, is scarce of such rebellions, which perhaps can be explained in terms of caste — it is fundamentally antithetical to any meaningful unity of the exploited and the oppressed. Recall that Mao adapted his Marxism-Leninism to the realities of China's history, China's potentialities; "learn truth from practice" was his message. Surely a party [CPI (Maoist)] that stems from a political tendency that, over the last 40 years, has done its best to take the Indian revolution forward might like to take a hard re-look into the abyss that is India — its history, its potentialities.

The Maoists must keep in mind that the scientific validity of the Maoism they uphold will be judged in the first instance in India by its contributions to correctly explaining Indian social reality. There is a lot they have had a hand in this respect, for instance, in emphasising the parasitical reliance of Indian capital on the state for its self-expansion, expressed in the notion of *bureaucrat* capital. Or, in stressing the powerful role of the state in the very making of the Indian big bourgeoisie (of course, the "state's" fostering of the ruling classes more than the other way round, going back to ancient times, is an insight from the eminent historian D D Kosambi). The Maoists have also helped us to see the post-1956 official "land reforms" as having led to the partial amalgamation of the old rural landowning classes into a new, broader stratum of rich landowners, those not setting their hands to the plough, including an upper section of the former tenants, all of whom, despite the various markets, have yet to rid themselves of various "semi-feudal" practices and pre-capitalist elements of culture. Also, it is the Maoists who, in their practice, correctly do not even try to differentiate the rural poor into "agrarian proletariat" or "landless peasantry", knowing very well that the same very poor household can be categorized in one or the other at various points in time. And, in organising the "agrarian proletariat"/"landless peasantry" along with the poor and middle peasants, and a section of the rich peasants, they insist on factoring in the caste question, despite their knowing how highly problematic and painfully difficult such a getting together can be. Also, it is the Maoists more than others who first grasped the brutal character of the dominant classes and the leaders of the political parties they have co-opted, the very same categories whose forebears had taken power in the name of Gandhian non-violence. All this is knowledge essentially derived from their practice; and, needless to say, in keeping with Mao's legacy, the content of practice and knowledge has to go on continuously rising to a higher level.

The party [CPI (Maoist)] has come in for a lot of condemnation for its violent activities, including killings. The violence however has to be viewed in the context of the undeclared civil war that is underway in the areas of its influence, for instance, in Dantewada in the state of Chhattisgarh. The government is implementing a barbaric counter-insurgency policy, which includes the fostering of a network of informers and combatants among the civilian population, right from the village level upwards — a state-supported, state-sponsored, and even state-organised so-called people's resistance [called Salwa Judum (SJ)] against the Maoists. Entire villages have been evacuated and the villagers forcibly dumped into relief camps, and this, in the circumstances of large-scale acquisition of land by private corporations in what is a mineral-rich region.

The last four years have witnessed violent attacks, loot, destruction, intimidation, rape and killing on an unprecedented scale principally by the SJ; indeed, the latter has even forcibly mobilised the displaced into its ranks. Undoubtedly, the killing is by both sides, but the big difference is that the Maoists, generally when they target specific state representatives, or even informers, they first warn them to desist from the anti-people activity they are undertaking. Those guilty of rape, torture, deaths in custody, or responsible for "encounter" killings are singled out so that others may, out of fear of such reprisals, desist from acting thus. As far as the SJ representatives are concerned, any person who joins them is targeted, not because of any personal enmity, but because of the role that the SJ has been playing in the undeclared civil war.

More generally, the violence also has to be seen in the context of the close de facto nexus between economic and political power at the local and regional levels; the dominant classes, through various means, exercise a degree of control over the police and the judiciary, which increases the chances of violent confrontation between the contending classes.

Those who deliberately, falsely depict the Maoists as "devotees of violence", choose to suppress the fact that the violence of the oppressed (and the Maoists who now lead them) has been always preceded and provoked by the violence of the oppressors (and the state and private forces that back them). To claim, as some liberals do, that the violence of the oppressed is "morally equivalent" to that of the oppressors, is to endorse the reactionary state, which backs the oppressors. And, in this age of the management of public opinion, the "programming" of what the public thinks, sees and reads, the "facts" that are disseminated are artificially separated from a whole host of other relevant facts, never allowing the public to discern the "real" present.

But, while acknowledging that antagonistic contradictions between hostile class-based organisations will lead to violence, it is a Maoist tenet that guerrilla actions ought to be subordinated to "mass-line" politics — the Maoist guerrillas should give precedence to winning over the mass of the people in their base areas and, in consequence, in the surrounding areas — and work towards a better balance ("proportionality") than ever before between means and ends. Regarding the resort to violence in the revolution, to the extent that I have absorbed their writings, it would be fair to say that Marx and Engels might not have disagreed with the use of violent methods by the revolutionary forces in India today. The dominant classes could never be expected to give up their control without employing all the repressive power at their command. It is useful perhaps to recall that Marx's response to the "crimes and cruelties alleged" against the "insurgent Hindus" of 1857 was to set out an account of the daily violence "in cold blood" of British rule in India.

As to the false claim that the Maoists have no mass support in their areas of influence, one has only to listen to perceptive yet sensitive, independent observers who know the situation on the ground. The state forces are much stronger (as far as armaments and numbers go) than the Maoist guerrillas, and yet the tribal peasants support the latter. Why do these peasants take the risk of supporting the underdogs, even when they know that when the guerrillas are vanquished, they, as their supporters, will be at the mercy of the state forces, and will most probably perish? If, at the risk of death itself, the peasants choose the guerrillas, surely there must be something more significant going on over here.

Besides India, Maoism is a political force to reckon with in Nepal, the Philippines, and Peru. The Nepali Maoist leaders have been imaginative — their ideas of some combination of the "Chinese" (triumph in the countryside and spread to the cities) and the "Russian" (victory in the cities and spread to the countryside) models of revolution, and of "21st century democracy" (multi-party competition as long as all agree by the goals of "new democracy") are appealing.

But these theories are being put to a severe test in practice. The Unified Communist Party of Nepal (Maoist), given its relative strength vis-a-vis "the enemies" of democracy and their friends and masters outside the borders of that small country (above all in India), seeks to utilize the bourgeois republic as a stage in mustering the force of the impoverished masses and nationalist intermediate strata to proceed towards NDR.

What then of the future of Maoism and the renewal of socialism that it promises? Frankly, "whatever chance there may have been that the revolutions of the 20th century could or would provide successful working models of socialism" have long since been extinguished; "socialism, we are told, has been tried and failed". But, as Marx was the first to show, the obstacles to a better future cannot be meaningfully addressed within the framework of capitalism.

The challenge then is to revive and renew the legacy of socialism. In this, can Maoism illuminate the way? Maoism has its roots in Marx who was, above all, a *radical* democrat — he demanded the reincarnation of community and mass solidarity; he dreamed of the communion of human beings with nature; he stressed the dialectic of liberation; he looked forward to a just society alongside "rich individuality"; and, as Paresh Chattopadhyay (2005) reminds us, he insisted on the removal of commodity exchange, the division of labour, the state,... But, then, Lenin too, in his *State and Revolution* appeared as a thoroughgoing democrat, though he introduced into his conception of socialism elements that are antithetical to the "association of free individuals" — wage labour and state (Ibid).

Mao and the Chinese Maoists too gave the impression of being revolutionary democrats, that is, if one were to go by the 20 million people marching through the streets of various Chinese cities in the last week of May 1968, the demonstrators mainly chanting the slogan: "long live the revolutionary heritage of the great Paris Commune". Indeed, Marx's interpretation of the Commune was then deemed relevant to the revival of the revolution in China, something that found a place in the famous "Sixteen Points" of 8 August 1966. "Let a hundred flowers blossom, let a hundred schools of thought contend" was not merely intended policy for the promotion of progress in the arts and sciences, but one of ushering in a flourishing socialist culture, at least that was the claim. Thus, given the *radical* democratic streak running from Marx to Mao, the best thing that Maoism could do is to commit to the promise of *radical* democracy; after all, while it is true that there cannot be liberty in any meaningful sense without equality, for the rich will certainly be more "free" (have more options) than the poor; so there also cannot be equality without liberty, for then some may have more political power than others.

6

Ethnic Identity, Conflict and Nation Building in Bhutan

Ethnic identity has become a significant source of instability in a modern state. The source of threat posed to the modern state can be attributed to the internal socio-political disturbances due to the evolving identity of a community as a nation, which has produced certain disturbing trends that resulted in instability. The process of nation-building has proved to be an uphill task for the elites of modern nations. To create a balance between ethnic identity (primodist group identity) and national identity with the right mixture of diversity of ethnic diacritics within a state has proved to be a challenging task.

The identity of the state with any particular group or groups residing inside a single dominion makes the deprived groups (groups outside the preview of such inclusion) perceive that they are being dominated by others which makes assimilation difficult. In this complexity of nation building, minority groups often feel marginalised, which further strengthens the feeling of alienation. This, if not taken care of in time, might lead to a situation where the very foundation of the state security is jeopardised. In the context of South Asia, there are many communities who were initially marginalised. But due to growing awareness about their rights, these groups have become more vocal in putting forward their demands, sometimes resorting to seccessionist movements which has posed a great challenge to security. South Asia can be described as an ethnic mosaic which can be considered as the potential source of any future conflict based on ethnic identity rather than nationality. Bhutan is no exception to this environment. A country which was known for its peaceful serenity has become a cauldron of ethnic conflict.

Bhutan is a plural society having different ethnic and linguistic groups and two major religions i.e. Buddhism and Hinduism. The recorded history of Bhutan dates back to the 7th century. Another important aspect which should be mentioned here is that like the Nepalese, the present ruling ethnic group, the Ngalongs, are an offshoot of the Tibetans. The present ruling elites had migrated from Tibet around this time. According to Michael Aris, an expert in Tibetan history, "If one were to apply the label of 'indigenous' to any people in Bhutan...one would be tempted to focus on a very small community of jungle-dwellers...known as the 'toktop'...They were once a people who appear to have spread over the whole country and who have now all but disappeared under the impact of fresh migration or military defeat from the north."

The national identity as conceived by the elites of Bhutan is synonmous with Drukpa identity (the followers of the Drukpa Kargyup sect of Buddhism). The term Drukpa is very loosely defined and has a broad parameter "...the different ethnic groups in western, central and eastern Bhutan are called Drukpa because of their shared religious beliefs not because they form a single culture or ethnicity...In common usage, however, the rubric term Drukpa has slowly begun to be synonmous with Bhutanese..." Mostly all the Ngalongs, Sarchops and other smaller communities like the Khengs, Brokpas, Doyas, Lepchas, etc. practise Buddhism and Lhotshampas (southern Bhutanese of Nepali origin) practise Hinduism. Thus, there is a greater degree of socio-cultural variation which stems out of religious practice. The conflict which started initially as a problem of illegal migration turned into a protracted ethnic conflict having far-reaching implications for the peace and internal stability of Bhutan.

The recent conflict in Bhutan has exposed the inner contradictions in the Bhutanese society. The tiny Kingdom which wants to come out of isolation and build a strong nation has been caught between the dichotomy of nation building and the ethnic aspirations of a section of population who are of migrant origin. In the present context, the whole gamut of the conflict stems from different interrelated factors. The factors which are gaining importance in the context of Bhutanese plural society are national identity vis-a-vis ethnic identity of the citizens and various constituents of the concept of national integration and conflict arising out of implementing this integrationist policy in a plural society.

HISTORY OF NEPALESE SETTLEMENT

Before going into details of the present crisis, it is important here to discuss the history of the Nepalese settlement in the foothills of Bhutan because lately many of those who were driven out of the country for various reasons have been categorised as illegal immigrants. Thus, it is pertinent here to trace the year of their settlement to arrive at a logical conclusion that they are a part of Bhutanese society and polity and thus an integral part of the Bhutanese national identity. The Nepalese migration to Bhutan had started in the 19th century, more specifically after the Treaty of Sinchula in 1864. Nepalese migration to Bhutan is closely associated with the Bhutanese migration to Sikkim, Darjeeling and Duars of Assam. Most of the Nepalese came to these areas as plantation workers or to work in various development projects undertaken by the British administration. Moreover, as recorded in history, it was Kazi Ugyen Dorji, the Prime Minister of Bhutan, who was in charge of the southern foothills of Bhutan, who had encouraged the Nepalese settlement in Bhutan because of labour shortage. The economic transformation brought about by the industrious Nepalese in Darjeeling and adjoining areas made Dorji employ the Nepalese for the twin purpose of development of southern Bhutan and to fulfill his commitment to pay annual rent to the central government in Bhutan. All these factors cumulatively, along with the reluctance of the Bhutanese to settle in the malarious, hot and humid part of southern Bhutan, led to the choice in favour of the Nepalese. Successive British missions that travelled through Bhutan to negotiate with the Bhutanese rulers to open up a trade route to Tibet have revealed the presence of the Nepalese in Bhutan since the early 19th century. The early mission undertaken by British Political Officers Charles Bell and J.C. White also noted the presence of the Nepalese in the western valley. Among other officers who travelled to Bhutan for various reasons and have recorded the presence of the Nepalese, are Major W.L. Campbell, F.M. Bailey, Williamson, B.J. Gould, Capt C.J. Morris.

In addition to this there are some government documents which register that though the British had no official role in bringing the Nepalese to Bhutan, it was Ugyen Dorji who encouraged Nepalese migration, perhaps after being subjected to the British pressure. The dissidents of Nepali origin, however, claim the settlement of the Nepalese as much before the recorded history of the British or the government. They have cited that many Nepalese artisans from Kathmandu went to Bhutan to build monasteries. Among 108 monasteries built by them, Paro Kiyachu and Bumthag Jamphel Lakhags are the most significant. It is believed that these artisans settled in the valleys of eastern and central Bhutan. This source also claims that when Guru Padmasambhava came to Bhutan to preach Buddhism, he brought an entourage of Nepalis who later settled in Bhutan. There are others who believe that the first Shabdrung brought Nepalis by requesting King Ram Shah to send troops to guard the frontier of Bhutan. The government sources confirm that "since the reign of Deb Minijier Tempa (1667-1680), Newari craftsmen who were renowned for their artistic skills in metal work were commissioned by Bhutan for execution of religious objects and casting of statues." But there is no evidence of these people settling in Bhutan. Moreover, the claim made by the refugees is not supported by any historical fact about their settlement in Bhutan. Thus, it is safe to rely on the British mission reports.

Before detailing the perception of Bhutanese elites regarding the constituents of national identity, one should be well versed with the fact that the concept of a separate identity for both the communities in Bhutan emanates from their religion and culture. The Government of Bhutan at a point of time described Hinduism as compatible. Thus, while restrictions were put on activities relating to Islam and Christianity, there was a sense of accommodation towards Hinduism. In spite of their presence in Bhutan for more than a century, the Nepalese have maintained their unique tradition and culture. This is because the identity of the Nepalese as a distinct ethnic group stems from the fact that they belong to a different religious, lingual and socio-cultural group. Moreover, the Nepalese "as a distinct cultural group, are very proud of their tradition and, in fact, they look to Nepal and India as the centres of their civilisation, historical achievements and religious pilgrimage. As the Nepalese elite castes abhor beef, polyandry and widow remarriage prevalent among the Brugpa Lamaists, and they themselves practise ritual purity, personal and food pollutions, there is definitely a cultural gulf between the two communities."

Policy of Accommodation

The policy of the Bhutanese government can be compartmentalised into two distinct phases i.e. policy of accommodation (1958-80) and policy of absorption (1980 onwards). The Lhotshampas were first conferred citizenship of Bhutan in 1958. It was decided in the National Assembly that "the Nepalese of Southern Bhutan should abide by the rules and regulations of the Royal Government and, pledging their allegiance to the King, should conscientiously refrain from serving any other authority (such as Gorkha). They should submit a bond agreement to this effect to the Government." The explicit reference to the Gorkha in the pledge reflects the susceptibility of the Bhutanese elites towards the loyalty of the southern Bhutanese.

Citizenship rights to the Lhotshampas not only gave them legitimacy but conferred on them political and economic rights at par with other communities of Bhutan. The National Assembly (Tshogdu) which was established in 1953 gave representation to the Nepalese for the first time in 1958, thus including them in the decision-making process. The southern Bhutanese were represented in the Bhutanese civil services at par with the ethnic Bhutanese. In the National Assembly, other than Dzongkha, the national language, the debates were translated into English, and Nepalese. The national official newspaper of Bhutan, Kuensel, also has three editions—English, Dzongkha and Nepalese. Till 1988, the Nepalese were free to study in their mother tongue and teaching was imparted in Nepali. The Nepalese were also taken in the Army and police and were included in the Cabinet and judiciary. There was no restriction on the Nepalese to open pathsalas to learn Sanskrit or to celebrate Hindu religious holidays and maintain their culture, tradition and wear their unique dress.

Till 1980, the government never interfered with the social life of the Lhotshampas. However, the situation across the border made the Bhutanese government nervous. The Gorkhaland movement essentially directed at the gratification of ethnic aspirations of the Nepalese in India, oscillating between the demand for autonomy and seccesionism under the current of Greater Nepal, sent alarming signals to the Bhutanese elites. Sikkim's merger with India was the historical fact which gave vent to such an apprehension. To quote Dawa Tshering, the Foreign Minister of Bhutan, "...just a century ago there were no Nepalese in Darjeeling hills and Sikkim, areas contiguous to us. The imperial gazetteers are historical proof of that. Now they constitute the overwhelming majority, they have political power and they are undisputed leaders in the region. This is a historical experience for us." The demographic threat in the case of Bhutan was portrayed as a security threat to its existence as a small nation having a unique identity. "They want to take over" one official lamented, referring to the apprehension of the Nepalese forging a common political entity which might see "...Bhutan to be a part of Greater Nepal."

Apart from the abovementioned factors, what added to their discomfort is the geographical contiguity of southern Bhutan to the Nepali dominated areas of India. Moreover, the Nepalese were suspected to have revolutionary ideas because of their close interaction with the Indians and Nepalis living beyond the border, and the democratic environment that prevails in those countries. It made the region politically vulnerable to the influence of neighbouring countries. The Nepalese are politically more conscious and outward looking people compared to the ethnic Bhutanese who are more conservative due to the lack of political education and political socialisation. According to Leo E. Rose, their political orientation can be attributed to the following reasons:

"They are recent immigrants, stemming from the very different (and in some respect antagonistic) Hindu cultural and value system and are generally resistant to integration into Bhutan's tradition social community and political culture...their more natural line of association runs south and west rather than north. Moreover, a few of the Nepali Bhutanese have been socialised in Indian political values—democratic, Marxist and Hindu orthodoxy—either before migration to Bhutan or as a part of their education across the border in India...The political traditions of Bhutan, including perhaps those surrounding the monarchy, are not deeply ingrained in the Nepali Bhutanese and their loyalty to the system is sometimes questioned."

The Nepalese political orientations were evident in the early Fifties. The influence of the freedom movement of India and later the fall of the autocratic Rana regime in Nepal, provided the Lhotshampas with much needed impetus to their limited political exposure and they formed the first political organisation known as "Jai Gorkha Solidarity Front." The objective of the organisation was to protect the interest of the southern Bhutanese' largely agricultural needs. The movement fizzled out because of its limited appeal and the fear that it might affect their land ownership rights in Bhutan.

The present crisis which has emerged as a challenge to the security of Bhutan is the dichotomy between ethnic identity and national identity. The Bhutanese identity emphasises the Dzongkha language, the dress code of the major communities i.e. Kho and Kira, typical Bhutanese dress, and other etiquette that are included in the cultural edict known as Driglam Namzha which was introduced as the theme of the Sixth Five-Year Plan. However, a reference to culture and customs was made during the fiftieth National Assembly. It may be pointed out here that the policy of nationalistic cultural "orientation" had started even as early in 1977. It was decided to adequately acquaint the graduates educated outside Bhutan with the Bhutanese programme of socio-economic transformation. The identity of the Nepalese stems from their distinct socio-cultural and religious beliefs, their distinct language, food habit and dress.

Policy of Absorption

To construct a framework for one King, one country and one people, Bhutanese nationalism with its unique ingredients of Ngalongs culture and way of life was introduced. Justifications for the policy were wrapped with apprehensions of a small country facing demographic threat from people of migrant origin. As a result of the introduction of various partisan policies to preserve its sovereignty and culture as described by the King, the people who till the late Eighties had perceived themselves as a part of the Bhutanese socio-political system, suddenly felt that they were being alienated in different sectors of the government and that their loyalty was suspected in spite of their presence in Bhutan for more than a century. A major shift in the policy towards the Lhotshampas took place in the late Eighties. As has been discussed elsewhere, the early Eighties saw tumultuous political activities in Nepal and by the Nepalese in India.

Marriage Act of 1980

Keeping in mind the relations resulting from marriages between the Nepalese on either side of the international boundary which encourages further immigration, the government introduced the Marriage Act, 1980, restricting marriage with non-Bhutanese by laying down certain penalties in terms of promotion and other benefits. It is important to mention here that earlier, to encourage inter-ethnic marriages between Drukpas and Lhotshampas, the government which had announced a cash reward of Nu 5,000 increased to Nu 10,000 if the marriage lasted for five years. But this policy failed to achieve the anticipated results due to various socio-religious constraints which prescribe the marital relationship within the Nepalese community. The Nepalese perceived this as a policy aimed at them because it is they who mostly have marriage relations outside Bhutan because of caste and other considerations. Thus, the Marriage Act was largely resented by the Lhotshampas because it affected them. One of the provisions of this Act stated: "Promotion shall not be granted to a Bhutanese citizen married to a non-Bhutanese beyond the post she/he held at the time of his/her marriage." This provision had a retrospective effect of being effective from June 11, 1977. Such a person shall not be promoted beyond the post of a subdivisional officer. Moreover, any Bhutanese citizen employed in the National Defence Department or in the Ministry of Foreign Affairs shall be removed from such services after his/her marriage to a non-Bhutanese.

They shall not get facilities enjoyed by other citizens. Moreover, they are not entitled to education or training abroad. However, later it was clarified by His Majesty that a non-national spouse "would be granted special residential permit and would be entitled to health, education, and other social benefits extended to the citizen of the country."

The grant of special residence permit is limited to marriages prior to the coming into force of the 1985 Act and not to those which took place thereafter so as to prevent anybody adopting the method of marriage as a means to migrate. This was perceived by the Lhotshampas as a move to prevent them from getting married outside the international boundary.

Citizenship Act of 1985

The Citizenship Act of 1985 put up more hurdles regarding both acquisition and termination of citizenship. It is more rigid and stringent compared to the 1977 Citizenship Act as far as naturalisation is concerned. Contrary to the 1977 Act, where single Bhutanese parentage was required for granting of citizenship, the 1985 Act stated that only in cases where both the parents are from Bhutan, a child born to such parents will be a Bhutanese citizen by birth. Other significant provisions of the 1985 Citizenship Act are in case a non-national marries a Bhutanese national, the offspring of such marriage and the spouse can apply for Bhutanese citizenship. For the non-Bhutanese spouse, it includes 15 years residency, ability to speak, read and write Dzongkha proficienttly, possessing a good moral character and having no record of acting or speaking against the King, country and people. Moreover, the government has the power to reject any application without citing any reason.

The rules for termination of citizenship are ambivalent in nature. The 1985 Citizenship Act lays down two conditions. Apart from making annual registration in the Census Department compulsory, the clause relating to the termination of citizenship reads that "any citizen of Bhutan who has acquired citizenship by naturalisation may be deprived of citizenship at any time if that person has shown by act or speech to be disloyal in any manner whatsoever to the king, country, people." This clause affected the Lhotshampas because many of them are naturalised citizens. It is interesting to note that through this clause, the government curtailed any dissent whatsoever to the policies undertaken in the name of national integration.

The Census Exercise of 1988

The problem assumed the present proportion when the 1988 census was taken only in the five southern districts of Bhutan. The census exercise of 1988 sent shock waves to the ruling elites of Bhutan. The census result of Samchi district in southern Bhutan revealed that its population had almost doubled within a period of ten years. The basis of this census exercise was the 1985 Citizenship Act. On the basis of it, people were divided into seven categories. Categorisation was done by a committee of 12 persons, including three village elders. However, as the refugee sources put it, "The village elders were allowed little or no role and very few southern Bhutanese were included in the census team." Some people who were previously given Bhutan citizenship identity cards during the 1979-1981 census exercise, were categorised as illegal immigrants and were required to leave the country. The basis of ascertaining citizenship was "any documentary evidence whatsoever (land ownership deeds or document showing sale/gift/inheritance of land, tax receipt of any kind, etc.) showing that the person concerned was a resident in Bhutan in 1958 and is taken as a conclusive proof of citizenship." Thus, people who had been residing in Bhutan for generations were declared illegal immigrants because of non-possession of such documents. There is a possibility of many people not having tax receipts because there was a system of paying tax in kind. Many people who live in Bhutan do not own land, because due to the government's policy, many southern Bhutanese known as Sukumbis were given land and settled in 1970. These people could not prove their residency before 1958. Though there were southern Bhutanese as a part of the census team to give credibility to the team verifying identity during the census exercise, as a scholar has put it "The state selects and nominates Nepalese to the various formal bodies, who are more pliable and do not necessarily represent the popular feelings of the Nepalese."

Policy of Driglam Namzha

The sense of security that emanated largely from the growing Lhotshampas population, made Bhutan apprehensive about its identity as a distinct nation, its culture and Mahayana form of Buddhism which the Bhutanese consider as unique and exclusive. Apprehensions surfaced over whether illegal migration of Nepalese to Bhutan can alter the ethnic composition of the Bhutanese society and reduce the Drukpas and other ethnic groups to the status of minority in their own country. The government realised the dangerous implication it can have for the identity of Bhutan with its unique Mahayana Buddhism and culture. To deal with this, the Bhutanese programme of Driglam Namzha was introduced in the form of a Royal Khaso (decree) on January 16, 1989, as a part of the Sixth Plan document. This cultural edict, as explained, includes "such virtues as respect for teachers, the sovereign, parents and elders; the institution of marriage and family, civic duties and behaviour that keep together the strands of the Bhutanese social fabric emanate from the source." Supporting the policy of integration, the King of Bhutan stated, "Our culture and tradition provide us with a unique identity to help us to protect our sovereignty. That is why we give so much attention to them. We must feel Bhutanese. Otherwise we will not be able to survive."

In a bid to assimilate the Lhotshampas, many measures were undertaken. In 1988, the programme started with the concept of "one nation one people." It was clarified that "since Bhutan is neither an economic nor a military power, so the only factor we can fall back on which can strengthen Bhutan's sovereignty and security is our identity, our different identity, we are really the last bastion of Himalayan Buddhism." Justifying such a need for a national identity in Bhutan, the King pointed out that there is a tendency among our people to identify themselves more closely with nationalities of other countries...in a large country (ethnic) diversity adds colour and character to its national heritage without affecting national security, but in a small country like ours it adversely affects the growth of social harmony and unity."

To gauge public mood, the government held a referendum in 18 districts of southern Bhutan. Though it was claimed later that the cultural edict was accepted overwhelmingly by the Lhotshampas, later popular resentment in the form of public demonstration proved that the government was wrong in the assessment of the people's opinion. The discrepancy between the real feelings of the people and the posture taken in front of government officials was due to two reasons. First, the people were too scared to articulate their opinion. Second, the representatives of the people are not elected through any kind of democratic means. From 1980 onwards, election of people's representatives was discouraged. Instead, District Administrative Officers were made to nominate them. Thus, the 1990 demonstration by the Lhotshampas against cultural imposition proved that the government was not given true feedback regarding the people's opinion. Moreover, it can be further inferred that the present system of government, without a free Press, political parties and freedom of speech and expression, does not leave much scope for ventilating of grievances.

A dress code was introduced as a part of the national integration scheme. While applicable only on formal occasions, in practice it was required to be worn everywhere "except by the Bhutanese operating modern machinery in workshops, factories, etc., where the use of Kho was inadvisable...Any person violating this rule was to be arrested and was liable to imprisonment." This dress code was not acceptable to the Lhotshampas because it was inconvenient for them to wear in the hot and humid weather of the Terai region. Moreover the material used for making this dress was quite expensive. It was not that the representatives of the

Lhotshampas in the National Assembly did not ventilate the reluctance of the people to abide by the dress code. But the government did not pay any attention to their opinion. If the dress code is not followed, there is fine of Nu 500 for the first offence, Nu 1000 for the second, and rigorous imprisonment if the same offender is caught for the third time.

Dzongkha was made an important language by reducing the use of other languages though Bhutan is a multilingual country. According to Leo E. Rose, "It is a language of administration, and the lingua franca of the country—at least to the extent there is one. It is also the language used (along with the Tibetans) within the Drukpa religious establishment, which makes it a medium of communication on a limited but important scale throughout most of the country...it is language of home in western Bhutan...The linguistic character of western Bhutan reveals that Dzongkha is generally understood only by those people who live in the vicinity of the Dzong itself...the government officials from outside usually require an interpreter to communicate with the people of their area of jurisdiction." It was made the working language in the National Assembly in 1980 though Nepali was used in the deliberations. However, from time to time, certain sections of the National Assembly members had demanded that only Dzongkha be used in the National Assembly. The government took measures to strengthen the use of Dzongkha. "It was resolved that correspondence, accounts, signboards of offices, house numbers and milestones would as far as possible be written in Dzongkha." Moreover to reduce the use of Nepali, the teaching of Nepali in the southern Bhutan schools were stopped in 1988 when the New Approach to Primary Education (NAPE) was introduced. The reason for dropping this language as explained was, "Nepali is the national language and lingua franca of another country...was only serving to accentuate the dichotomy of two distinct national cultures in Bhutan." Text-books were prepared by the Department of Education to educate people in the national language and adequate grace marks were given for the students of southern Bhutan in Dzongkha. The government, however, maintains that until 1988, Nepali was being taught upto grade five in all the primary schools in the south as a third language and not as a medium of instruction.

GRIEVANCES OF THE SOUTHERN BHUTANESE

In the National Assembly there is no proportional representation for the ethnic Nepalese. Though the exact ethnic break-up of the population is not available, one can be sure about the disproportionate representation of the southern Bhutanese. In a 151-member National Assembly, the southern Bhutanese have only 16 representatives and only one of them is serving as a Cabinet Minister. His Majesty, the King of Bhutan, accepted the unfairness of the representation when he said in an interview, "In the south, the representation is not fair. When my father established the National Assembly in 1953, no one had an idea about it and nobody wanted it. So, when he forced its creation, the seat representation was done on an adhoc basis. We had no census. It definitely needs to be changed in accordance with the demographic distribution in the districts." The under-representation of Lhotshampas does not give them any weightage in the decision-making process as they can always be overriden by the majority belonging to the Sarchop and Ngalong community. There is no secret ballot system and most of the legislations or important policies are approved through consensus. Hence, the present National Assembly which is packed by such nominated representatives is seen by many in southern Bhutan as nothing more than a rubber stamp Assembly. The King "is still not only the Head of the State but the ruler of the country, and the decision-making process continues to be concentrated in the Palace." The paternalistic and populist postures attempt to endear the King to the average subject. The young graduates of the National Voluntary Service attribute their selection, stipend, maintenance, guidance and ultimate awards, then postings, increments, promotions and overall career to the King. The rural folk, are obliged to the royal sovereign for all developmental activities or special welfare programmes because such steps are new to them. Thus, the King has a mass support base among his citizens regarding policies because the people are hardly exposed to any idea about democracy or government by the people. In this kind of society, political socialisation and political education are highly improbable propositions. "It was not that most Bhutanese were resistant to modern concepts, they never heard of them." The absence of mass media for their exposure to the world outside has been systematically delineated. The ban on satellite television helps in the survival of the present system. The strengthening of feudal elements in policies can be exposed from the following facts. The no-confidence motion against the King which was initially adopted during King Jigme Dorji's rule by the thirtieth National Assembly in 1969, was increased from two-third to 50 per cent in the thirty-sixth National Assembly. Later this was rejected by the same National Assembly in its thirty-ninth session and the representatives of the Assembly accepted, and affirmed their faith in a hereditary King. Though Bhutan shed its isolation and started the modernisation process in the early Sixties "...the Bhutanese were determined to be selective about those facets of modernisation that would be introduced in Bhutan. Such total alien institutions as political parties were, of course, anathema." Thus, it is the Lhotshampas who are politically more informed through their interactions across the international boundary.

The Nepalese also have a series of religious grievances. The monk body is represented in the National Assembly. But considering the fact that a good number of Bhutan's citizens are Hindus, a request for a representation of a Hindu pandit was turned down citing limited membership of the Assembly. Dussera was declared as a national holiday only in 1980. However, the government banned Kirtan Sanghs in 1988.

The Lhotshampas feel that they are under-represented in the civil services. In 1960, the bureaucracy was modernised and was more organised. By 1972, there were a number of departments, organised on a more "modern basis that exerted substantial authority on virtually all subjects. Decision-making became the virtual monopoly of the Thimpu 'boys' who, on most occasions paid little attention to the views of local leaders scattered all over the country or even their representatives in the National Assembly." The data of regionwise representation in the civil services indicates a bias in favour of the northern Bhutanese since the Lhotshampas are more educated than other Bhutanese In twelve dzongkhags (district), there are 120 schools with 36,798 students and enrolment ratio is 40 per cent, in five southern dzongkhags and one dungkhag (sub-division) there are 80 schools, 31,054 students and enrolment ratio is 81 per cent. In the civil services, the northern Bhutanese constitute 73.50 per cent and the southern Bhutanese 26.50 per cent. Lhotshampas maintain that "the top positions inevitably go to Drukpas."

Protest and Eviction

All the above reasons were enough to ignite the growing disillusion and dissatisfaction of the Nepalese towards the Royal Government. The census exercise of 1988 based on the 1985 Citizenship Act changed the fate of many Bhutanese from citizens of Bhutan to non-national or illegal immigrants. It is pertinent here to point out that import of labour has been banned since 1971 in government and private organisations except for the Ministry of Trade and Industries which was permitted to import labour "for imparting training...and take the responsibility for the imported labour." It was further decided that such labour cannot use land and should be transferred every year. All these precautions establish the fact that with such cautiousness on the part of the government, it was not easy for the non-nationals to settle in Bhutan in such large numbers as the ruler of Bhutan claims whenever any reference to the Bhutanese refugees in Nepal is made.

Demonstrations were organised against the Citizenship Act of 1985 and the census exercise of 1988 which put many people in the bracket of illegal immigrants. It is pertinent here to point out that there is no freedom of speech and expression in Bhutan as per law. In the past when a proposal to extend the right of freedom of speech and expression was made, it was rejected by the National Assembly because "most of the members felt that granting of freedom of speech and expression to the people, although good in principle, was premature in view of the general backwardness of the people and their lack of consciousness...it was resolved that the public would not be granted freedom of speech at present." To express their dissatisfaction, the Lhotshampas, in a strongly worded pamphlet, circulated as the voice of the oppressed people of Bhutan, asserted the ethno-cultural distinction and superiority of the Nepalese settled in southern Bhutan. The pamphlet titled, The Gorkha People of Southern Bhutan, Must Unite and Fight for our Rights stated: "We Nepalese have a far rich tradition and culture which is derived from the oldest religion in the world which is Hinduism and that our Nepalese-Hindu culture is immensely more superior to the cheap and concocted version of Sino-Tibetan customs, the Drukpa are so proudly calling Diglam Namzha."

It further warned the government against any cultural imposition and stated, "We the Gorkhas of Southern Bhutan are not only the majority but we also have seventeen million brothers and sisters in Nepal and over 10 million in India...there is every possibility that the borders of the Gorkha state...will join...we Gorkhas must unite together and create another Gorkha state in Bhutan and extend the borders of Gorkha states along the Himalayas which has always been the rightful home of our people."

The pamphlet was explicit about the threat in its contents and warned that the King "will soon go to the way of his late uncle, the Chogyal of Sikkim...If the present racist policy of Bhutanisation is not stopped, as one large and strong fist that will strike a lethal blow and once and for all remove the evil Drukpa regime." It further stated that "we must call upon the support of our brothers and sisters in Nepal and India in the liberation struggle against the despot Drukpa King and his corrupted Drukpa government." To succeed in its tactics to voice its protest against the government policies, Bhutan People's Party (BPP), a political party in exile now, had used violence and forced the people to come for the rally organised by it against the cultural imposition. The party President, R.K. Budhathoki, a former employee of the government put forth the 13-point demand to the King on August 26, 1990. Later, two Councillors of the Royal Advisory Council from southern Bhutan, Teknath Rizal and B.P. Bhandari, presented a petition to the King charting out the grievances of the Lhotshampas. However, the government, terming them anti-national, arrested and later released them, and they took refuge in Nepal. Later, Rizal with the connivance of the Communist government in Nepal, was abducted brought back to Bhutan where he is still languishing in jail.

The government came down heavily on the demonstration which was organised in the tiny town of Chirang in southern Bhutan to express genuine dissatisfaction. This led to loss of life and property. Many people left Bhutan and took refuge in India and were later shifted to the refugee camps in Nepal maintained by the United Nations Commission for Human Rights (UNCHR). Many people who were just present during the demonstration out of curiosity were evicted since they were considered as conspirators in these anti-national activities and were made to sign voluntary immigration forms. Moreover, as has been pointed out earlier, the Bhutanese Citizenship Act has laid out in clear terms that any person who by act, speech or deed is considered to be disloyal to the King, country and people, will forfeit citizenship. This is also evident from a circular of the Home Ministry that reads, "Any Bhutanese national leaving the country to assist and help the anti-nationals shall no longer be considered as a Bhutanese citizen. It must also be made clear that such people's family members living under the same household will also be held fully responsible and forfeit their citizenship." There were recent reports in Keunsel that the government is planning to evict relatives of the so-called anti-nationals.

For Bhutan, the security implications are much larger. The terrorist activities committed by the dissidents inside Bhutan have become a major security threat to a tiny kingdom like Bhutan with limited resources, an under-developed economy and a very small security force. According to a government report:

"Since 1990, 913 families were robbed...destroyed 29 schools, 12 health units, 5 agricultural service centres, 4 animal husbandry facilities, 45 police and custom checkposts and offices, forest range offices and government houses... they had burnt down or destroyed 60 village houses, hijacked 64 vehicles and destroyed 36. They had also destroyed 15 rural drinking water schemes and more than 63 km of irrigation channels at the Takali and Lalai irrigation project which had been constructed for the benefit of the people of Gelephu. The Ngolop terrorists had assaulted 667 Bhutanese people, embushed and attacked the security forces 66 times and had killed a total of 71 Bhutanese citizens."

Some of the terrorists are even operating from the camps of Nepal which strengthens the evidence of such cross-border diaspora involvement. However, the accusations and counter-accusations by both the parties involved has worsened the situation. The former Nepalese Deputy Prime Minister, Madhav Kumar Nepal, made a statement saying that "Bhutan will suffer the same fate as Sikkim if it wants to protect its nationalism by driving out Nepalese."

The implications of the present problem can be gauged from the fact that most of the subversive activities which were carried out by the BPP and other organisations had the tacit help of the transnational ethnic actors.

The Chhatra Sabha, and the Gorkhaland Liberation Organisation are suspected of giving some of the rebels arms and guerrilla training, just as the Akhil Bharatiya Gorkha League extends moral support. Apart from this the local population and the leftist elements in the Duars and in Darjeeling and Kalimpong, have sought the support of, and assistance from, Nepal, particularly from the radical Marxists. Recent reports indicate that "...apart from supplies of medicines and rations, arms are being smuggled to the BPP...some sections of the BPP are making all possible efforts to procure arms and explosives both from Nepal and through contacts with militant elements in the north-eastern region of India."

Ventilating a similar kind of threat perception, BNDP President R.B. Basnet, said, "Bhutan is a strategic area and the Government of India would not like any kind of disturbances like the present one. If the Government of India does not help to resolve the crisis, there is a possibility of a Pan-Nepali movement." However, the movement is in a formative stage and mobilising Nepali public opinion in India will depend on the future political agenda of the disgruntled groups in the Duars of India. It is not only the leaders but the people in the refugee camps and especially the younger generation, who are feeling restless that the time is running short for the movement to be resolved peacefully. "If the government does not give a decisive push towards the establishment of democracy, one can visualise a sharp increase in terrorist activities in Bhutan as a means to achieve success against the repressive regime. This repressive measure, if continued further, may drive the people to overthrow the Monarchy and establish a Republic."

The current situation is that in spite of seven rounds of bilateral talks that have taken place between Nepal and Bhutan, it still evades an early solution. Though both the governments had agreed upon the categorisation, the change in the stance and the intransigent policy pursued by the parties involved are important reasons why the solution is still a distant dream.

The present conflict which has assumed such proportions can be attributed to the vigorous integration postures that are adopted by nation states. The policy to absorb a particular ethnic group by dissolving their ethnic identity is not viable and can produce conflict as has happened in the case of Bhutan. The pre-1985 policies, as pursued by Bhutan, had given the southern Bhutanese space to keep their ethnic identity intact.

The language and dress of the Nepalese was never a threat to Bhutan's unique identity—why did it became so significant suddenly? It is the democratic aspiration which scared the elite, not the demonstration by the southern Bhutanese. Referring to the refugees in the eastern Nepal camps as illegal immigrants is not going to solve the problem. It amounts to non-recognition of the problem. Bhutan has to look into the problem realistically and has to be more accommodative and sympathetic in its approach towards this problem. Any tough stand on its part will provide only temporary relief. The hundreds and thousands of refugees in the neighbouring country who have many grievances against the government, might be led to align with terrorist groups operating in this part which will compound a major security threat to the country and the ruling elites.

BUILDING PRODUCTIVE CAPACITIES TO CREATE GLOBALIZATION WORK FOR LDCS

The BPoA calls for the building of productive capacities as being vital for engendering sustained economic growth and alleviating pervasive poverty in the LDCs. As LDCs are constrained deeply by extremely low productivity levels, it is deemed to be particularly important that LDCs improve their competitiveness in international markets in goods and services in order for them to benefit meaningfully from trade openness and globalization and avoid the risk of increased marginalization from the global economy.

As defined in the UNCTAD LDC Report 2006, productive capacities here refer to the productive resources, entrepreneurial capabilities and production linkages which together determine the capacity of a country to produce goods and services and enable it to grow and develop.

As with many LDCs, Bhutan has been plagued by extremely low levels of productivity in its non-hydropower sectors of the economy. Bhutan's industrial and export base still remains very narrow, lacks depth and is highly exposed to single market and single commodity risks.

There is also a clear recognition that productivity levels in Bhutan's industry, manufacture and agriculture sectors have been poor and largely explain their weak levels of growth over the decade.

The share of agriculture, livestock and forestry sector has declined from about 40% of GDP in the mid nineties to 18.5% in 2008. Similarly, the manufacturing sector has declined from around 16% of GDP between 1990-95 to around 5% of GDP over the last five years. Moreover, both the manufacturing and agriculture sectors have not generated sufficient quality employment with labour force participation declining in these sectors. Some key supply side constraints responsible for the productivity gap in Bhutan pertain to the weak economic infrastructure including inadequate road access exacerbated by the rugged mountainous terrain, low level of technological base and weak human resources.

Physical communications

The weak strategic infrastructure has always posed a major challenge that has chronically impeded economic and industrial development in Bhutan. Moreover, various national poverty studies clearly reflect a strong co-relationship between road connectivity and poverty incidence. The inadequate road and air transport links to both external and domestic markets have been a critical constraint, a situation exacerbated by the mountainous and rugged terrain.

Road transportation costs are therefore high with haulage costs for certain products exceeding the value of the product itself. These high transportation costs combined with the poor dependability of roads due to their vulnerability to landslides and adverse climatic conditions make it extremely difficult for local industries to compete efficiently in producing goods. Transportation further adds considerably to inflate import expenditures for various commodities, materials and goods thereby raising living costs and development expenses considerably. Additionally, the weak air transport system, including the absence of domestic air services, has proved to be a major bottleneck for the further development of the tourism sector and high value niche exports.

In view of these reasons, the Royal Government has consistently accorded a high priority to the development of socio-economic infrastructure. As in past years, a large share of the capital expenditures has been earmarked for infrastructure development. Over the Tenth Plan, infrastructure development will receive about 36% of the total capital expenditures.

About 25% of the total capital expenditures alone have been earmarked for the expansion of the road network, which does not include local government budgets that have considerable allocations for the development of feeder and farm roads in local communities. On the basis of the road infrastructure expansion activities, the Royal Government anticipates that 85% of the rural population will live within half a day's walk from the nearest road head by the year 2013.

At present, international air convey is confined to one single airport at Paro. Domestic air services too have not yet started. However, despite these air transport bottlenecks air passenger traffic and air freight has grown manifold since 2001. The Royal Government plans to start up another airport at Gelephu and will also initiate domestic air services with the participation of the private sector. The development of various domestic airstrips with short take off and landing facilities are being explored currently in Trashigang and Bumthang. Airport facilities and infrastructure including air navigational aids are further expected to be enhanced at the Paro International airport. Expanding air connectivity and access will be particularly important within the context of Bhutan's plans to enhance international tourism including the promotion of Bhutan as a well being and MICE destination and emerging as a regional centre of excellence for educational services.

By 2010, the Golden Jubilee Rail Link will place Bhutan on the global railway map with a railhead in the border town of Phuentsholing connected to the Indian town of Hasimara. Feasibility studies are also to be undertaken for rail connections between other border points with India. This critical railway link with India will help reduce exports and import costs and further boost bilateral trade with India.

The adequate development of ICT infrastructure is deemed highly important for enhancing productive capacities in Bhutan. The Royal Government fully appreciates that without the effective utilization of ICT Bhutan could be effectively marginalized in the global economy and will be unable to take advantage of the opportunities of globalization. There is also the clear recognition that Bhutan cannot afford to be caught on the wrong side of a global digital divide and that ICT holds enormous potential to help the country overcome its considerable geographic and terrain challenges.

Currently, all twenty districts and 199 of the 205 sub- districts are connected to the national fixed line telecom network. Mobile coverage has reached 107 geogs with the plan to provide full coverage to all of the sub districts by the end of 2013. Fixed-line tele-density has increased from 2.8% in 2002 to 4.6% in July 2008 and mobile tele-density as of July 2008 has reached 36% since its launch in November 2003. Fixed-line tele-density has increased from 2.8% in 2002 to 4.6% in July 2008 and mobile tele-density as of July 2008 has reached 36% since its launch in November 2003. As such, with regard to fixed line tele-density Bhutan with 4.6 lines per 100 inhabitants is near the BPoA target of 5. In terms of mobile tele-density, it is close to levels in developing countries and much higher than the average for LDCs. The startup of a new telecom service provider in the country in 2008 has further helped enhance mobile coverage networks, telecommunication and drive down consumer costs through competition. Internet connections have doubled from about 5,000 to 10,000 since 2003 which reflects a ratio of 1.5 connections per 100 inhabitants. This however is considerably below the BPoA target of 10 connections per 100. Internet usage and connections should increase though once the

Increasing computer literacy among students in high institutions and 50% and in junior and high schools by 25% by 2015

No data available on computer literacy levels in educational institutions Royal Government establishes a nationwide ICT infrastructure backbone that is fast, affordable and future proofed to the extenting average telephone density to 5 main lines per 100 inhabitants connection to 10 users per 100 inhabitants by the year 2010 possible. Following this and the planned expansion of internet bandwith and connectivity, Fixed line Teledensity (%) Mobile Teledensity (%) (%) Bhutan will potentially have one of the world's highest internet bandwith per inhabitant. Additionally the Royal Government plans to enhance last mile access of ICT connectivity down to the village level which will help prevent the emergence of a rural-urban digital divide.

A regional development that will further enhance Bhutan's ICT networks is the SASEC information superhighway. Under this regional project, Bhutan along with Bangladesh, India and Nepal will share an information superhighway by 2011 with these countries directly linked to one another with high speed optical fibre cables. The project will not only contribute to cross border connectivity but will considerably enhance Bhutan's ICT human resources and help bridge the urban-rural digital divide. Under this project, 30 communication information centres (CICs) and an ICT Research and Training Institute are to be established in Bhutan.

A major constraint and challenge in promote ICT development in Bhutan is the critical lack of human capacity in the ICT sector. To address this, the Royal Government proposes to establish an IT Park and an ICT centre of excellence and has actively promoted the establishment of private IT training institutes. Additionally, IT literacy has been introduced in all schools as a tool subject with efforts to equip all Higher and most Secondary grade schools with computers. Computer science and computer application subjects are being taught. There is however no available data at present regarding IT literacy. Currently there is an average of 24 computers per school in 62% of all schools in Bhutan (335 schools). 184 schools (35%), most of them community primary schools do not have any computers as many of these schools do not have access to electricity. In terms of internet connectivity, 25% of public schools and 81% of higher secondary schools had working internet connections. With the rural electrification programme reaching close to universal levels and last mile ICT access down to village targeted to be achieved by 2013, it is expected that most schools will have better access to computers and the internet and IT literacy levels will improve importantly.

Power

Bhutan's hydropower capacity at present stands at 1,488 MW up from 422.8 MW in 2001. Most of the energy generated has always been exported to India with hydropower exports comprising about 45% of the total exports in 2008 and contributing to about 40% of national revenues. National electricity coverage as of 2007 stood at 70% of all households as compared to 54% in 2001. It is envisaged that Bhutan will attain electricity for all within this decade.

The development of energy infrastructure notably for the harnessing of Bhutan's hydropower resources has fundamentally transformed the landscape of Bhutan's economy. As such, the further expansion of hydropower development on an accelerated basis remains at the core of Bhutan's economic development strategy. The Royal Government is envisaging the scaling up the total hydropower capacity in Bhutan to over 10,000 MW by 2020 with a power protocol being signed with the Government of India to that effect in 2009.

An empowered joint group has been constituted to fast track the implementation of the hydropower projects agreed upon between the two countries. For the medium term, the Royal Government has targeted the doubling of hydropower capacity to 1,602 MW with the immediate construction of the Punatshangchhu I. By 2013 it is expected that the energy sector will comprise over 15% of GDP and contribute to over 36% of national revenues. The attainment of electricity coverage by 2013 is 100% of the total population is another critical target to be achieved over the next few years with even the possibility of attaining the goal of electricity for all by 2013. Raising this to near universal access levels through the rural electrification programme will require the targeted electrification of about 40,000 rural households. In view of the accelerated hydropower development programme and the major RE programme, the Royal Government is actively considering the establishment of hydropower training institutes to build up adequate local capacity.

Send abroad Infrastructure

Bhutan as a landlocked country has considerable trade transit constraints. To facilitate exports and ease such transit constraints, the Royal Government intends to establish dry ports in the regional industrial and economic hubs of the country and develop industrial parks and special economic zones – most of them along the border areas with India. This will boost Bhutan's manufactured exports to external markets and help double the share of manufacturing sector in the national economy. Additionally the expansion of export infrastructure will promote a greater degree of economic integration with the Indian, regional and global economy and draw on the advantages that such integration provides. However, due to resource gaps several of these activities may have to be financed through a private public partnership model.

Sustainable sightseeing

Tourism is a rapidly growing services sector for Bhutan, particularly in terms of its contribution to generating employment and foreign exchange. Promoted and managed in a highly sustainable manner, tourism is also viewed as an effective catalyst for conservation of the environment and for the promotion of local diversity and culture in Bhutan. Moreover, the promotion of community based tourism and forms of eco-tourism are expected to support sustainable rural livelihoods and reduce poverty while also serving to advance environmental conservation activities and awareness in rural communities.

While the total volume of tourism remains extremely small, Bhutan enjoys an exclusive and exotic profile in the global tourism and travel market. The country has consistently been voted among the top travel destinations in the world several times over the last decade in 2005, 2008 and most recently in 2009.

In 2001, international tourist arrivals amounted to 6,393 contributing gross earnings of about US$ 9.2 million. Both tourist arrivals and gross earnings have increased importantly since even as Bhutan continues to pursue its high value low impact tourism policy.

In 2008, 27,636 international tourists visited the country contributing US$ 39 million in hard currency excluding revenues generated for the national airline. This figure however does not include non dollar paying regional tourists nor does it factor in downstream revenues generated from tourism activities. Under the Tenth Plan projections, visitor arrivals are projected to increase to about 100,000 by 2013 with the tourism sector contributing to 9% of total national revenues. However, the aspiration is to overachieve these targets considerably in a sustainable manner and without lowering the quality of the visitor experience. The Royal Government will continue to maintain a sharp focus on the niche market of high value tourism.

Scaling up the number of international tourists will clearly require a commensurate expansion in tourism infrastructure, products and services. Notably, existing air travel bottlenecks that limit tourist arrivals will have to be addressed urgently and to this end the development of the proposed second airport in Gelephu will greatly help ameliorate tourist access constraints. The expansion of air passenger capacity of the national airline Druk Air is also clearly essential. To mitigate the impact of large inflows of tourist arrivals, the Royal Government will address the highly seasonal nature of tourism in Bhutan through evening out visitor arrivals in both time and space. The further improvement of tourism services through human resource development remains another critical challenge, particularly in the context of the policy objective of sustaining high value tourism.

PROMOTE CHILD HEALTH AND CONTINUED EXISTENCE

Infant and under-five mortality rates are widely regarded as among the best measures of a nation's health. The BPoA has set targets of reducing infant mortality rates (IMRs) to below 35 per 1,000 live births and under-five mortality rates (U5MRs) below 45 per 1,000 live births by 2015.

Bhutan has enjoyed notable success in scaling down the high child mortality rates that it once suffered from in the past. Between 1990 and 2000, IMRs declined by one third and by 2008 had come down by over 55% from the base year to 40.1 per 1,000 live births.

Likewise the under-five mortality rates have declined to 61.5. On the basis of the current pace progress and the sustained levels of intervention, Bhutan is on track with regard to both targets.

Infant deaths in Bhutan are attributed to infectious diseases such as diarrhoea, respiratory infections and malnutrition. The high incidence of low birth weights is also an important underlying factor affecting the survival of infants as it is a critical determinant of an infant's chance of survival and health growth. The LBW incidence in Bhutan declined from 24% in 1998 to below 9.3% in 2006 and 2007. However, the LBW data needs to be interpreted with some caution as this pertains only to institutional recorded births in hospitals (70%) and in basic health units (30%).

A major reason explaining the success in improving the situation of child health and survival in Bhutan is the highly successful immunization programme. Bhutan achieved universal primary immunization in 1991 and has successfully maintained these high levels of child immunization since. Immunization coverage was maintained at 94.5% in 2008. This consistent and high level of immunization coverage in Bhutan reported at 95% for TB, measles and DPT is close to coverage levels in developed countries. This achievement was recently recognized in November 2009, when Bhutan along with five other countries received a global award from the Global Alliance for Vaccines and Immunization (GAVI) for best performance in maintaining high immunization coverage.

With regard to the goal to eliminate excess and preventable mortality among girl infants and children, there are no known cases of child infanticide or cultural preference for boys over girls. As such there is no discernible pattern of poorer health conditions or higher mortality rates among female infants and children. However, the low levels of adult female literacy, poor hygiene and nutrition, limited access to emergency obstetric care and skilled birth attendance can impact on the further reductions in infant mortality in Bhutan. The Royal Government to this end is strengthening efforts to promote institutional deliveries, improve skilled birth attendance and enhance breast feeding advocacy that will help sustain progress towards improving child health and reducing mortality rates.

Nutritional Status of Young family

In Bhutan infants are usually breast feed up to two years (median duration 23 months), but exclusive breast-feeding is not widely practiced. The recent NNIYCFS 2009 Survey revealed that 91.4% of mothers in Bhutan initiated breast feeding within one hour and that exclusive breast feeding was done by 86% of mothers upto the first month. However, only a mere 10.4% of infants were exclusively breast fed for upto six months and 36.9% upto four months. The Royal Government implemented a breast feeding policy in 2002 that advocates a four month exclusive breastfeeding approach but this may now have to be reviewed in light of recent findings strongly advocating a six month exclusive breast feeding period. With regard to complementary feeding for six to nine month infants, the survey indicated that 89.6% were given complementary food (mainly rice powder and infant formula milk) in addition to being breast fed.

The NNIYCFS 2009 indicates that acute undernourishment (wasting) is not a major problem at the national level although it has increased from 2.6% (1999) to 4.6% (2009). However, the distribution of acute malnutrition reflects regional variation with areas that may require relevant interventions.

Underweight and stunting prevalence has decreased over the years on the basis of the NCHS standard but progress has been below expectation. Once again regional variations exist including rural-urban differences for underweight and stunting. With regard to the main BPoA indicator of child malnutrition, namely the prevalence of underweight children, this has been brought down from 18.7% in 1999 to 11.1% in 2009, a reduction of 40%.

The survey data further reveals that Bhutanese children's anthropometric measurements lie close to the WHO median for weight-for-height Z-score and Height-for–age Z-score at 6 months of age.

It is only after 6 months that the deviation from the median occurs and widens as the child becomes older. At present around one third of Bhutanese children are still short for their age as compared to other children around the world but they have the potential to grow as tall as them. The most likely factors that appear to cause child stunting are chronic dietary deficiencies, frequent infection and poor feeding practices over prolonged periods of time.

Bhutan has done extremely well with regard to improving its micronutrient deficiency situation. Iodine Deficiency Disorder (IDD) was once widely prevalent but in 2003, Bhutan became a "Normal Iodine Nutrition Country" and salt coverage at the household level stood at 98.4% in 2008. Moreover, the micronutrient deficiency of Vitamin A is also no longer a public health problem though iron deficiency resulting in anemia still remains a concern among pregnant women. Iron deficiency anemia in pregnant women was estimated to be about 60%.

Improving motherly Health

Bhutan has enjoyed sustained success in reducing the maternal mortality ratio attributed to the growing network of free maternal services which is integrated with childcare and a trained cadre of village health volunteers. Antenatal coverage (at least one visit) in Bhutan today has touched 88% up from 51% in 2000. The MMR has declined from 5.60 in 1990 to 2.55 per 1,000 livebirths in 2000. Currently no proper survey has been initiated to assess MMR levels but the Royal Government has set a target of reducing it to below 1.4 per 1,000 live births before 2015 with the principal strategy revolving around enhancing institutional deliveries. In terms of skilled birth attendance, this has increased from 15% in 1990 to 24% in 2000 and was estimated at 66% in 2008.

Contraceptive prevalence rates (CPR) serve as a useful proxy measure of access to reproductive health services that are clearly essential to meeting many of the BPoA goals such as child mortality, maternal health and HIV/AIDS and even gender equality. The CPR rates in Bhutan though have not increased importantly and are still very low at 35.4% in 2008. Additionally, even with the widespread accessibility to reproductive health services there is less than an optimal utilization of these services, particularly in rural Bhutan. This is mainly attributed to cultural factors and the lack of awareness. To remedy this, the Government is working to promote the wider acceptability and awareness of modern maternal health services and tackle related issues such as the low levels of literacy and educational attainment among women. The rapid expansion of Emergency Obstretic Care facilities will also help improve reproductive health care services and reduce maternal mortality further.

Expanding Primary teaching and Literacy

Educational indicators have improved over the last decade at all levels. Gross Primary and Net Primary Enrollment Ratios have gone up to 115.7% and 91.8% in 2008. The proportion of students starting grade 1 who complete grade five has also increased from 75.8% to 93.6% between 2001 and 2009. In terms of gender equity, at the primary and secondary level, Bhutan has achieved full parity with a gender parity index of 1.02 for NPER. Girls enrollment stands at about 50% at every level of basic education with 49.6% even at the higher secondary level. Additionally, the performance levels and survival rate for girls in schools have been equal if not better than for boys over the last few years.

Adult literacy levels in Bhutan though remain weak, particularly of the older generation, most of who missed out on schooling as educational facilities in the country were extremely limited. Adult female literacy rates too are a important thirty percentage points lower than for men. The literacy levels of the youth at 74.4% though are much higher due to the important growths in school enrollment over the years. Female youth literacy rates (68.5%) are about ten percentage points than for men. The gender disparity in literacy levels both at the adult and youth levels are likely to even out over time due to sustained female enrollment in primary education. The situation of low adult literacy rates, particularly for women, is being addressed through the active promotion of non-formal education programmes where female participation is very high. Of the 13,160 NFE learners in 2009, around 70% comprise female learners and many classes often consist entirely of women. In recognition of the growing success of the NFE programme, Bhutan was awarded the UNESCO Confucius Literacy prize in 2009 for its holistic approach to literacy and its success in reaching remote areas. Over 140,000 men and women have benefited from the NFE programme that was initiated in 1990 by the National Women's Association of Bhutan. The success of the NFE programme and the high numbers of school enrollment will help in the achievement of the Tenth Plan target of 70% adult literacy by 2013.

Access to Improved Source of eating Water

The Bhutan Living Standards Survey 2007 reflected that 90.9% of the Bhutanese population had access to an improved water source. Even in rural areas, access to improved source of drinking water coverage levels are now at 88% and all districts have upwards of 80% coverage levels with the exception of the least populated district, Gasa. These near universal levels of coverage have been due to the successful implementation of the Rural Water Supply and Sanitation (RWSS) Programme that was initiated in 1974 when rural access to safe drinking water was at less than 5%. The primary goal is to reach and maintain universal coverage for safe drinking water with the primary interventions focusing on increasing the number of public tap stands in rural areas largely through the normal gravity fed water supply system (99%) and through rainwater harvesting and alternative means (1%).

Notwithstanding these high access levels, there are several critical issues that need to be addressed urgently. Many of the older water supply schemes are now in dire need of repair and maintenance. Quite a number of the schemes also appear to be failing due to a drying up of springs and other water sources. Moreover, the RWSS Management Information System data for fifteen districts in 2006 revealed that 40% of the rural water schemes are functioning well, 33% are working with some minor problems, 17% are functioning with need for repairs and improvements and 10% were totally non-functional and require reconstruction. The coverage gains could therefore be severely compromised if the repair, maintenance and rehabilitation of many of the older water supply schemes are not addressed effectively and quickly. An important lesson learnt for Bhutan has been that any future expansion of rural water schemes must necessarily take into consideration the allocation of resources and planned activities for their regular upkeep without which their long term sustainability and functionality is at stake. As such, on the basis of the MDG Resource Needs Assessment and Costing Report (2006-2015), more than 75% of the total outlay for water supply schemes is to be earmarked for recurrent expenditures for the maintenance and upkeep of these schemes. The other constraints of enhancing access to improved sources of drinking water pertain to the feeble sense of community ownership, the substantive lack of capacity and the frequent communal disputes over water rights.

FOSTERING A PEOPLE-CENTRED POLICY STRUCTURE

Bhutan has taken critical steps to combat poverty and ensure sustainable and equitable development. At the heart of its development approach spanning several decades has been the quest to achieve Gross National Happiness (GNH) which comprises four key pillars and provides a wholly people-centred policy framework. The first of the four pillars of the GNH development policy framework pertains to sustainable and equitable socio-economic development. Bhutan has enjoyed notable success in achieving a high level of economic growth that has helped it progress rapidly towards realizing many of its sustainable development goals and MDGs.

Additionally, the Royal Government of Bhutan through its five year development plans prioritized and addressed a range of poverty concerns broadly through an expansion of social services, rural development and income generation activities. The fight against poverty in Bhutan is currently being addressed even more directly and aggressively than before. The Tenth Five Year Plan (2008-2013) has a strong MDG and pro-poor orientation with poverty reduction as the core theme and development objective. Moreover, the current five year development plan establishes clear poverty reduction targets and mainstreams poverty alleviation as a cross-cutting theme with all sectors integrating this objective into their sector specific plan perspectives and programmes. This clearly reflects the strong commitment of the Royal Government to align national priorities and the development planning framework with international development goals such as the BPOA and the MDGs.

Real GDP growth in Bhutan over the period of review (2001-2010) on average is estimated at 8.5%, taking into account the provisional and projected estimated growth rates for 2009 and 2010. Projected growth estimates indicate that the economy between 2008 and 2013, coinciding with the current plan period, will be 7.7% though the target growth rates have been set at 9%. This sustained growth pattern has been fueled by the rapid expansion and growth in the hydropower and construction sectors which together currently comprise more than one third of the economy or 37% of GDP in 2007. Additionally, the electricity sector (23.4%) for the first time overtook the agriculture sector (18.6%) as the main contributor to GDP. The enormous spike of 19.7% growth in 2007 occurred on account of the commissioning of all six turbines of the Tala Hydropower project that saw the electricity sector grow by as much as 138.5%.

The rapid growth of Bhutan's economy has been underpinned by the exceptionally high rates of savings and investment. Gross investment measured in terms of Gross Domestic Capital Formation (GDCF) as a percentage of GDP has been at 53% over the decade between the review period of 2001-2010.

This exceeded the high level of capital formation over the 1990-2000 decade that on average stood at 44% of GDP. These very high rates of capital formation are explained by the dominance of the hydropower sector which is highly capital intensive. Additionally, this high rate of capital formation is likely to continue up to 2020 in view of the mega power projects planned for implementation to reach the targeted 10,000 MW hydropower capacity.

Incremental capital-output ratio (ICOR) is rising fast in Bhutan and has a lagged aspect to it. This is explained by the massive physical infrastructure being created in connection with the hydropower projects with capital formation occurring several years preceding the flow of output. This is also partially a consequence of Bhutan's high cost of adding physical infrastructure due to its rugged and mountainous terrain and tyranny of distance factors that escalate capital expenditure and development costs in providing economic and social services equitably. The high rates of capital formation and ICOR are expected to remain persistent features of the Bhutanese economy in the medium term.

Important of Bhutanese Poverty

As with the MDGs, reducing poverty levels among LDCs is a critical goal of the BPoA and one that has strong linkages in achieving the other identified development goals and targets.

Bhutan has made important improvements in reducing income poverty, measured by the percentage of population living below the national poverty line. Poverty incidence has declined from 36.3% in 2000 to 23.2% in 2007. As such, the country is well on track towards realizing its poverty reduction targets well before 2015 with the national Tenth Plan target to reduce poverty levels to below 15% by 2013. The decline in poverty levels has been made possible through rapid economic growth and effective redistributive programmes including sustained social investments. However, poverty continues to be a predominantly rural phenomenon with 98% of the poor in Bhutan residing in rural parts of the country which is exacerbated by human poverty conditions and relatively poorer access to social and economic services.

The poverty gap and poverty severity ratios also provide a useful perspective on poverty in Bhutan. Available data for the years for 2004 and 2007 indicate moderate reductions in the poverty gap and poverty severity ratios which declined from 8.6% to 6.1% and 3.1% to 2.3% respectively.

The poverty gap and poverty severity ratios for rural areas in Bhutan have also declined from 10.5% to 8.1% and 3.8% to 3% respectively reflecting a slightly lower decline rate than at the nation aggregate. The BPoA affirms the importance of eradicating hunger not only as an important goal in itself but emphasizes its critical linkages to all of the other BPoA goals too.

These include better prospects for a healthier population and its well being, reduced disease burdens, better maternal and child health, enhanced educational attainment, improved productive capacities and for the sustainable use of environmental and natural resources. Within Bhutan too, there is a clear recognition that meaningful achievements in combating hunger and food insecurity will help secure important and tangible benefits in terms of sustainable development including sustained economic growth and poverty reduction.

For the Royal Government, any form of hunger or food deprivation would be unacceptable and deeply inimical to the country's GNH development approach and for this reason the Body Mass Index (BMI) is an important measure of happiness and well being within the GNH index.

According to the PAR 2007, about 5.9% of the Bhutanese population suffer from food poverty and consume less than 2,124 Kilocalories a day. While this does not represent a high degree of hunger incidence, it has increased importantly as compared to figures available for 2003 when only 3.8% of the population lived below the minimum level of dietary energy consumption.

Moreover, certain districts are known to face a high degree of food vulnerability and seasonal food deficit. Both the BLSS 2007 and the VAM 2005 reports indicate certain districts such as Samtse, Samdrupjongkhar, Monggar, Zhemgang and Trashigang have much higher levels of population suffering from food poverty. The NNIYCFS 2009 Survey also indicates a important statistical variation in the malnutrition of children in different regions of the country with the eastern and central regions worse off than the western region. Rural-urban disparities are also clearly apparent in the nutritional situation of children. It is highly likely that there exist numerous communities across Bhutan that do experience important levels of food insecurity and seasonal food deprivation and therefore higher degree of child malnutrition that are often masked by relatively low levels at the national level.

At the national level, there has been a important reduction in the prevalence of underweight children. On the basis of the NCH Survey undertaken in 1999, 18.7% of under-five children were deemed underweight for their age. The most recent NNIYCF Survey in 2009 based on the new WHO child growth standards deemed that only 11.1% of children suffered from underweight problems. However, stunting among children due to chronic malnutrition has declined only marginally by three percentage points, though the basis of measurement over the two surveys differs. On the basis of the NCH Survey methodology, stunting in children in 2009 would have declined to 30.2%. The other concern is that the prevalence of wasting among children has increased from 2.6% to 4.6%, even though the latter is still relatively low.

CHORTENS ARCHITECTURE IN BHUTAN

Chortens, known as 'stupas' in India, are quite common in the countryside of Bhutan. Thousands of chortens can be found all over the country, at crossroads, near a dzong or a monastery and even on high mountain passes. They range from being very small and just two meters in height to being huge and over ten meters in height. Serene and peaceful, chortens are religious monuments that are built in a precise way and are a receptacle for worship or offering. Chortens were originally built to keep the relics of the Buddha and other Buddhist saints but with time, building a stupa is considered a pious thing to do and the builders and those who pay to make a chorten are believed to earn merit for it. Chorten or a stupa is considered to support faith and represent Buddha's Body.

Chortens or stupas also symbolize the five elements of the Universe. Its square base represents earth, the dome represents water, the shaft represents fire, the crescent represents air and the circle represents ether. One of the five 'Jina' (also known as Dhyani Buddhas or primordial Buddhas) corresponds to each of these elements. For religious and didactic reasons, the chorten has always been an object of faith and devotion for the entire Buddhist world. All the major gompas or monasteries have their own chortens, preserving the remains of the Head or Senior Lama. The walls of the chorten are painted from inside with murals, each telling a different story. Sometimes thick prayer walls called 'mani' connect chortens. Chortens may be built in various ways. The most common one in Bhutan is called 'Khangtseg, that' or house chorten, which is simply a building with a square base, enclosed on all four sides sealing sacred objects and relics inside it and perhaps an ornamental roof.

There is a wooden square known as 'sokshing' that acts as the central post of the chorten, around which it is built. It is adorned and has inscriptions of sacred text representing the vital principle and 'life spirit' of the chorten. While building a chorten, there are special rituals and ceremonies for each stage of work as it commemorates the death (Parinirvana) of the Buddha Sakyamuni and his spiritual progress towards enlightenment.

The other types of chortens are Chendebji or Chorten Kora that follow the model of Bodnath in Nepal, made up of lime washed stone and are huge; smaller Tibetan style chortens; and pure Bhutanese square chortens or stupas with four-sided roofs. The red stripe below the roof called 'khemar' mark the religious nature of chortens, just like dzongs.

FOLK HERITAGE MUSEUM

Inaugurated by Her Majesty, the Queen Ashi Dorji Wangchuck on 28th July 2001, Phelchey Toenkhyim or the Folk Heritage Museum at Thimphu provides you a glimpse of lifestyle, items and artifacts of Bhutanese villages and rural households. Besides the display, the museum also organizes demonstrations of rural traditions, skills, habits and customs, educational programs for children and research and documentation on rural life of Bhutan. The museum building itself is one of the star exhibits of the library. It is a restored three-storey traditional rammed mud and timber house that resembles the average rural household in the Wang area during the mid-19th century, complete with typical household objects, domestic tools and equipments that were used by rural families of that period.

The age of the building proves how durable and long lasting, the building materials used in those times, were. The activities of the museum follow a seasonal rhythm, just like the activities of a true rural household, offering you something new to see, every time you visit Phelchey Toenkhyim. The rural setting and flavor has been well-preserved and you can see paddy, wheat and millet fields here, a traditional water-mill with mill stones more than 150 years old, traditional style kitchen gardens with vegetables that were grown over the past 100 years and the famous traditional hot stone bath. Native trees and plants that had domestic uses in Bhutanese rural household are being grown here in an effort to keep indigenous knowledge about the use of natural resources alive and have a patch of greenery, right in the heart of the capital city of Thimphu.

Tourists may also avail the special offers of the museum at a nominal fee and advance booking of at least one week. They include demonstrations of the traditional way of extracting oil or Markhu Tsene, brewing ara or Ara Kayne, roasting rice or Zaw Ngowni and pounding rice or Thom Dhungni within the museum premises and organizing an open air buffet lunch and dinner offering a taste of the traditional cuisine at the museum. The menu for such arrangements is available at the Museum and consists of a variety of traditional food items from all parts and regions of the Kingdom of Bhutan. However, lunch and dinner arrangements are only arranged for groups with five or more than five members at a time. Phelchey Toenkhyim or the Folk Heritage Museum at Thimphu closes only on government holidays. The museum remains open from 10:00 am to 4:30 pm from Monday to Friday, from 10:30 am to 1:00 pm on Saturdays and 11:30 am to 3:30 pm on Sundays.

7

Naxalism Conflict in South Asia

HISTORY OF NAXALISM CONFLICTS

By July 1948, 2,500 villages in the south were organised into 'communes' as part of a peasant movement which came to be known as Telangana Struggle. Simultaneously the famous Andhra Thesis for the first time demanded that 'Indian revolution' follow the Chinese path of protracted people's war. In June 1948, a leftist ideological document 'Andhra Letter' laid down a revolutionary strategy based on Mao Tsetung's New Democracy.

1964

CPM splits from united CPI and decides to participate in elections, postponing armed struggle over revolutionary policies to a day when revolutionary situation prevailed in the country.

1965-66

Communist leader Charu Majumdar wrote various articles based on Marx-Lenin-Mao thought during the period, which later came to be known as 'Historic Eight Documents' and formed the basis of naxalite movement. First civil liberties organisation was formed with Telugu poet Sri Sri as president following mass arrests of communists during Indo-China war.

1967

CPM participates in polls and forms a coalition United Front government in West Bengal with Bangla Congress. This leads to schism in the party with younger cadres, including the "visionary" Charu Majumdar, accusing CPM of betraying the revolution.

Naxalbari Uprising (25th May): The rebel cadres led by Charu Majumdar launch a peasants' uprising at Naxalbari in Darjeeling district of West Bengal after a tribal youth, who had a judicial order to plough his land, was attacked by "goons" of local landlords on March 2. Tribals retaliated and started forcefully capturing back their lands.

The CPI (M)-led United Front government cracked down on the uprising and in 72 days of the "rebellion" a police sub-inspector and nine tribals were killed. The Congress govt at the Centre supported the crackdown. The incident echoed throughout India and naxalism was born.

The ideology of naxalism soon assumed larger dimension and entire state units of CPI (M) in Uttar Pradesh and Jammu and Kashmir and some sections in Bihar and Andhra Pradesh joined the struggle.

July-Nov: Revolutionary communist organs 'Liberation'and 'Deshbrati' (Bengali) besides 'Lokyudh' (Hindi) were started.

Nov 12-13: Comrades from Tamil Nadu, Kerala, Uttar Pradesh, Bihar, Karnataka, Orissa and West Bengal met and set up All India Coordination Committee of Revolutionaries (AICCR) in the CPI (M).

1968

May 14: AICCR renamed All India Coordination Committee of Communist Revolutionaries (AICCCR) with Comrade S Roy Chowdhury as its convenor. The renamed body decides to boycott elections. Within AICCCR certain fundamental differences lead to the exclusion of a section of Andhra comrades led by Comrade T Nagi Reddy.

1969

April 22: As per the AICCCR's February decision, a new party CPI (ML) was launched on the birth anniversary of Lenin. Charu

Majumdar was elected as the Secretary of Central Organising Committee. AICCR dissolved itself.

May 1: Declaration of the party formation by Comrade Kanu Sanyal at a massive meeting on Shahid Minar ground, Calcutta. CPI (M) tries to disrupt the meeting resulting in armed clash between CPI (M) and CPI (ML) cadres for the first time.

By this time primary guerrilla zone appear at Debra-gopiballavpur (WB), Musal in Bihar, Lakhimpur Kheri in UP and most importantly Srikakulam in Andhra Pradesh.

May 26-27: Andhra police kill Comrade Panchadri Krishnamurty and six other revolutionaries during a crackdown on Srikakulam struggle in Andhra Pradesh sparking wide protests.

Oct 20: Maoist Communist Centre was formed under Kanhai Chatterjee's leadership. It had supported Naxalbari struggle but did not join CPI (ML) because of some tactical difference and on the question of the method of party formation.

1970

April 27: Premises of Deshabrati Prakashan, which published Liberation and its sister journals, were raided. CPI (ML) goes underground.

May 11: The first CPI (ML) congress is held in Calcutta under strict underground conditions. Comrade Charu Majumdar is elected the party general secretary.

July 10: Comrades Vempatapu Satyanarayana and Adibatla Kailasam, leaders of Srikakulam uprising are killed in police encounter during the crackdown. Comrade Appu, founder of the Party in Tamil Nadu was also killed around September-October. The Srikakulam movement in continued in Andhra Pradesh till 1975.

Leading lights of literary world of Telugu like Sri Sri, R V Shastri, Khtuba Rao K V Ramana Reddy, Cherabanda Raju Varavara Rao, C Vijaylakshmi with others joined hands to form VIRASAM (Viplava Rachayithala Sangam) or Revolutionary Writers Association (RWA). Artistes from Hyderabad inspired by Srikakulam struggle and the songs of Subharao Panigrahi form a group — Art Lovers – comprising the famous film producer Narasinga Rao and the now legendary Gaddar.

1971

In the background of Bangladesh war, the Army tries to crush the ultra-left movement in West Bengal. Uprising in Birbhum marks the high point of this year.

Art Lovers change its name to Jana Natya Mandali (JNM) late this year. It joins Communists and start propagating revolutionary ideas through its songs, dances and plays. It functioned legally till 1984.

1972

July: Charu Majumdar is arrested in Calcutta on July 16. He dies in Lal Bazar police lock-up on July 28. Revolutionary struggle suffers serious debacle. CPI (ML)'s central authority collapses.

August: 'Pilupu' (The Call), a political magazine was launched in Andhra Pradesh.

Kondapalli Seetharamaiah reorganises the AP State Committee of Communist Revolutionaries following killing or arrest of the 12-member AP State Committee.

1973

Fresh guerrilla struggles backed by mass activism emerge in parts of central Bihar and Telangana, now a part of Andhra Pradesh.

1974

July 28: The Central Organising Committee of CPI (ML) was reconstituted at Durgapur meeting in West Bengal. Comrade Jauhar (Subrata Dutt) was elected general secretary. Jauhar reorganises CPI (ML) and renames it as CPI (ML) Liberation.

March: Andhra Pradesh Civil Liberties Committee (APCLP) was formed again with Sri Sri as president.

August: Andhra Pradesh state committee was reconstituted with Kondapalli Seetharamaiah representing Telangana region, Appalasuri (coastal AP) and Mahadevan (Rayalseema).

October 12: Radical students union was formed in Andhra Pradesh. It faced brutal suppression but surged again after emergency was lifted.

1975

Following declaration of emergency on June 25 and the following repression on ultra-leftists and others, the Central Organising Committee in its September meeting decided to withdraw a "common self-critical review" and instead produce a tactical line 'Road to Revolution'. But it did not unity among the cadres. Armed struggles were reported from Bhojpur and Naxalbari.

1976

CPI (ML) holds its second Congress on February 26-27 in the countryside of Gaya, in Bihar. It resolves to continue with armed guerilla struggles and work for an anti-Congress United Front.

1977

Amidst an upsurge of ultra-leftists' armed actions and mass activism, CPI (ML) decides to launch a rectification campaign. The party organisation spreads to AP and Kerala.

February: Revolutionaries organise Telangana Regional Conference in Andhra Pradesh and seeds of a peasant movement are sown in Karimnagar and Adilabad districts of the state. The conference decided to hold political classes to train new cadres and to send "squads" into forest for launching armed struggle. Eight districts of Telangana, excluding Hyderabad, were divided into two regions and two regional committees were elected.

May: Bihar and West Bengal representatives of Central Organising Committee resign at a meeting. Andhra Pradesh representative fails to attend the meet due to the arrest of Kondapalli Seetharamaiah. The Central Organising Committee is dissolved.

1978

Rectification movements (CPI ML and fragments) limits pure

military viewpoint and stresses mass peasant struggles to Indianise the Marxism-Leninism and Mao thought.

CPI (ML) (Unity Organisation) is formed in Bihar under N Prasad's leadership (focusing on Jehanabad-Palamu of Bihar). A peasant organisation – the Mazdoor Kisan Sangram Samiti (MKSS) is formed.

'Go To Village Campaigns' are launched by Andhra Pradesh Party of revolutionaries to propagate politics of agrarian revolution and building of Radical Youth League units in Andhra Pradesh villages. It later helped in triggering historic peasant struggles of Karimnagar and Adilabad.

Sept 7: The famous Jagityal march is organised in Andhra Pradesh, in which thousands of people take part.

Oct 20: Andhra Government declares Sarcilla and Jagityal 'disturbed areas' giving police "draconian" powers.

1979

From April to June, Village Campaign was for the first time organised jointly by RSU and RYL in Andhra Pradesh. The two organisations also expressed solidarity with National Movement of Assam.

Between 1979 to 1988, MCC focused on Bihar. A Bihar-Bengal Special Area Committee was established. The Preparatory Committee for Revolutionary Peasant Struggles was formed and soon Revolutionary Peasant Councils emerged. Two founding members of MCC passed away-Amulya Sen in March 1981 and Kanhai Chatterjee in July 1982.

1980

April 22: Kondapalli Seetharamaiah forms the Peoples War Group in Andhra Pradesh. He discards total annihilation of "class enemies" as the only form of struggle and stresses on floating mass organisations.

Mass peasant movement spreads in Central Bihar.

CPI (ML) puts forward the idea of broad Democratic Front as the national alternative. It was part of a process to reorganise a centre for All-India revolution after it ceased to exist in 1972.

The central committee was formed by merging AP and Tamil Nadu State Committees and Maharashtra group of the CPI (ML). Unity Organisation did not join. The tactical adopted by the committee upheld the legacy of Naxalbari while agreeing for rectifying the "left" errors.

CPI (ML) Red Flag is formed led by K N Ramachandran.

1981

CPI (ML) organises a unity meet of 13 Marxist-Leninist factions in a bid to form a single formation to act as the leading core of the proposed Democratic Front. However, the unity moved failed. The M-L movement begins to polarise between the Marxist-Leninist line of CPI (ML) (Liberation) and the line of CPI (ML) (People's War).

First state level rally is held in Patna under the banner of Bihar Pradesh Kisan Sabha beginning a new phase of mass political activism in the state.

1982

Indian People's Front (IPF) is launched in Delhi at a national conference of CPI (ML) (Liberation). At the end of the year the third Congress of CPI (ML) is organised at Giridih (Bihar), which decides to take part in elections.

1983

Peasant movement in Assam shows signs of revival after allegedly "forced" Assembly elections. IPF plays a crucial role in this regard.

An all-India dalit conference is held in Amravati (Maharashtra) to facilitate interaction with Ambedkarite groups.

1984

CPI (ML) and other revolutionaries try to woo Sikhs towards joining peasant movement following Operation Bluestar in June and country-wide anti-Sikh riots after Indira Gandhi's assassination in Oct 31 the same year.

1985

People's Democratic Front is launched in Karbi Anglong district of Assam to provide a "revolutionary democratic orientation to the tribal people's aspirations for autonomy". PDF wins a seat in Assam Assembly elections bring about the first entry of CPI (ML) cadre in the legislative arena.

Jan Sanskriti Manch is formed at a conference of cultural activists from Hindi belt at New Delhi.

1986

Bihar govt bans PWG and MCC

April 5-7: CPI (ML) organises a national women's convention in Calcutta to promote cooperation and critical interaction between communist women's organisations and upcoming feminist and autonomous women's groups.

April 19: More than a dozen "landless labourers" are killed in police firing at Arwal in Jehanabad district of Bihar.

1987

PDF gets transformed into the Autonomous State Demand Committee.

1988

CPI (ML) holds its fourth Congress at Hazaribagh in Bihar from January 1 to 5. The Congress "rectifies" old errors of judgement in the party's assessment of Soviet Union. It reiterates the basic principles of revolutionary communism – defence of Marxism, absolute political independence of the Communist Party and primacy of revolutionary peasant struggles in democratic revolution.

CPI (ML) ND is formed in Bihar by Comrade Yatendra Kumar.

1989

May: The founding conference of All India Central Council

of Trade Union (AICCTU) is held in Madras. Key resolutions are passed at this meet.

November: More than a dozen "left supporters" are shot dead by landlords in Ara Lok Sabha constituency of Bhojpur district in Bihar on the eve of polls.

CPI (ML) (Liberation) records its first electoral victory under Indian People's Front banner. Ara sends the first "Naxalite" member to Parliament.

1990

In February Assembly election, IPF wins seven seats and finishes second in another fourteen. In Assam too, a four-member ASDC legislators' group enters the Assembly. Special all-India Conference is held in Delhi on July 22-24 to restructure the party.

August 9-11: All India Students Association (AISA) is launched at Allahabad. It opposes VP Singh's implementation of Mandal Commission recommendations.

Oct 8: First all-India IPF rally is held in Delhi. CPI (ML) (Liberation) claims it to be the first-ever massive mobilisation of rural poor in the capital.

CPI (ML) S R Bhaijee group and CPI (ML) Unity Initiative are formed in Bihar. The former is still active in east and west Champaran.

Andhra Pradesh Chief Minister Chenna Reddy lifts all curbs on naxal groups. Naxalites operate freely for about a year but observers say it corrupted them and adversely affected the movement.

1991

In the May Lok Sabha elections, Indian People's Front loses Ara seat but CPI (ML) retains its presence in Parliament through ASDC MP.

1992

Andhra Pradesh bans People's War Group

CPI(ML) reorganises the erstwhile Janwadi Mazdoor Kisan Samiti in South Bihar as Jharkhand Mazdoor Kisan Samiti (Jhamkis).

May 21: Chief Minister N Janardhan Reddy bans PWG and its seven front organisations again in Andhra Pradesh.

Dec 20-26: CPI (ML) organises its fifth Congress at Calcutta from Dec 20 to 26. CPI (ML) comes out in the open and calls for a Left confederation.

1993

AISA registers impressive victories in Allahabad, Varanasi and Nainital university elections in Uttar Pradesh besides in the prestigious Jawaharlal Nehru University in New Delhi.

CPI (ML) launches a new forum for Muslims called 'Inquilabi Muslim Conference' in Bihar.

1994

February: All India Progressive Women's Association is launched at national women's conference at New Delhi.

Indian People's Front is dissolved and fresh attempts are initiated to forge a united front of various sections of Leftists and Socialists with an anti-imperialist agenda.

Interactions among various Communists and Left parties intensify in India and abroad to revive the movement drawing lessons from Soviet collapse.

1995

A six-member CPI (ML) group is formed in Bihar Assembly. Two CPI (ML) nominees win from Siwan indicating the expansion of party's influence in north Bihar.

May: N T Ramarao relaxes ban on Peoples War Group in Andhra Pradesh for three months. PWG goes in for massive recruitment drive in the state.

July: CPI (ML) organises All India Organisation Plenum at Diphu to streamline party's organisational network.

Revolutionary Youth Association (RYA) is launched as an all-India organisation of the radical youth.

1996

Five members of ASDC make it to Assam assembly. An ASDC member is re-elected to Lok Sabha. Another ASDC member is elected to Rajya Sabha. ASDC retains its majority in Karbi Anglong District Council and also unseats the Congress in the neighbouring North Cachhar Hills district in Assam.

CPI(ML) takes initiative to form a Tribal People's Front and then Assam People's Front

CPI (ML) joins hands with CPI and Marxist Coordination Committee led by Comrade A Roy to strengthen Left movement.

CPI (ML) initiates the Indian Institute of Marxist Studies. Armed clashes between ultra-leftists and upper caste private armies (like Ranvir Sena) escalate in Bihar.

The Progressive Organisation of People, affiliated to revolutionary left movement, launches a temple entry movement for lower castes in Gudipadu near Kurnool in Andhra Pradesh. It emerges successful.

1997

CPI (ML) organises a massive 'Halla Bol' rally in Patna. A left supported Bihar bandh is organised as part of "Oust Laloo Campaign" in view of the Rs 950-crore fodder scam.

1999

CPI (ML) Party Unity merges with Peoples War.

Naxalites launch major strikes. CPI (ML) PW kills six in Jehanabad on February 14. MCC kills 34 upper caste in Senai village of Jehanabad.

Dec 2: Three top PWG leaders killed in Andhra Pradesh leading to a large scale brutal naxalite attacks on state forces.

Dec 16: PWG hacks to death Madhya Pradesh Transport Minister Likhiram Kavre in his village in Blalaghat district to avenge the killing of three top PWG leaders in police encounter on Dec 2.

2000

PWG continues with its revenge attacks. Blasts house of ruling Telugu Desam Party MP G Sukhender Reddy in Nalgonda district in Andhra Pradesh in January.

In February it blows up a Madhya Pradesh police vehicle killing 23 cops, including an ASP. It destroys property worth Rs 5 crore besides killing 10 persons in AP in the same month.

Dec 2: PWG launches People's Guerrilla Army (PGA) to counter security forces offensive.

2001

April: CPI (ML) celebrates 32nd anniversary of its foundation in Patna on April 22 and gives a call to rekindle 'revolutionary spirit of naxalism'.

July: Naxalite groups all over South Asia form a Coordination Committee of Maoist Parties and Organisations of South Asia (CCOMPOSA) which is said to be first such an international coalition. PWG and MCC are part of it.

As per the Intelligence reports, MCC and PWG establish links with LTTE, Nepali Maoists and Pakistan's Inter-Service Intelligence to receive arms and training. Naxalites bid to carve out a corridor through some areas of Madhya Pradesh, Andhra Pradesh, Bihar, and Uttar Pradesh up to Nepal.

Nov: MCC organises a violent Jharkhand Bandh on Nov 26.

Dec: Naxalites, mainly in AP, Orissa and Bihar celebrate People's Guerilla Week hailing the formation of PGA on Dec 2. The week unfolds major violence in the three states during which a plant of Chief Minister Chandrababu Naidu and the house of an Orissa minister is blown up.

ROOT CAUSES OF CONFLICT

Conflict is a universal and permanently recurring phenomenon within societies. But the question to ask is, what triggers violence?

Unfortunately no single general theory of conflict exists. H.L. Nieburg has argued that violence is a natural form of political behavior, that the threat of inflicting pain by restoring to violence will always be a useful means of political bargaining within domestic and international society; that the threat of resorting to force demonstrates the seriousness with which the dissatisfied party sets forth its demands against the satisfied, the establishment. 9 Karl Marx is known for his assertion that conflict arise inevitably out of socio-economic change. Moderate political elements as to Marx; prove too weak to strike viable compromises between those who agitate for rapid change.

In a society such as Nepal, in transition from traditional to modern, active monarchy to democracy, the causes of conflict are many. Conflict between forces seeking change and those resisting it has been ongoing since the dawn of democratic awakening in the 1940s. After the declaration of the Peoples War by the Maoist, Nepal became a country under siege with violence. What actually triggered that violence? Some see social inequality and exclusion of a large section of the population from the structures of political power and the sharing of resources by the traditional ruling elites as the underlying causes. There have been a lot of similar debates put forward as to gauge the root cause of Maoist Insurgency in Nepal. "There is however widespread consensus as to the root causes of the conflict in Nepal. The main grievances, all closely related to each other include inequitable socioeconomic and political access, bad governance/corruption and widespread poverty. These issues are used by the Maoists to justify their challenges to the legitimacy of the government, and all contribute to motivate certain sectors of the population to join or at least support their movement and their cause."

The new political order set up after 1990 failed to include all sections of Nepali society, and the nationalities and Dalits (untouchable caste) remained – and they felt they were –outside both mainstream politics and the reach of development programs. Traditional regional disparities continued and far flung areas like districts of Karnali Zone remained under-represented in politics, planning and the development processes. Meantime, the gap between the people in the villages and the cities and between the rich and the poor continued to widen. Nepal in the 1990s experienced relative prosperity in the urban areas, but the redistribution of wealth and opportunities remained skewed, resulting in increased unemployment.

It did not take long for the insurgency launched simultaneously in three mid-western mountain districts of Rolpa, Rukum, Jajarkot, Gorkha in the West, and Sindhuli in the East to spread. By the year 2000, Maoist violence had left no district unaffected and by mid January 2001, the Maoists had declared the formation of a provisional revolutionary district government in Rukum, Jajarkot, Sallyan and Rolpa districts. There are many theories on why the influence spread as fast as it did. Some attribute the spread of rebel influence to the involvement and support of the excluded groups – mainly women, minorities and the Dalits – but there is not enough evidence to isolate this as main reason. As noted by the Saubhagya Shah, the epicenter of the insurgency - the Rapti Zone in the mid-western Nepal – is not the most backward region in the country. He argues that "if social and economic marginalization alone were responsible for the emergence of the Maoist Movements, the hill districts of Karnali, Seti and Mahakali zones would be far more likely candidates, not only because of their grinding poverty and chronic food shortage, but also because of the nature of their terrain and their remoteness from the state centers. Even though difficult to generalize, what is almost clear now is that the spread of Maoist influence has strong social and economic roots including the exclusion of the poor and the marginalized by the State, as opposed to it being only and ideological and "law and order problem", or "terrorism", which was the initial government response to this conflict.

From one perspective, the Maoist insurgency in its mid-western stronghold areas can be seen as a renewal of an age old confrontation between the Thakuri Raj and the radical left. The Thakuris (descendants of the rulers of the old principalities) and their clients had long dominated this area, and the nature of their rule at local level was repressive. This was in accord with the authoritarian regime at the center during the party less Panchayat system (1962-1990). Even after the restoration of democracy in 1990, the former Panchas survived, reviving their power base under a new guise by responding to the Nepali Congress's Policy of incorporating the traditional social and political elites in its schemes of party building during the early 90s. However, the sense of popular empowerment that spread after the successful 1990 *jana andolan* (People's Movement of 1990s) introduced a new power against the traditional forces. Both the CPN (UML) and the CPN (Maoist, formerly the UPF) emerged as the most influential left forces in the people's fight against various forms of the Thakuri Raj in this region. The equation among the left forces has changed in favour of the CPN (Maoist) as a consequence of the UML's movement from the left towards the center, while the Congress Party is constantly heading towards the right from the center of the political spectrum in the country. The local Thakuri –centrist alliances in the mainstream parties' has never been strong under the democratic set-up, and it deteriorated during the period of hung parliament (November 1994 to May 1999). Because politics was concentrated at the center in the game of government making and unmaking, the parliamentary parties grossly ignored the need for the party building at the grassroots level. Having this as the most appropriate time for a long drawn-out people's war. Lund and Mehler divide the root causes of conflict into four main areas with sixteen sub-areas. Nearly all of the causes mentioned are present in Nepal.

Imbalance of Political, Social, Economic and Cultural Opportunities

"In terms of caste and ethnic break-up, the country is essentially a conglomeration of minorities, with the two largest groups comprising 16 percent (Chhetri) and nearly 13 percent (Bahun) of the population. None of the other groups constitute more than 10 percent of the population. ...Regardless of the reality on the ground, Nepal is usually represented as a Hindu kingdom where different castes as well as ethnic, linguistic and religious groups have co-existed peacefully. ...However, the subordinate groups are beginning to question this picture of tolerance and pluralism. Particularly since the restoration of multi-party democracy in 1990, when the open political atmosphere allowed the emergence of an energetic movement of ethnic assertion, whose leadership might regard Nepal as a pluralistic society, but one that is characterized by hierarchy, dominance and oppression." "As early as 1992, British scholar Andrew Nichson had warned in an article entitled 'Democratization and the Growth of communism in Nepal: A Peruvian Scenario in the Making': 'The future prospects of Maoism in Nepal will...depend largely on the extent to which the newly elected Nepali Congress government addresses the historic neglect and discrimination of the small rural communities which still make up the overwhelming majority of the population of the country...[which] means that a radical shake-up of the public administration system is in order to make both more representative of the ethnic diversity of the country and more responsive to the needs of peasant communities."

Another notable characteristic of Maoist movement is the degree of women's participation in guerrilla ranks. Women's political participation in the past had been limited to electoral areas, especially in voting and occasional candidacy in elections. It is a big surprise that Nepali women have now joined guerrilla organization taking up arms.

It is a subject of analysis and study that Why many rural women have been a part of Maoist Movement? What specific life experiences convinced or compelled the women to take part in Maoist activities? Although it is very difficult to verify the exact number but it is reported that women constitute anywhere between thirty and forty percent of Maoist military force, which according to conservative estimates, total at least 10,000 people.

Among female military personnel, it is reported that most come from ethnic and Dalit groups, but there are also women from the Bahun-Chhetri castes. Ideologically, the Maoist claim to favour an end to the patriarchal organization of the society. In Nepali context, it appears that this position is exemplified by their demands for equal rights for women to inherit ancestral property.

In the well-known forty-point demand submitted to the government just before the declaration of people's war, one point deals exclusively with the' patriarchal exploitation and discrimination against women should be stopped. Daughters should be allowed access to parental property'. However, the full liberation of women and gender equality is to be achieved only in a classless or communist society. Such a position is widely explained by the Maoist to women through political classes, cultural programs, and the party media and mass print media. So women are another interest group which Maoist have time and again addressed women needs to attract them to their activities, this new phenomenon must not be taken lightly.

INDIA'S NAXALITE CONFLICT

India's Naxalite movement has been described by the Indian Prime Minister Manmohan Singh as "the single biggest internal security challenge ever faced by our country". The conflict claimed at least 4,800 lives over the 2005-2010 period.

India's Naxalite conflict provides an ideal testing ground for the theoretical predictions of this paper for a number of reasons. First, the Naxalite conflict has seen high levels of targeted violence against civilians, who account for more than one third of the total number of casualties. Second, due to the reliance of the Naxalite affected areas on rain-fed agriculture, exogenous variation in rainfall can be exploited to identify the impact of labour productivity shocks on the intensity of violence. Third, the Naxalite conflict affects a large number of districts and its actors have asymmetric financial capacities. Observers indicate that the rebels heavily rely on taxation of the local economy, whereas the government relies on a much broader tax base. Interestingly, the Naxalites operate in areas that include (but are not limited to) districts that produce key mineral resources. These mineral resources should make the rebels' local tax base more independent from local agricultural labour market conditions. Hence, variation in mineral resource wealth can be used to identify the differential impact of labour income shocks on violence, as required by the theoretical framework.

To test the predictions of the theoretical framework, we collect a data set of annual casualty numbers at the district level between

2005 and 2010. These conflict outcomes are combined with Kharif season rainfall data, data on mineral resource wealth, and key socio-economic and environmental controls. Importantly, the data set allows for casualties to be attributed to three categories: civilians, security forces, and Maoists. In support of the subsequent reduced form approach,

The key result of this paper is that lower Kharif rainfall boosts Naxalite violence against civilians, regardless of the resource environment. This funding is consistent with the idea that rebels use violence against civilians to counterbalance the increased appeal of collaboration after scanty rainfall. For security force casualties, we find that violence only increases in response to negative rainfall shocks in those areas that produce key minerals. This funding is consistent with the idea that the rebels can only use a negative income shock to boost recruitment (and thus their fighting capacity against the government), if their tax base does not depend too much on local labour productivity. To shed further light on the mechanism that underlies these results, we use detailed incident information to break down civilian casualties into three groups: civilian collaborators; other civilian targets; and civilians who were not the intended target of the attack.

The drivers of targeted violence, by highlighting both the role of civilian collaboration and the importance of the rebels' tax base. These insights matter for the design of conflict resolution strategies. By offering rewards that are conditional on collaboration, the government may want to exploit negative income shocks to boost collaboration and weaken insurgents. My results suggest that this strategy could mainly put civilians at risk of retaliation, as the rebels can strategically respond by boosting violence against civilians.

The role of income shocks in conflict and research on the logic of violence against civilians. A growing body of research explores the targeting of the non-combatant population in civil conflict. The mechanism highlighted in this paper is close to the work of Kalyvas (2006), who analyses in detail how civilian collaboration relates to selective violence. Berman, Felter and Shapiro (2011) also consider the strategic interaction between governments, civilians, and rebels. These authors develop a model of retaliatory violence that is close to the framework presented in this paper, but they do not provide empirical evidence on such violence. The existing empirical evidence on targeted violence against civilians is mainly based on case studies and cross-sectional regressions. The first empirical contributions to explore the causes of variation in targeted violence against civilians versus the government in a subnational panel. In contrast to the existing literature, this paper explicitly links targeted violence against civilians to labour income shocks. This approach enables me to overcome key endogeneity concerns.

Several key contributions in the conflict literature share the focus of my paper on labour income shocks. Dube and Vargas (2011) show that a fall in coffee prices led to increased violence in the Colombian civil war. Miguel, Satyanath, and Sergenti (2004) find that negative GDP shocks, as instrumented by rainfall growth, explain the onset of civil wars in Sub Saharan Africa. Most of the theoretical arguments that link labour income shocks to violence rely on the idea that negative shocks reduce the opportunity cost of joining armed conflict. However, this view has been challenged in recent work by Berman, Callen, Felter and Shapiro (2011). These authors find that high unemployment is associated with reduced violence in the context of Afghanistan, Iraq, and the Philippines. They argue that high unemployment could mainly facilitate information gathering by counterinsurgency forces. My paper suggests that the relationship between labour income shocks and violence against the government crucially depends on the structure of the rebel's tax base. For the opportunity cost channel to dominate in response to a negative labour income shock, the rebels need access to external sources of funding. Therefore, my analysis can account for the conflicting findings on the relationship between income shocks and violence in the existing literature.

Finally, this paper aims to contribute to the understanding of India's Naxalite insurgency. It is well established that civil conflict hampers economic development, and previous work has suggested that the Naxalite conflict has indeed reduced economic growth in the affected states. This consideration gains even more relevance because the districts affected by Naxalism are among India's poorest regions. Given the particular developmental challenges faced by India's so-called "Red Corridor", the importance of understanding the logic of Naxalite violence can hardly be overstated. While existing work points at factors that explain the susceptibility of districts to Naxalite activity in the long run, these studies cannot account for the variation in the intensity of different types of conflict over time. However, understanding the dynamics of conflict and the strategic behaviour of its parties is crucial for the design of effective conflict resolution strategies. This paper is the first contribution to explore the causes of changes in the intensity of Naxalite violence within districts over time. It is also the first study to highlight the logic of Naxalite violence against civilians.

SEVERAL REASONS FOR THE NAXALITE CONFLICT

There are several reasons for why the Naxalite conflict provides an ideal testing ground for the theoretical arguments set out in the theoretical framework.

First, information is important in this conflict. Maoists and the Government clearly compete for civilian collaboration. While certain offcials deny the existence of informers (possibly in an attempt to protect civilians from reprisals), the Government openly offers substantial rewards for tip-offs that lead to the death or arrest of Maoists. Certain state governments (possibly with the support of the Centre) are thought to have encouraged civilians to join militant groups that help the police to collect information and assist them in operations. Finally, the state governments have also rolled out several programmes to encourage low ranking Maoists to surrender and provide information. In line with the theoretical framework, the Naxalite groups react to these attempts to elicit collaboration (or desertion) by explicitly threatening to kill or destroy the property of police informers:

"The CPI-Maoist reportedly issued a press release at Chintapalli village in the Visakhapatnam District, blaming the Police for turning the Girijans (local tribals) into informers by spending huge amounts of money and warned that the properties acquired by the surrendered Maoists, after taking up the job of Home Guard, would be destroyed.[...]".

When the Maoists resort to violence against civilians, their punishments tend to be highly visible and brutal: "CPI-Maoist cadres killed two people, including a village head, at a [kangaroo court] in Jamui District after funding them "guilty" of helping the Police. Reports said that a group of armed Maoists killed Babuli village head Ashok Das and his close associate [...]. "Their throat was slit by Maoists to send a message of harsh punishment to others," informed the Police."

A second key characteristic of the Naxalite conflict is its asymmetric nature. The theoretical framework clearly assumes asymmetric reliance on local labour productivity. This assumption seems reasonable for a large number of intra-state conflicts, including the Naxalite insurgency. The last quote (referring to "huge amounts spent on informers") reflects the fact that the Government (both at the state and the Union level) can draw from a large and stable tax base to fund anti-Maoist operations. Moreover, counter-insurgency strategies are In contrast, the Naxalites need to tax local economic activity (and agricultural output in particular) to fund their activities:

"ANI reports that the CPI-Maoist is collecting INR 10,000 from each farmer as 'tax' in the Jamatara District. The farmers are being forced either to pay up or to stop tilling their fields."

A third characteristic of the Naxalite conflict is that mineral resources are an important component of the Naxalite's tax base in certain districts. On 20 May 2010, the Maharashtra State Home Minister R. R. Patil openly accused the mining industry of funding Left Wing Extremists (LWEs). Newspaper reports provide anecdotal evidence on the modus operandi of the Naxals:

"Early last year, the Maoists blasted pipelines of a leading steel company cutting through Chitrakonda in Malkangiri district. Within a month, the company's infrastructure in the same place was targeted again. A guest house was set ablaze. A pump house, control room and property worth several lakhs of rupees were damaged. Then the attacks stopped. Police sources said this happened only after Rs 2 crore went into the Maoist purse. Illegal mining in states such as Orissa and Jharkhand is a rich source of revenue for the Maoists." (Times of India, 2011)

In conclusion, civilian collaboration is important in this conflict, the tax bases of the Government and the rebels are asymmetric, the rebels need to tax agricultural activity, but mineral resources provide variation in the structure of the rebels' tax base within this conflict. Hence, this setting offers an ideal testing ground for the hypotheses that were set out in the theoretical framework.

Relies on Violence Data

This paper relies on violence data from the South Asia Terrorism Portal (SATP). The SATP combines newspaper reports on Naxalite activity into daily incident summaries. These summaries typically provide the district (and sometimes village) in which the incident took place and the number of casualties on each side of the conflict (civilians, Maoists and security forces). Based on this information, I construct variables for the number of casualties, for three categories (civilian, security forces and Maoists) at the district-year level.

The analysis will be restricted to those states that are confronted with significant Naxalite activity over the period under study. One limitation of this dataset is that it does not systematically include casualties who do not immediately succumb to their injuries. An additional limitation is that the number of Maoists casualties is hard to verify and the reports often highlight that these numbers are based on police sources. One can imagine that security forces have an incentive to overstate the number of Maoists they killed or to include innocent civilians who are wrongfully targeted in police actions. These concerns are addressed to some extent by the police policy of disclosing the names and the ranks of any killed Maoists to add credibility to its reports. Unfortunately, the data-set does not include state violence directed towards civilians, in spite of wide-spread claims of atrocities being committed by state forces. Of the three types of violence reported in the dataset, Maoist violence is probably the most prone to errors.

However, none of the key results are based on this variable. With regards to civilian casualties, it is possible that news on Maoist violence does not reach newspapers if it occurs in isolated communities. Civilian casualties only include deaths thought to be inflicted by Maoists, although it cannot be ruled out that some casualties are wrongfully attributed to the Maoists. The type of casualties which is probably the least prone to misreporting are government casualties, as these are highly visible. Again, these casualties only include deaths inflicted by Maoist groups.

Data on mineral output are obtained from the ministry of Labour and Employment. I focus on three minerals which are linked to Maoist activity in the SATP incident lists: iron, bauxite and coal. For iron and bauxite, I rely on production data from 2005-2006. For coal, production data from 2003 are used. To reduce endogeneity, these minerals are evaluated at India-wide 2004-2005 prices. The use of iron and bauxite data for years after the baseline may still give rise to endogeneity concerns if production responds to violence. Furthermore, Naxalite extortion is often linked to illegal mining activity, which could depress the official output data in affected districts. These concerns are addressed by reporting key results for mineral production dummies (which should not capture any endogenous output responses on the intensive margin) and for an alternative measure of mineral production.

Rainfall data were collected from the Indian Meteorological Department (IMD), for the years 2004-2010. For several districts, rainfall data is not available, in particular for non-monsoon months. To address this problem I restrict my analysis to rainfall in the main monsoon season (June-September). This approach has the additional advantage of focusing on rainfall shocks that are directly linked to the main crop growing season, while rainfall outside of the growing season could have more ambiguous effects on agricultural productivity. Monsoon rice (Kharif rice) accounts for the bulk of the rice production in the region under study. To deal with missing rainfall data in the Kharif months.

To confirm the validity of the use of rainfall, annual rice production data were collected for the period 2003-2007 from the

Indian Department of Agriculture. These production data correspond to fiscal years (e.g. 1 April 2003-1 March 2004) and are assigned to the earliest calendar year. This creates the maximum overlap with the fiscal year and it ensures that the main harvesting season during any given fiscal year is assigned to the calendar year in which the crops were fed. Due to missing observations, the resulting rice production panel is unbalanced and incomplete.

As additional controls, I collect 2001 census data at the district level on population, the size of the tribal population, the size of the scheduled caste population and literacy. Furthermore, I also collect forest cover and area data from the Ministry of Environment and Forest.

As rainfall information is missing for several districts (even for monsoon months) and as certain districts were split over the 2001-2010 period, I merge districts to create a balanced panel of violence outcomes and explanatory variables. 207 districts are merged into 167 districts based on four criteria. First, 2001 census districts that were split during the 2001-2010 period are remerged to their 2001 boundaries. Second, districts with missing rainfall information are merged with the closest district that has rainfall information available (based on the distance between district capitals). Third, the largest urban districts (Bangalore, Kolkota and Mumbai) are dropped from the analysis. Fourth, for a small number of districts, rainfall is used of a district in a neighbouring state. To avoid merging districts across state borders, these observations are treated independently. The resulting data set contains a balanced panel of 167 (merged) districts.

Empirical Strategy

The paper employs rainfall shocks as exogenous determinants of agricultural productivity. While this approach has successfully been employed for the study of violence in the context of Sub-Saharan Africa (Miguel et al., 2004), the relationship between rainfall and economic activity is not straightforward in less arid regions. Nevertheless, Burgess et al. (2011) have confirmed the importance of rainfall shocks for agricultural wages and productivity in the Indian context.

Interpretation

The main results indicate that lower rainfall results in more violence directed against civilians, regardless of the presence of mineral resources. This funding is consistent with the theoretical model develop. Negative economic shocks could boost the willingness of civilians to collaborate with the government. Hence, the rebel group may find it optimal to increase its punishments of civilian collaborators or defectors in order to discourage civilians to pass on information to the government. By killing civilians in targeted attacks, the Maoists show that they have invested in suffcient retaliation capacity to locate and punish informers.

In line with this interpretation, the communication of the Maoists in the SATP Timelines underlines the importance that the Maoists attach to motivating civilian deaths. To justify attacks on civilians, the rebels often leave notes on the bodies of victims, they hold public trials, or they even contact the press directly. Moreover, they often rely on brutal execution methods to add further visibility to their attacks against civilians.

For approximately 30% of casualties, a motive is not explicitly referred to. Focusing on casualties for whom a motive is recorded, a large majority is referred to as (suspected) collaborators. Police informers (29%), members of mainstream political parties that oppose the Naxalites (31%), surrendered Naxalites (2%), and members of vigilante groups (7%) account for a total of 69% of the casualties for which information on the motives of the attack is available. Strikingly, failure to meet extortion demands only accounts for 3% of the civilian casualties. The bulk of the remaining casualties fell victim to "untargeted attacks". These are incidents in which the civilians were not the intended target of the attack. The main results are shown separately for killings of civilian collaborators and victims of "untargeted attacks". In support of the mechanism highlighted in this paper, the main results appear to be driven by attacks on collaborators. In contrast, untargeted civilian killings follow exactly the pattern of security force casualties. The latter finding suggests that civilians suffer the indirect consequences of increased violence against the government. The fact that the main results are driven by targeted attacks on civilian collaborators adds further credibility to the main mechanism of this paper. Finally, there is also anecdotal evidence that illustrates how droughts affect the alliances between Naxalites and the civilian population:

"After some 30 villages in Korchi area of Gadchiroli district deffed the Naxal boycott of government-run employment-generation schemes, the revolt has spread to more drought-hit villages in the region, say high-level police offcials. Special Inspector General of Police (Nagpur range) Pankaj Gupta told The Indian Express yesterday that clusters of villages, gripped by a severe drought, had chosen to take on Naxalites rather than let go of an option for alternate employment. Gupta, however, didn't divulge the location of the villages which number over 20. This, he said, may prompt Naxalites to upset their plan." (Indian Express, April, 2003)

For security force casualties, the main results are consistent with the idea that the rebels' tax base shapes the relationship between labour income shocks and conflict. If the rebels' tax base is sensitive to the rainfall shocks, the rebels may not be able to exploit a negative shock to increase recruitment. This argument could explain why rainfall shocks do not lead to higher government casualties inflicted by Maoist attacks in non-mining districts. The fact that rebel groups respond to negative shocks with increased violence against the government in mining districts, is consistent with the interpretation that the rebel group's tax base is less reliant on agricultural output in these districts.

Underlying these interpretations are a number of implicit assumptions that may require further justification. First, I assume that the fighting capacity of the Maoists is increasing in the number of fighters deployed against the government. This assumption (which is common to most "opportunity cost" models) seems reasonable in the context of the Naxalite conflict. The SATP Timelines indicate that most Maoist attacks on the government involve a substantial number of fighters, and bombs are mainly used to create initial confusion, after which the rebels attack the security forces with guns. A second assumption that is implicit in the theoretical framework is the assumption that different Maoists groups operate independently. At first sight, this assumption could be too strong, as the main Maoist outlet (CPI Maoist) is in theory an integrated party movement that is led by a secretary general. However, the reality of guerilla warfare does not allow for signiûcant organisational integration, as the CPI (Maoist) Central Committee highlights: "[t]he essential principle forming the basis of our Party structure is political centralisation combined with organisational decentralisation." Thus, the key military units operate at a lower level, in so-called the "Sub-Zonal, Zonal/District Commands". These units can independently stage attacks and they focus on geographic areas that broadly correspond to districts analysed in this paper. Moreover, these local command units are closely linked to the local party organisations that play an important role in gathering financial support for the Naxalites.

Alternative Explanations and Robustness Checks

The main results are consistent with the model develop and the anecdotal evidence. This subsection addresses the extent to which alternative mechanisms can explain the observed patterns.

Violent Appropriation

The main results are driven by retaliation against civilian collaborators. However, these results could still be consistent with appropriation theories if the true motive of targeted killings is not accurately recorded in the SATP reports. A negative relationship between shocks and violence could be observed if Maoists increase their appropriation activities in response to bad shocks and if violence is proportional to appropriation. From a theoretical perspective, this interpretation would require the civilian population to have assets that do not depend too strongly on local economic conditions. However, these theories cannot explain why violence against the government and violence against civilians would react differently to income shocks in the absence of natural resources. Moreover, if the rebels strategically choose the extent to which they loot civilians (as in Azam, 2006), the presence of natural resources should mitigate the impact of negative productivity shocks on violence against civilians. We find no evidence of such a mitigation effect. While the Maoists clearly tax the local economy and they do this under the threat of violence, the violence that results from appropriation may have a different logic than the lethal violence that this paper investigates. The SATP timelines provide ample anecdotal evidence on the importance of lethal violence against informers. The Maoists communicate openly about civilian casualties and they typically refer to their victims as police informers. Even if the victims of violence did in fact refuse to pay levies to the Maoists, this open communication suggests that the intensity of violence against civilians could be driven by the rebels' goal to optimally deter (and punish) collaboration.

Incapacitation and Precision of Attacks

Berman *et al.* (2011a) find that higher unemployment inhibits insurgent attacks against security forces. These authors hypothesise that high unemployment makes civilians more willing to share information with counterinsurgency forces. They also argue that the resulting incapacitation effect might force rebels to switch towards less precise attacks that inflict more "collateral damage". In the context of India's Naxalite conflict, the incapacitation effect appears to be weak. The positive sign of the impact of rainfall shocks on security force casualties is not signiûcant at conventional levels (and only positive in the absence of mineral resource wealth). The theoretical framework offers one explanation of why the incapacitation effect is limited: the rebels may effectively prevent collaboration by increasing violence against civilians. Furthermore, the theoretical framework and the empirical findings suggest that the incapacitation effect could be outweighed by the opportunity cost channel if the rebel group has access to external sources of funding.

In principle, the increase in civilian casualties that is observed in response to negative shocks could still be the result of a change in violence technology and decreased attack precision. However, such a collateral damage interpretation cannot explain the impact of rainfall on *targeted* civilian casualties. The results on *untargeted* civilian casualties suggest that indirect victims follow the pattern of attacks against the government. This suggests that if there is decreased precision, it is not the results of incapacitation (as argued by Berman *et al.*, 2011a). While the elasticity on untargeted casualties is larger than the one on government casualties (which implies reduced precision), violence against the government goes up in response to negative productivity shocks in mineral rich areas. Incapacitation would predict that government casualties go down in response to negative income shocks.

Police Activism

A third alternative explanation for the main results relies on the activities of the police forces. Mining districts might have greater police presence, which offers more opportunity for the rebels to respond to rainfall shocks with increased violence against police forces. Hence, negative rainfall shocks could lead to more violence against civilians in any district and to violence against the security forces in those districts with a large security force presence. This explanation seems unlikely to drive the results, as higher police activity in mining district would mainly lead to higher levels of violence against the security forces in any given year.

In an extreme version of this argument, violence against the police should be zero in non-mining districts. However, mining districts only account for 40% of the districts that see any police casualties. Furthermore, the proportionality of the impact of rainfall shocks to the average levels of violence against the police is already accounted for by the multiplicative fixed effects in the Poisson model.

This argument can also help to address concerns that Maoist violence against the police is purely driven by the aspiration to control mineral resources. Again, one would expect this channel to operate through higher levels of violence, which are accounted for by the fixed effects. Nevertheless, it remains possible that mining regions face types of police activity which are not captured by average levels of violence against the police but do shape the incentives for rebels to attack the security forces in response to a productivity shock. One way to account for the possibility that mining regions would be more prone to police activism. The salience of police activity by the number of incidents in which the Maoists suffered casualties in the baseline year (2005). If my results are driven by the differential impact of rainfall in districts with higher police activity, the coefficient on the interaction term of rainfall and baseline maoist casualties could pick up the differential effect of mineral resource wealth. However, the coefficient on the interaction term is estimated to be very small, while the coefficient on the interaction term with mineral wealth retains its magnitude and significance.

Mining Activity

The current analysis cannot provide direct evidence on taxation by rebel groups, which is the key mechanism within my framework that explains the differential impact of rainfall shocks in mining regions. The Maoists publicly campaign against mining activity on the grounds that mines lead to pollution and the displacement of the tribal population. Rebel groups in mining regions are thought to bank on the wide-spread resentment against mining activity. The first order effect of grievances against mines should operate through average levels of violence, which are accounted for by the fixed effects. However, the adverse impact of mining activity on rural communities could inspire certain alternative explanations of the observed differential impact of rainfall in mining regions. In particular, rebel groups could be more effective in recruiting from mining regions because of two reasons. First, it may be that a given rainfall shock has a larger impact on agricultural productivity of potential recruits as a result of environmental degradation or displacement. This channel could even be strengthened through political economy factors. If districts that produce minerals have weaker political institutions, this could exacerbate the impact of a given rainfall shock (as suggested in the ordered conflict model of Besley and Persson, 2010). While the analysis cannot fully rule out this possibility, the estimated rice production function failed to pick up any differential effect of rain on agricultural output in mining regions. Furthermore, a political resource curse interpretation is undermined by the fact that key policies are set at the state level and all selected states (with the exception of Bihar) produce key minerals. A second channel that relies on the environmental impact of mining activity is the possibility that grievances against mines create an additional incentive for individuals to join the Maoists. While these channels are different from the pure budget constraint mechanism as presented in the theory, the main difference could be one of interpretation. First, if the impact of rainfall shocks is more severe in mining regions, this could affect the communities who are considered for recruitment (for instance, the tribal population) more than the tax base of the rebel group. Hence, this channel could formally be equivalent to the mechanism proposed earlier. Similarly, the grievance against mines could create an additional pull factor which makes the rebel group's budget constraint less dependent on local economic conditions. In this sense, the grievance mechanism could be understood within my theoretical framework.

It is possible to test the importance of the tribal population explicitly. If the conflict between mines and rural communities mainly affects tribal groups (as suggested by Kujur, 2009), one could expect the grievance effect of mines to be stronger in tribal areas. To test this hypothesis, I include a triple interaction of mineral wealth, the share of the tribal population, and rainfall in the baseline model. The coefficient on the triple interaction term should be negative and signiûcant (for security force casualties), if the effect of rainfall shocks in mining districts is larger for tribal districts. This should be the case if the impact of mining mainly operates through the grievances of the tribal population. However, the coefficient on the triple interaction is insigniûcant.

NAXALISM-FACT, FICTION AND FUTURE

Overcoming the Hamletian dilemma, the Andhra Pradesh Government has, at last, clamped a ban on the activities of the Peoples War Group, a Naxalite outfit, which has been responsible for disturbed conditions in Rural Andhra Pradesh particularly in the Telangana region, bringing to a halt all developmental activities.

Civil liberties groups, of trampling on the rights of the innocent people. A call for State wide bandh has been given for August 8,

1996, Judging by past experience, considerable public property will be destroyed and may be a few lives will be lost. It is necessary to ponder over the Naxalite movement in the country at this juncture to evaluate the action taken by the Government of A.P. and the response by interested parties.

Peoples War Group is said to work for the welfare of tribals and rural poor. Conceptual clarity is sine qua non for arriving at valid conclusions and viable policy options, while dealing with a complex socio-economic problem like Tribal/Rural Backwardness.

One should avoid the temptation of equating the symptoms of the deep-rooted malady with the manifestation of parasitical infestation. The treatment for the malady and clearing of the parasitical infection are distinct and separate.

It is worthwhile to ponder whether amelioration of the conditions of Tribal/Rural poor would cause the disappearance of Naxalism from political scene automatically, or conversely, assisting the growth of Naxalism would ensure the removal of Tribal/Rural poverty. The answer is in the negative as both are not interrelated.

Communist Ideology of Marxist-Leninist Variety

Naxalism is a political ideology and it is not a socio-economic movement aimed at the betterment of Tirbal/Rural poor. The social and their geographical location provides a 'classic situation' for Naxalites to test out their ideological tactics of guerrilla warfare, Peoples War and Rural based Revolution. Assuming that the 'Tribals' lot improves, Naxals would simply shift their scene of operations to where 'exploited classes' exist and geographical conditions are conducive to guerrilla war. Naxalism is a brand name for Communist ideology of Marxist-Leninist variety, which burst out on the Indian scene as a radical romantic, revolutionary political creed in the Spring of 1967.

Debunking Parliamentary Democracy and swearing by the tenet that the political power flows through the barrel of the gun, openly swearing allegiance to Chairman Mao, a well thought out political strategy had a premature birth in West Bengal in the ideal conditions of chaos that prevailed after the fall of the unpopular Congress Ministry. Euphoric at their unexpected success, the United Front, in its policy statement of March 1, 1967, proclaimed support to all downtrodden people in their legitimate struggles to ameliorate their conditions. Police were asked not to interfere in 'class actions'. Marxist Leninists chose the Siliguri area for launching their revolution, not by accident.

The area was close to Nepal, Bangladesh, Sikkim and Tibet was less than 100 miles away. Populated by over 1.25 lakh tribals in a compact area of about 250 sq.miles, the area was a classic case of exploitation by landlords, money-lenders, and simmering discontent. Tribals had risen in revolt in the past also in 1939 and 1959. Police were rendered ineffective by political directives and violence as a means of social and economic change was put into operation with gusto. The 'Spring Thunder' broke over India and the Communist Party of China hailed these developments as the 'front paw of the revolution'.

As Naxalbari movement started showing signs of success and was being replicated in other parts of the country, even an indulgent West Bengal Government had to crack the whip to control the damage. But it was too late. Sporadic revolts broke out in violent form in many parts of the country. Exulting at the spread of the message of revolution, a Coordinating Committee and later a party was formed to synchronise and coordinate localised violent struggles into a Mass Movement, and Naxalism was accepted as the brand name for CPML with the basic ideology of:

a. Complete rejection of the ethics of Parliamentary Democracy,

b. Emphasis on uncompromising class war,

c. That political power can be won only through violence- 'political power flows through the barrel of the gun', and

d. Harass, weaken and vanquish the enemy (here the established authority), thereby create 'liberated areas' as an inspiring prelude to the people's war of liberation.

Four point plan of action for guerrilla struggle consisting of:

a. Setting up liberated zones,

b. Building up Peoples Army from the core of Guerrillas,
c. Encircling the cities from country side, and
d. 'Kill one and frighten thousands'-the theory of annihilation of class enemies.

The real aim of Naxalites is neither the domain of economics nor social welfare. it is a political movement having its goal as the seizure of political power i.e., State power. Agrarian uprisings with the help of landless peasants and poor tribal using guerrilla warfare tactics have their ultimate aim in capturing state power and then establishing a totalitarian regime. Charu Mazumdar summed up nicely the aim: "Militant struggles must be carried on not for land, crops, etc. but for the seizure of State Power". The basic doctrines of guerrilla warfare avoid the strength of the enemy and strike at his weak points; hide and seek the enemy; appear as good Samaritan to the poor masses by robbing Paul to pay the poor Peter; gain credibility by executing hated enemies of the poor etc., are fully practiced by the Naxals.

It is a figment of imagination to describe Naxalism as a label for downtrodden agrarian and tribal poor. Equally so to describe the tribals living in the contiguous forest areas of Orissa, A.P., M.P. and Maharashtra as Homogeneous Tribal Society and to say that Naxalism is a problem existing coterminous with the Homogeneous Tribal Society. The fact is, that Naxalism exists as a political ideology beyond the tribal belt. The front organisations of Naxalites among students, workers, intellectuals etc. would believe the fact that Naxalism is only a tribal movement. Naxalism exists in tribal area because : (1) Existence of discontentment; (2) availability of forest area suitable for guerrilla tactics, (3) inaccessibility of these areas to the enemy-the police and (4) non-existence of worthwhile grass root administrative machinery.

Another fiction circulating among well meaning people is that administrative process is the cause for naxalism as it is anti-tribal and non-responsive to the needs of tribals. There may be inadequacies, lack of involvement and dedication on the part of administrative machinery but to say that nothing was done for the tribals by the administration is far from the truth. By the same token, the description of police as abettors to exploitation of tribals by vested interests and feudal elements is a fiction. Police are a law enforcement agency. The law specifies the areas where police can act. Murder, Arson, Loot, Extortion, Kidnapping, Sabotage are prescribed by law. Once they are committed, the police are to step in. Extenuating circumstances, if any, can be taken notice of only by the Judiciary. For example, if a harassed debtor uses violence against a usurious money lender and causes him serious injuries, police have to take action against the perpetrator of violence. The reason for the same can be adjudged as just or otherwise only by a court of law.

Effective and efficient law enforcement would appear to the uninitiated as Police siding with the 'haves' and against the 'have nots'. Law is always reactive and seldom proactive. Police have to enforce the law as it stands on the statute book. It is not their's to reason why.

In a guerrilla war situation, where new personnel of the forces of law and order operate, certain excesses are bound to happen. One cannot in a war situation discern between a friend and a foe. Where it is a question of life and death, the one who pulls the trigger faster survives. As a trained force, the police come out more successful. In such situations innocent persons may also get killed.

There are provisions in the law and administrative procedures to determine whether such deaths were justified and were not the result of premeditated malice. None can support fake encounter deaths or violence against innocent people by the police. They are required to be put down with an iron hand. The wrongs can not make one right. Naxalite killings cannot be an excuse for fake encounters and police excesses. Conversely, alleged police excesses can not be the rationale to support naxal violence.

There are many self appointed rights groups to articulate vociferously against state terrorism and police excesses. One is surprised to find these elements remaining mute when it comes to the question of excesses and crimes by Naxalites. Why this double standard? Is it fear psychosis of possible reprisals by

Naxals or a tacit approval of Naxalite ideology. One can understand the affected party, the Naxalites, demanding the removal of ban. But, one is at a loss to know why law-abiding citizens and intellectuals clamour for this.

Tribal and rural development has lagged behind by many decades and urgent steps are to be taken to render justice to them swiftly and efficiently. Unless this is done, conditions in these areas would be ripe for any violent groups to exploit. Positive steps are to be taken to:

a. Eliminate Benami holdings in Tribal/Rural areas,

b. Assign surplus land to landless poor,

c. Ensuring payment of minimum wages to the tribals/rural poor,

d. Supply of essential commodities at subsidised rates,

e. Tribals should be allowed to collect, sell and utilise minor forest produce. This right should be well publicised among tribals and harassment of petty forest officials should stop,

f. ensure abolition of Bonded Labour,

g. Provide drinking water, medical, educational, and irrigation facilities,

h. Provide easy credit facilities and eliminate money lenders,

i. Establish a specially structured GIRIJAN Organisation which can function multi-dimensionally and initiate all pro-developmental activities under one roof. Plethora of organisations/corporations only confuse the tribals,

j. Impart training in simple skills to the tribal youth to enable them to play a useful role in their community,

k. Create a simple and unified Criminal Justice System in the Tribal areas to render instant justice to the community,

l. Improve communications. All weather-Roads, Wireless, telephone facilities, postal facilities,

m. Special T.V.Radio Programmes in Tribal dialects to educate the tribals, and

n. Forest contracts are to be given only to tribal cooperatives.

Police Activities

(1) Order and security are prerequisites for economic development. Hence police presence in Tribal areas is not only necessary but to be strengthened.

(2) Instead of increasing armed police, specially trained civil police personnel should be posted in Tribal hamlets/villages to assist the tribals in their developmental activities and to prevent their exploitation by outsiders. The activities of police in tribal areas are to be closely monitored to prevent abuses.

(3) Large number of tribal youth are to be inducted into police service. Their training should be specially catered to developmental activities in Tribal area. They should function as catalysts for change.

(4) All past charges levelled against Police are to be enquired by a Judge of the High Court and excesses coming to notice to be punished as per law.

P.W.G. should convert itself as Peoples Welfare Group and give up violence. If there is a genuine change of mind, Naxalites would be welcomed with open hands to enter the main stream of life. But if it is only a play to fool the government, the bluffs will be exposed soon.

8

Threat of Terrorism in South Asia

TERRORISM—A THREAT TO DEMOCRACY

The terrorism according to United Nations can be defined as:- "Any action that is intended to cause death or serious bodily harm to civilians or non-combatants, when the purpose of such an act, by its nature or context, is to intimidate a population, or to compel a Government or an international organization to do or to abstain from doing any act.

"Terrorism" is an ambiguous term whose definition implies a political act. Over the years, the term has been used more frequently, and today it often seems to be synonymous with "evil". Generally speaking, the term "terrorism" can be used to describe a "systematic use or threat of violence in order to achieve political goals". But this definition does not address some of the problematic aspects of the phenomenon, and does not differentiate between terrorism and other forms of political violence, such as revolution, uprising and guerrilla warfare. Terrorism is subjective. One person's terrorist is another's revolutionary crusader. Terrorism in its modern interpretation is a new word for cruel criminal acts. Terror can be committed in the name of Good – but basically it is a way to fight for political goals in a criminal manner. Indeed, disputing the claim that it is important to define terrorism in order to effectively battle it, some argue that clearly defining terrorism and making it a singular criminal offence may serve to authorize the deprivation of the human rights of the suspects. Regardless of the definition of terrorism, democracies must be beware of the danger of transforming the war on terrorism from a means of defending democracy to one that undermines its foundations. Terrorists have killed people of all nationalities, faiths and backgrounds. Terrorists aim to achieve objectives through intimidation and fear. They assert that "end justify means", no matter what the cost in human life and suffering.

Since past, we have encountered several main types of terrorism:

1. Acts of terrorism committed by the state against internal or external opposition.
2. Acts of terrorism committed in order to oppose the state or in order to promote national independence.
3. Acts of fundamentalist terrorism, which is an expression of a struggle between religions or cultures.

Some examples of terrorist acts involve:

- The use of explosive devices and suicide bombers
- The assassination of political, military or media figures
- Hostage taking
- The hijacking of airplanes or other vehicles
- The destruction of infrastructure and communications
- The use of chemical, biological and nuclear weapons

Their methods, too, are different. Because they recognize no common bonds with people who have different beliefs, they are prepared to kill indiscriminately. Indeed, mass murder is their explicit objective, their measure of success in their terms, and their methods of recruitment bear more comparison with self-destructive cults than political movements.

Democracy lies in the hearts and minds of people. It permeates those hearts and minds, so that no one allows them to be usurped by force or in any other way. Democracy is a condition in which the vast numbers of people who comprise a nation — and ultimately the world — submit themselves to institutions of law of their own making, and in which they care about each other and the planet on which they live. Democracy is not only an idea; it is also a set of values (freedom, equality and brotherhood) and a way of governing." Terror" in the sense of a "terror-regime" is originally another way of governing-without democratic values. It is a thread against democracy which is not threaded as criminal acts but as something, that can suspend democratic rights in societies.

Democracy is not a form of government but a set of principles that guide how we govern ourselves. Terrorism is merely a method of utilizing fear as a means to an end. Therefore, Terrorism cannot destroy the principles of democracy. Terrorist can and indeed are attempting to cause us to ignore those principles as we cater to our fears that terrorism brings. It is when we abandon the principles, even in the short term that will bring the ultimate demise of Democracy. So we should not allow ourselves to publically fear terrorism but instead, we should discipline ourselves to allow the principles of Democracy and peace to prevail. I believe that even a terrorist desires peace. The question is who gets to lead the peace, the people or the terrorist?

Terrorism poses a direct and indirect threat to democracy. The direct threat is a result of terrorism's capability to undermine the fundamental security that nations and international organizations are supposed to provide their citizens, which is the foundation of the legitimacy of a government. Terrorism also poses a direct threat to the basic human rights of life and property. But the indirect threat to democracy is by far the most dangerous. The war on terrorism challenges the democratic institutions of the nations and their ability to ensure the security of their citizens without harming innocent people. The terrorist attacks signal a turning point not only in the intensity of global terrorism, but also a warning to any enlightened democracy that wishes to combat the threat of terrorism.

Democracy is traditionally seen as a panacea to provide security and civil liberties to citizens and avoid political extremism or terrorism provoked by un-redressed grievances. The oft-cited theory of democratic peace holds that democracies do not wage war against each other. Democracy is in crisis; insecurity is on the rise and the threat of terrorism is equally menacing in newly democratizing and long-democratic countries. Terrorism, and equally the fight against terrorism, pose a dual challenge to recent and long-established democracies: terrorism undermines a cherished goal and objective of democracy, that of providing citizens with security and the rule of law; and in responding to terrorism, democracies risk undermining the values of democracy such as the rule of law and human rights that are central to their existence and legitimacy.

Terrorism's greatest power lies in the arbitrary nature of its victims and in the large amount of coverage it receives in the media. Today, in addition to "conventional" terrorism, there are also the risks of the use of weapons of mass destruction and cyber-terrorism. The ability to use diverse methods in order to wreak havoc indicates that although terrorism has not yet become an existential world threat, if we didn't wake up then, that day is not far-off.

In my views, Terrorism can both destroy and build democracy. Throughout past, the oppressed and abused have used such means as were available to them to strive to attain social justice and gain individual dignity based on liberty, freedom and full access to democratic rights of citizenship. The means have often been inhumane but the character of the struggle is as much determined by the resistance of those in power as the selected means of the terrorist. In Zimbabwe the threats of the Zanu-PF thugs against all opposition voters destroyed the validity of the last two-three elections there. But making the most inspiring sights in the modern world for democracy to be seen, the peoples rose above the threats of terrorists and millions queued patiently to cast their ballots despite the physical perils involved in going to polling stations. This happened in Afghanistan after the fall of the Taliban and of course then again in Iraq in December 2005.

While Islamic fundamentalist terrorists see an undemocratic religious state as the fulfillment of their earthly goals, this is one type of terrorism. Other types of terrorism can create democracy-for example, the African National Congress had an armed wing, led by Nelson Mandela, which easily falls under the category of terrorist. Indeed, 'Free Nelson Mandela' records and T-shirts could fall under the category of glorification of terrorism. Yet this very organization and this very terrorist leader were responsible for leading South Africa to democracy.

In Sri Lanka, the ongoing war between the Tamil Tigers and the Colombo administration is in danger of undermining the nation's fragile democracy. Similarly, in the Gaza strip, Algeria and most obviously Pakistan, terror and the threat of terror are a serious impediment to nurturing a viable, democratic state. By contrast, the voters of Spain responded to the Madrid train bombings with a bravura display of popular sovereignty. And in Northern Ireland it was the ballot box and not the Armalite that brought the struggle to an end.

We cannot rely exclusively on military power to assure our long-term security. Lasting peace is gained as justice and democracy advance. In democratic and successful societies, men and women do not swear allegiance to malcontents and murderers; they turn their hearts and labor to building better lives. And democratic governments do not shelter terrorist camps or attack their peaceful neighbors; they honour the aspirations and dignity of their own people. In our conflict with terror and tyranny, we have an unmatched advantage, a power that cannot be resisted, and that is the appeal of freedom to all mankind."

Freedom of speech, freedom of the press, and the right to peaceably assemble, serve to empower citizens, legitimize debate, and provide alternatives to violence. The fair and independent judicial systems present in liberal democracies play a similar role. A truly independent judiciary is a vital check on executive power and a protector of those exercising their rights to free expression. Ensuring that no group is above the law also gives average citizens a greater stake in their political systems. Absent these democratic attributes, we find conditions that in some instances give rise to sympathy for terrorism. This is especially true in nations where demagogues who preach the language of hate under the guise of religion are the only alternatives to corrupt or brutal elite. Today, the danger to us comes not exclusively from dictators who make war directly upon us, our allies, and our interests — it also Proceed from dictators who create an atmosphere so poisonous and so brutal that evil sprouts and motivates a small but radicalized cadre to terrorism.

To counter terrorism, we seek genuine representative government that brings liberty and democracy to all of a country's citizens, including those who often have been excluded — especially women. Women have a critical role to play in democracy, in civil society, and in ensuring that democratic ideals are instilled in future generations. Our long-term strategy is to strike at the heart of terrorism by depriving it of its shelter, its recruitment grounds, and its foot soldiers. We will do this in no small measure through the avid promotion of democracy and freedom. I believe that this can be achieved because we have developed a highly successful model of integration which enables people of all backgrounds and faiths to prosper and live together within the safeguard of common values. Our society is itself an affront, and a reproach, to the ideologues who believe that only their way of living life is the right one. And make no mistake: The threat we face is ideological. It is not driven by poverty, or by social exclusion, or by racial hatred. Those who attacked London in July, those who have been engaged in terrorist networks elsewhere in the world, and those who attacked New York in 2001 were not the poor and dispossessed. They were, for the most part, well educated and prosperous.

Unlike the liberation movements of the post-World War II era, these are not political ideas like national independence from colonial rule, or equality for all citizens without regard for race or creed, or freedom of expression without totalitarian repression. Such ambitions are, at least in principle, in many cases have actually been negotiated. However, there can be no negotiation about the re-creation of the Caliphate; there can be no negotiation about the imposition of Sharia law; there can be no negotiation about the suppression of equality between the sexes; there can be no negotiation about the ending of free speech. These values are fundamental to our civilization and are simply not up for negotiation. It is equally wrong to claim, as some do, that the motivation of terrorists and their allies is driven by some desire to seek justice in the Middle East—the part of the world where progress has been most difficult to achieve in the past 30 years. I do not accept this in any respect.

We suggest that the best way to contest this threat is by building and strengthening the democracy of our society, by isolating extremism in its various manifestations, by strengthening the legal framework within which we contest terrorism, and by developing more effective means to protect our democracy.

First, in each of our societies, we need to strengthen our democracy. That means promoting a society which is based upon the true respect of one individual for another, one culture for another, one faith for another, one race for another. It means promoting the view that democracy is the means of making change in our societies, and it means working to strengthen our democracy so that young people from all communities can see the ways in which their engagement in our societies can bring about democratic change and reduce the alienation which can make individuals prey to those who seek to destroy us.

Second, we need to take steps to isolate extremist organizations and those individuals who promote extremism. In so doing, it is essential for us to work closely with the mainstream faith communities and to understand their preoccupations. In our country, we need legislation which outlaws incitement to religious or race hatred and makes it clear that glorification of terrorism is not a legitimate political expression of view. We wish to encourage faiths to pursue their faith openly and directly. We should intend to attack the foci of extremist organization, whether they are in training camps, in prisons, in bookshops, or in places of worship. We should, work with international allies where appropriate, to identify the networks and individuals who are promoting extremism, and use legal power to disrupt and weaken them. We should intend to remove from the India those foreign citizens who are using their time in our country to promote extremism, though this course is not legally straightforward. All of these measures will further isolate and weaken those extremists who wish to promote terrorism as an appropriate form of activity.

Third, we need to strengthen the legal framework within which we can address these issues. I assert throughout all this the need to retrain and strengthen our human rights and the values which underlie them. But I say at the same time that the right to be protected from the death and destruction caused by indiscriminate terrorism is at least as important as the right of the terrorist to be protected from torture and ill-treatment. I believe that our peoples expect not only the protection of individual rights, but also the protection of democratic values such as safety and security under the law. We need a legal framework which seeks to address the difficult balance in these rights. We cannot properly fight terrorism with one legal hand tied behind our back, or give terrorists the unfettered right to defend themselves as they promote and prepare violent attacks on our society. For that reason, we should propose legal changes in our country which outlaw acts preparatory to terrorism and terrorist training.

Fourth, we need to strengthen our ability to control our borders. That means doing our best to harmonize the biometric data on passports, visas, ID cards where they exist, and perhaps even driving licenses. This is a substantial agenda to contest the threats we face, but I believe it to be essential for us.

Democracy is the strongest form of society and the most resilient. It is the aspiration of peoples throughout the world. Through democracy, extremist terrorism will be defeated. As we face the challenge of terrorist attack, most recently in Delhi again last Saturday, it is our duty to analyse and then determine the means by which this threat can be best contested. We have to clarify the values and society which we are defending; identify the threat with which we have to deal; and set out the central means by which we need both to contest those who seek to destroy us and to build the solidarity and determination which we need to succeed.

The most important conclusion to draw from this analysis is that there is not some particular government policy decision, or even some overall policy stance, which we could change and thus somehow remove our society from the terrorist firing line. Their nihilism means that our societies would only cease to be a target if we were to give up all those values of freedom and liberty which we have fought to extend over so many years.

We all know that our society, based on these values, will continue to evolve and develop. But we also know that the achievements we do have are based on centuries of struggle. The societies which we have built, with the values which they embody, are not slight or passing. They are deeply rooted and profound. However, it is the case that these are absolutely enormous changes in one generation, which proves that change for the good can happen and, moreover, that it can happen in very many cases without violence or bloodshed. And the fight for democracy is at the core of this change.

It can be lastly concluded that terrorism can not be a threat to democracy but democracy can be a weapon to fight against terrorism. I assert that the single most important weapon that we have in defending the societies from which we come is our determination and our solidarity.

NATURE OF THE THREAT

When one considers the ways in which BT might be carried out, the first rule should be that we do not know who the possible terrorist will be, his or her motivation, or the wherewithal that may be available for the attack. Thus, attacks to incapacitate selected persons to gain attention, or to cause serious illness for revenge might have a very different approach than attacks designed to cause mass casualties. An effort by a disgruntled clinical laboratory worker could have a very different scope than one by a well-funded non-state organization or a state-sponsored group. Parenthetically, the failure of the Japanese Aum Shinriko cult to succeed with biological terrorism should not provide much comfort concerning the need for state sponsorship given the manifest ineptitude of the perpetrators.

The second issue is the dissemination of factual information concerning the real dangers of such an attack. Some would argue that the less said the better. Unfortunately for this approach, US society does not respond without facts and public opinion supporting programs. This means that the actual dangers must be explained to the public and responsible political leaders without inflammatory rhetoric or divulging detailed methods for the assaults, and we must take the chance that plain-speaking might motivate some to undertake the very actions we are trying to prevent. Furthermore, discussion of the facts may help the public, media, and health authorities respond in a calmer and more rational fashion than was observed with the aerosol anthrax attacks of 2001.

If we consider the methods by which microbes might be delivered to a target population there are multiple routes. Direct inoculation, infection of natural vectors or reservoirs and loosing them on the target population, or infection of a few persons and counting on their spreading the infection even further are some possibilities. If we focus on terrorist strategies that can inflict mass casualties none of these possibilities is highly feasible today with the exception of the use of smallpox, a virus that is well-known to spread from human to human after a long and successful career in that evolutionary niche. If we conclude that other organisms must be delivered directly to the target host, we should also consider water, food, and aerosols as potential vehicles of infection. Contaminated water from wells and storage containers has been associated with outbreaks of disease, but the odds are against this approach for causing mass casualties because of the dilution factor, chlorination, and the usual treatment of water before consumption in this country. Food-borne pathogens have caused many outbreaks in the US and are a major cause of morbidity and mortality. Even though our distribution system is highly centralized, food items are usually not consumed synchronously except at special events. Improved surveillance of food-borne disease and newer methods of molecular typing of offending organisms should provide a counterweight to the wide dissemination of contaminated food. If a few cases are recognized and traced to a food source, warnings and recalls may well serve to protect us.

The over-all societal impact of any one of these dissemination methods could be considerable, regardless of the actual health damage. We have case studies already, including non-lethal

Salmonella infection of a few hundred citizens (Torok et al., 1999), Sarin gas attacks with only 20 deaths, food tampering, and most recently anthrax delivered by letter or even anthrax hoaxes. Aerosols, however, are an important route of attack because of their ability to cause really large numbers of casualties. The deficiencies of aerosols such as dependence on metrological conditions, the unsuitability of most organisms for air-borne spread, and the technical demands may be counterbalanced in the hands of skillful perpetrators by the advantages of stand-off attack, silent spread of incapacitating or lethal disease, and wide-area coverage.

Aerosol Infections

Aerosol infection has long been recognized as a route of microbial transmission. Measles, influenza, smallpox, and tuberculosis are all known to be transmissible between patients by aerosols and additionally in the laboratory tularemia, rickettsiae, viral hemorrhagic fevers, and many other agents are threats to the microbiologist. Decreases in human tuberculosis and virtual elimination of diseases such as measles and smallpox from common medical experience as well as development of enhanced methods of protecting laboratory workers (ironically using technology developed during the US biowarfare program) have resulted in a loss of appreciation for this route of infection, but the US and Soviet BW programs were largely based on the properties of selected agents for causing large scale infection of human populations under the proper metrological conditions and with carefully developed methods of dissemination. Moreover, the terrorist could attack enclosed environments such as stadiums or large buildings in order to eliminate the meteorological factors that degrade a small particle aerosol.

Biological agents have not seen widespread use in warfare so it is not surprising that there is skepticism as to their efficacy. It is not appreciated that the US program in offensive biological warfare (terminated on November 28, 1969) rigorously tested each step in the link between a microorganism selected by several criteria and the delivery of a credible biological attack. Tularemia would be an excellent example because extensive information is available in the published literature, congressional hearings, and popular press. From the initial isolation of the organism by Francis and coworkers, it was notorious for causing infections in the laboratory, a frequent hallmark of aerosol infectivity. The aerosol properties were intensively studied and methods were found to enhance its stability in storage and in aerosols. Animals and later humans were challenged with graded doses of the bacterium delivered in different particle sizes to establish the quantitative properties of these aerosols. Open air dissemination was mimicked using a surrogate organism, *Serratia marscens*, and this confirmed that an organism with the aerosol stability and infectivity of *Francisella tularensis* could cause mass casualties over large geographic areas provided attention was given to metrological conditions. The areas affected could reach thousands of square kilometers. The resulting environmental transmission from the large number of different nonhuman mammalian and arthropod species that would be infected in a tularemia attack cannot be evaluated. Thus, there is little doubt that large numbers of human casualties could be caused by efficiently weaponized organisms readily available from nature.

A relatively small number of agents are suitable for causing literally thousands or hundreds of thousands of casualties, and this may provide a basis for prioritization of medical and other measures to deny the intent of terrorists. Biological toxins, even the highly potent botulinum toxin, and chemical agents are absent because of their relatively low potential to cause casualties whether evaluated on the basis of purified agent or the basis of the likely highest concentration practically achievable. It is impossible to list every possible agent and there are always discussions among experts as to whether some should be added or omitted. Toxins are inherently of lesser efficiency because they cannot match the killing or incapacitating power of the highly infectious organisms; the toxins have to produce their effects as delivered, but the infectious agents grow and produce toxins or other effects in the recipient's body. According to a WHO scenario several infectious agents would be expected to produce 35,000 to >100,000 casualties if 50 kg were delivered in a line source and carried down-wind over a populated area. In the case of some of the more stable agents, down-wind reach would exceed 20 km. The Office of Technology Assessment (1993) has published similar figures. It must be borne in mind that the US and Soviet programs prepared literally metric tons, not kilograms, of agent and that appropriate devices for delivering line sources or multiple overlapping point sources were available (Alibek, 2001; Sidell et al., 1997). Impact on the infected members of the population would depend on the agent used and the nature of the response (for example, alacrity of recognition of initial patients, public health and medical infrastructure, vaccine and antibiotic stockpiles). The additional impact that might be possible through modification of naturally occurring organisms by methods well within the reach of simple biotechnology including induction of antimicrobial resistance, enhancement of virulence by addition of toxin genes, or selection of more stable or virulent organisms is formidable. Issues surrounding the more extensive engineering of threat agents are beyond the scope of this discussion, however, it is important to note that the potential exists, but that there would probably be a need for human testing of any resulting candidate.

Properties of Small Particle Aerosols

The basic properties of aerosols must be understood to appreciate the way in which such weapons could be used. The optimum aerosol particle size is thought to be 1–5 microns. This size provides two critical properties: the particles do not settle out over a several hour time period but rather are truly airborne and are carried on wind currents or through heating, ventilation, and air conditioning systems (HVAC) and they are of an optimum size to reach the terminal respiratory bronchiole or alveolus of humans and deposit in those critical areas to set up infection. Generation of small particle aerosols requires energy as evidenced by classical examples such as laryngeal tuberculosis, the wide dissemination of rubella by a disco singer (Marks et al., 1981), or the persistent cough of the index case of a nosocomial Lassa fever outbreak (Carey et al., 1972). Such particle sizes can be achieved intentionally by generating a liquid aerosol with a spray device or by using an appropriately manufactured powder. The dissemination system for a liquid must have the correct relationship between viscosity and solids content of the liquid, air pressure, orifice diameter, and other variables to attain the critical particle size, as well as have the proper stabilizers in the solution to assure that infectivity is not lost. The dry powders are difficult to manufacture, but they are extremely dangerous because they can be prepared so as to aerosolize with minimal energy input and can be manufactured in very fine particle sizes. If the skills to prepare these particles are available, it may also be possible to formulate encapsulated weapons of greater biological stability.

It is obvious that the preparation and testing of such weapons requires microbiological skills to attain the high concentrations of organisms needed. Equally as important is the expertise for dissemination of liquid or powder aerosols in a stable form in the correct particle size. Such capabilities may be available from many people in different walks of life. Nonetheless, assembling the needed skill sets implies an organization with some resources, particularly as one moves into the powders and into greater quantities of agent. Practice or trials would be important to assure success, although, as the saying goes, "the proof of the pudding ...". Persons with previous experience in offensive biowarfare programs could be extremely valuable resources to such an endeavor.

When these aerosol clouds are generated, there is a period of instability and larger particles or agglomerates fall out near the dissemination device with considerable surface contamination possible. Once the small particle aerosols are formed, they will move with wind currents and traverse the landscape, being gradually diluted by mixing and decay. Because of their dependence on wind currents, aerosols may be diverted from their planned target; warming of the earth's surface after sunrise will result in their being carried to higher levels of the atmosphere unless inversion conditions are present. Loss of infectivity by biological decay will also occur, depending on stabilizers in the suspension medium, ultraviolet intensity, humidity, and temperature. They will enter buildings through HVAC systems, but the urban landscape profile may result in extensive disturbances of air flow. The ultraviolet light sensitivity of most of the organisms, combined with the meteorological needs, will favour the use of an evening, night time, or early morning, attack if done outdoors. Terrorist attacks may also be directed toward buildings or enclosed stadiums, making the air conditioning systems the obvious route of the delivery of the aerosol.

The extreme "fluffiness" or ease of aerosolization of the most dangerous powders is difficult to imagine. The material in the Hart Senate office building seems to offer an excellent example: all present in the room when the offending letter was simply opened had spores in their noses when tested 4 hours later; anthrax spores traveled to adjacent rooms through the HVAC; extensive surface contamination was present. Subsequent examination of the powder showed it to have a very high concentration of anthrax spores (reportedly 1012/g), finely dispersed particles, and it was readily aerosolized with the slightest disturbance. Undoubtedly, without antibiotic prophylaxis most of those in the room would have suffered inhalation anthrax. Had this material been introduced clandestinely into the air conditioning intake, there would have been no warning until the first cases were recognized, perhaps too late for therapy. The magnitude of the exposure can be seen from studies done by the Canadian Defence Forces (Kournikakis et al., 2001) in a simulation using only 1/10th the number of spores and 1/20th the estimated quantity of a readily aerosolized powder containing *Bacillus globigius* as a surrogate for *Bacillus anthracis*. In less than one minute, spores spread throughout the room in similar concentrations as observed at the site of the envelope opening. Testing of the filter from the respirator worn by the subject opening the letter yielded 80,000 infectious units, equivalent to an estimated 15-320 human LD50 for anthrax spores.

These principles governing airborne particles in the 1–5 micron range are essential in our response to the possibility of an aerosol attack. First of all, buildings with their HVAC may provide little protection against small-particle aerosols if currents of air bring a widely disseminated agent into the zone of their air intake. Indeed, the HVAC systems may provide a particular vulnerability to bioterrorism. Secondly, environmental sampling of surfaces or clothing in areas exposed to such aerosols or nasal swabs of potentially exposed persons will not predict if a person was infected with any certainty; finding agent in these situations demonstrates that an attack has taken place. Thirdly, surgical masks and similar defences are not effective against such small particles and only give a false sense of protection; highly efficient masks that can protect against small particles (e.g., N100 masks designed for medical staff working with tuberculosis patients) and which are properly fitted on trained personnel are needed (Lowe et al., 1999). Obviously, protective gear must be worn during the risk period, but these small-particle aerosols are odorless and invisible to the eye so the general utility of personal protective gear is limited.

Secondary Aerosols

The issue of secondary aerosols is an important one. Infectious agents on solid surfaces such as soil, counter tops, machinery are thought not to be subject to aerosolization unless considerable energy is applied. Studies of *Bacillus* spores have shown aerosols intentionally deposited on the ground are very difficult to re-suspend with ordinary traffic or even intentional beating of the surface.

Soil subjected to high air flow yields few particles in the dangerous 1–5 micron range (Chinn et al., 1990). These field evaluations show that even when the contamination of a surface reaches 107/meter2 the concentration above the surface, even with considerable disturbance, will be extremely low. Thus, in a field biowarfare situation there is little danger from secondary aerosolization. There is little experience with transfer of infectious powders from one solid surface to another or with the deposit of larger clumps of highly aerosolizable particles on hard solid surfaces. Surrogate infectious agents, fluorescent tracers or radioactive particles predict that highly concentrated biological agents (titers >109/g and perhaps as much as 1012/g) will extensively contaminate surfaces they impact and, if viable, pose a contact risk. Large quantities of organisms from dangerous powders can result in short-term presence of organisms in the external nares of exposed persons and the fall-out of larger particles can lead to environmental contamination near the site of dissemination.

The possibility of secondary aerosols in this situation is thought to be small, but application of high energy sources or the presence of physical clumps of particles could be problematic. The risk of aerosol infection to an exposed human would depend on the amount of material aerosolized and the infectious dose for humans. The actual amount of tularemia or Q fever required to infect 50% of exposed humans is known and is on the order of 1–10 organisms. For other organisms such as anthrax it is necessary to extrapolate from cynomolgus monkeys or other experimental animals.

In this case the lethal dose for 50% of animals is 8,000 spores by aerosol. The LD50 is determined by exposing animals to graded doses of the infectious agent and calculating the linear relationship between the logarithm of the dose increment and the increase in response of the target animals. This is usually done between 20–80% lethality and the LD50 calculated.

In fact the linearity can probably be extrapolated further to furnish at least an approximation of the risk from lower doses; in the case of anthrax, published values for the slope (Glassman et al., 1965; Chinn et al., 1990) suggest that inhaling a dozen spores could be risky in a small percentage of the population. These concepts are important to the practical management of situations in which a suspicious powder is involved. The physical properties of a readily aerosolized powder will be recognized by an experienced observer or by laboratory analysis. An ordinary dried culture of, for example, anthrax will not pose a great hazard beyond the readily recognized and treated cutaneous anthrax. Decontamination of a building needs to address the dangerous states of the contaminating organism. Safety is the goal, not "sterility". In the case of anthrax spores, significant quantities of aerosolizable particles is the criterion. Sterility is less important than being certain that any residual infectivity is earth bound.

Relative Importance of Different Agents

Consideration of the different bioterrorism agents and some of their properties is the first step to prioritize defences against them. Each has different properties as we see them today and thus each presents different threats and different opportunities for control. This discussion has been cast in terms of the worst case scenarios (effective broad-scale aerosol dissemination) but we must recognize that, although protection against this situation is important, the most likely eventuality is a less extensive or less successful attack. Fortunately, attention to the worst case is a step toward the more general solution, although the lesser eventuality should also be in the mind of planners. It is also important to note that biodefense efforts meld with the general struggle against infectious diseases. For example, strengthening the public health system will provide benefits regardless of whether a bioterrorist attack occurs. Money spent on communications within the public health system is long overdue. Planning will help in disaster response, regardless of the nature of the event. Perhaps much of the money spent on increasing smallpox vaccine stocks will eventually be "sunk costs" but we should not regard research and vaccine development on other agents as anything other than an benefit for human-kind. Smallpox provides a threat whose consequences are simply unacceptable, regardless of the probability of its use. Therefore we must develop clinician awareness, diagnostic systems, and stockpiles of existing vaccine that give us a validated countermeasure to deploy in case of attack. Whether additional antiviral drug and vaccine development is justified is a matter of prioritization against other threats.

Anthrax also is a special case. It is widely distributed in nature and thus readily available to terrorists in virulent form. The spores are extraordinarily stable on storage and in aerosols obviating many of the terrorist's research needs to develop an effective weapon. Inhalation anthrax is a fearsome disease if not treated early with effective antibiotics, and production of antibiotic-resistant anthrax is readily achieved. Plague and tularemia are both severe diseases but they require another level of sophistication in weaponization. Their cultivation in virulent form and their dissemination in stable aerosols is more difficult than for anthrax. The viral hemorrhagic fevers are essentially without therapy, have severe psychological impact, and carry a high mortality. Their production is still more difficult, but the technology is readily accessible to an experienced microbiologist. When considering the impact of limited or massive dissemination of the agents in tables 2-4 and 2-5, one must factor in the disruption of the health care system, the role of antibiotic resistance, the fear-factor in the population and medical staff, as well as the state of defensive preparations. One element that is often neglected is the influence of a communicable disease on travel and commerce. Any of these diseases could lead to severe disruptions in the free travel of U.S. citizens and others within the US and in international air transport systems. If the agent is also an agricultural pathogen, then internal movement of animals would be frozen and exports would be stopped, resulting in even more severe economic consequences.

Strategies to Confront the Problem

Any attempt to deal with BT should consider the entire spectrum of responses, including state and local organization supported by a comprehensive federal plan. The public health system will be the back-bone, but there will have to be participation of the entire society. Recognition by the clinician, laboratory diagnosis, and mobilization of countermeasures will all play a part. As noted above, the strategy should be tailored to each agent or group of agents. It must be emphasized that environmental detection and patient diagnosis of the specific agent employed are keystones of an improved response to the threat. Detection suffers from the need to be active at the time and site of an attack, so economics will probably limit its future usefulness to selected high risk venues.

Diagnostics are, in principle, more focused and also require the suspicions of informed clinicians; widely deployed they are a very significant expense. An additional demand on detection and diagnostics is the recognition of subversion of our defences by inducing resistance to anti-infectives or other protective modalities. Vaccine approaches are suitable for selected at-risk groups, particularly for specific high-priority BT agents. However, specific vaccines are not general remedies for the threat to the civilian population. The expense and difficulty of administration and the inevitable side effects will limit their widespread use. They remain important elements of our response in selected populations and specific circumstances.

Anti-infective drugs could be a very effective response if problems of drug development, drug-resistance, safety and efficacy testing, stockpiling, and distribution can be solved. Other supportive measures directed to bacterial toxins or the over-exuberant inflammatory responses induced by some viruses could be useful, as well.

Further definition of the Toll-like receptor family could open the way to broadly protective remedies that could be used in the event of BT attacks. Some agents pose sufficient problems to demand immediate and thorough attention. Smallpox, because of its track record of interhuman transmissibility and high case fatality, is clearly a first-echelon target. Anthrax, because of its ease of weaponization, deserves attention to the development of more effective therapy beyond antibiotics. Antitoxic strategies at the level of the toxin molecules as well as their down-stream effects should be developed in a very short time frame. Furthermore, the terrorist use of antibiotic-resistant strains should be anticipated. Plague and tularemia might seem to be resolved in principle because of the existence of effective antibiotics, but their relatively short incubation periods place high demands on availability of effective antimicrobials and the facility with which antibiotic resistance can be induced has important implications for defensive strategies. This is complicated because the log-normal distribution of incubation periods is "front-loaded" and because late treatment can fail even though the bacteria are eradicated. The viral hemorrhagic fever agents would induce widespread fear and even panic among the both general population and health-care providers. The arenavirus drug ribavirin should be stockpiled in modest amounts in the mean while, but more general strategies against the arenaviruses and other viral threat pathogens should be pursued.

Of course intelligence information and any dissuasion afforded by international agreements would be most welcome. We clearly cannot depend on these modalities to protect us completely. Many of the agents are widely available and so measures designed to limit their access are illusory in their effectiveness; anthrax is a case in point. However, limiting access to certain agents such as Ebola, Marburg, and smallpox viruses should be pursued. The equipment needed to produce limited amounts of biological agents is readily available and we cannot control or monitor access, but perhaps we can develop measures to track high output equipment and the movement of particularly sensitive expertise and genetic material. A strong research program and the industrial base to develop promising research leads into practical human countermeasures will be the best defence. One of the impediments, in addition to the perennial need for funding, is the lack of suitable containment laboratories. Furthermore, the diminution of expertise and suitable laboratories to study infectious aerosols is alarming. Another variable in play is the concern for limiting dissemination of research results; we have to be very careful not to suffocate our defensive effort with excessive secrecy unless the controls can be shown to add to our safety.

BETTER UNDERSTANDING OF BIOLOGICAL THREATS

Because they are our best protection against infectious disease, it is necessary that we continue to develop, approve, and introduce new vaccines against many naturally occurring infectious diseases and against some biological weapons threat agents. Yet the U.S. tends to focus its discussion of bioweapons vaccines and therapeutics on only a handful of potential agents, even though the former Soviet Union is known to have developed at least thirty biological agents for use as bioweapons. Alarmingly, it takes only two to three years to develop a biological weapon but, in the best-case scenario, eight to ten years to develop a new vaccine.

It has been suggested that live vaccines are too reactogenic for general use. But, for the purpose of boosting our biodefense arsenal, perhaps this issue requires reevaluation. In Russia, for example, all major vaccines—including anthrax, plague, and tularemia—are live vaccines. The United States had a good live plague vaccine and has a very strong live tularemia vaccine. The latter may not be approved for human use, but its protective efficiency is very high. Bioengineered vaccines are another possibility.

The use of alternate methods of vaccine administration must also be addressed. Biodefense vaccine administration techniques should not only be safe but must also provide for the vaccination of large numbers of people in a very short amount of time. Currently the U.S. focuses on injection vaccines, but there have been many studies on aerosol, inhalational, and oral vaccines. An aerosol plague vaccine, for example, can be used to immunize more than 1,200 people per hour, while a single operator can administer injection vaccines to only 20 to 30 people per hour. Inhalable plague, anthrax, and tularemia vaccines have all been extensively studied in Russia and have not shown any significant side effects.

This type of vaccine could work both systemically and locally, for example to induce mucosal immunity in the respiratory tract. However, though vaccines have proven extremely effective against infectious diseases in general, they are of limited utility in the defence against infections caused by biological weapons. Vaccination is a successful defence only when the target population is well-defined and can be identified well in advance of an attack; when the biological threat agents in the enemy's biological weapons arsenal are known; when vaccines for those agents have already been developed; and when the biological agents used are not genetically altered strains capable of circumventing a vaccine. Most military and nearly all terrorist scenarios will not meet all of these criteria. Therefore, vaccination of the general population against biological weapon agents is neither feasible nor advisable. In the context of biological weapons, the best use of vaccination is for troop protection, where both the target population and potential threat are more defined. Other, non-vaccine biodefense products need to be more seriously considered. In particular, over the past twenty years there has been extensive research on immunomodulators and their role in protecting against viral and bacterial pathogens. Although several such products have been developed that could potentially resolve many of our biodefense issues, none of them have been introduced yet into the field of biological weapons defence. In a biological attack, the target population would likely be large and poorly defined, the scale or even the fact of the attack may not be immediately apparent, and the biological agent used in the attack may not be immediately identified. For either military or terrorist use of biological weapons, creation of an aerosol cloud—usually accomplished by explosion or spraying—is by far the most effective mode for deploying biological weapons. This method can be used against large target areas and with practically any biological threat agent. Therefore, effective medical defence against biological weapons must incorporate protection against aerosol deployment. The nature of a biological weapons attack also dictates that the most successful medical defences will be prophylactic, rapid-acting, long-lasting, effective against a broad spectrum of threat agents, and relatively easy to deliver to a large population.

Finally, we need to re-examine our knowledge about the pathogenesis of bacterial and viral infections. For example, we still refer to the three major virulence factors in any discussion of anthrax. However, many other virulence factors may exist. My laboratory has conducted hundreds of experiments on anthrax lethal toxin, and thus far we have found no evidence whatsoever that it is capable of inducing normal healthy donor immune cells to produce any cytokines involved in the development of septic shock. Human endothelial cells are, however, relatively susceptible to the effect and the action of lethal toxin. It is becoming apparent that current theories on the role of anthrax toxin must be reexamined and revised. Our experiments have indicated that other overlooked anthrax virulence factors exist, including cell wall components and (possibly) hemolysins. Our work has indicated that the only factor of the anthrax bacterium capable of consistently inducing the mediators of septic shock seen in late-stage anthrax infection is a component of the cell wall skeleton, not lethal toxin, and that there exist many other overlooked exogenous and endogenous mediators which contribute in the development of anthrax sepsis and septic shock. Although these are preliminary data with which we are not able to make any final conclusions, they do highlight the need to re-examine the pathogenesis of anthrax. They may also explain why people die when antibiotics are administered in the late stages of infection: these cell wall skeleton components are very powerful inducers of septic shock mediators, and their concentration remains very high in the bloodstream after bacterial death. The preliminary work we have conducted to this point has led us to the belief that the most successful strategy for anthrax treatment would be dependant on the stage of infection (postexposure, lymphatic, systemic, or late-stage). It is our recommendation that a task force be established to more carefully analyse the events that occur during anthrax infection. It is very important that we re-evaluate our knowledge of pathogenesis and identify what we have missed in the field of protection and treatment of infectious diseases caused by biological weapons.

THERAPEUTIC COUNTERMEASURES TO BIOLOGICAL THREATS

As with vaccines, not only are therapeutics an integral component of our biodefense arsenal, but making it publicly known that we are producing a constant stream of new, innovative antimicrobials would serve as a very strategic form of deterrence. Several issues related to antibiotic, antiviral, antitoxin, and antibody research and development were identified and discussed during this session of the workshop. In light of the plethora of bioterrorist agents that could be used against us, of utmost importance is deciding whether we should focus our efforts on the development of broad-spectrum or agent-specific antimicrobials. For example, one possible antiviral strategy is the development of family-specific antivirals. Increasing evidence suggests that common antiviral targets exist. Our antibiotic arsenal is limited to only a handful of old antibiotics. Unfortunately, the general confidence in existing antibiotics and the complacency that was associated with infectious diseases in the 1960's resulted in a lag in producing new classes of antibiotics. There are about twenty-five antibiotics currently in the early phases of clinical development. However, none of these are new classes of antibiotics, and none are broad-spectrum. In fact, there has been only one new class of antibiotic developed in the past two decades, and resistance to it emerged before it came to market. This is alarming given the increasing accessibility of the tools and knowledge needed to develop antibioticresistant strains of bioterrorist agents.

There is concern that the situation will become ever worse with the recent FDA changes in clinical trial design requirements. It is expected that the increased cost associated with larger clinical trials will discourage companies from pursuing new antibiotic development, especially when there are other therapeutic interests vying for the same resources. Although the FDA attempts to balance the demands of a public health emergency with their needs as a regulatory agency and offers several accelerated routes to licensure, including the proposed animal efficacy rule, there is still a sense that these regulatory processes need to be streamlined even more in order to accelerate drug discovery and development efforts and provide more incentive for the pharmaceutical industry.

Our antiviral amamentarium is even more limited than our antibiotic arsenal. Cidofovir, for example, can only be administered intravenously and is highly nephrotoxic, making it unsuitable for mass casualty use. The clinical utility of ribavirin as an antiviral drug strategy for bioterrorist agents remains unclear. Antibiotics and antivirals are not the only potential therapeutic defense against bioterrorist agents. Basic research on the anthrax toxin system has led to some exciting prospects for antitoxin targeting. The most promising are the dominant negative inhibitors (DNIs), mutant forms of the protective antigen that block translocation of the virulence factors across the plasma membrane. Currently, DNIs are a very late stage product. If they can be proven efficacious in infected animal models, they could be produced and deployed very rapidly. There are several other approaches in much earlier stages of development. The use of recombinant monoclonal antibodies is another option which has been implicated for use against several biothreat agents, including anthrax, smallpox, and botulinum neurotoxins. For example, recent research has shown that a small mixture of recombinant monoclonal antibodies provides complete protection in mice against botulinum neurotoxin type A. Antibodies have several advantages as a bioweapons defense tool: they have been shown in multiple studies to be safe; ten have already been approved by the FDA and seventy more are in clinical trials, so their route to licensure is known; the technology and knowledge needed for production are readily available; their overall course through the discovery and approval process is much quicker than those of other types of therapeutics; and the technology platform used to produce and manufacture antibodies could be applicable to multiple agents.

Finally, scaling up research and development of all of these various potential therapeutics will require an evaluation of the availability of and need for additional laboratory capacity. In particular, there are a very limited number of BSL-3 and 4 labs where nonhuman primate studies can be conducted. Hope was expressed that in the future the FDA will accept rodent data in lieu of nonhuman primate data, if it can be demonstrated that the efficacy is the same in rodents as in nonhuman primates. This would allow for more testing in a greater number of facilities, although it would still require at least BSL-3 capability. Aerosol testing requires BSL-4 capabilities, as well as trained, vaccinated personnel.

TULAREMIA AND PLAGUE: ASSESSING OUR UNDERSTANDING OF THE THREAT

Yersinia pestis and *Francisella tularensis* are category A critical biological agents that pose a risk to national security because they could be easily disseminated (both agents) or transmitted person-to-person (*Y. pestis*), could cause a high mortality, and require special action for public health preparedness (CDC, 2000). Both agents have been weaponized as aerosols, the expected mode of delivery in a bioterrorist attack. Plague holds special concern because of its potential to cause panic, its contagiousness in the pulmonary form, its fulminating clinical course and high fatality, and the possibility that it could be engineered for plasmid-mediated resistance to multiple antimicrobial agents. Sepsis with either agent can result in catastrophic physiological consequences of compliment and cytokine cascade (systemic inflammatory response syndrome [SIRS]). Severity of illness is expected to require intensive medical care, including respiratory and other organ support that might readily overwhelm hospital response capacity (Inglesby et al., 2001). Pneumonic plague's contagiousness would require isolation and possible quarantine, which would complicate medical and public health management. A WHO model of the release of 50 kg of *Y. pestis* over a city of 5 million predicts 500,000 cases with 100,000 deaths when both primary and secondary transmission are considered; a similar model for release of *F. tularensis* predicts 250,000 persons incapacitated and 19,000 deaths.

Bioterrorism Aphorisms

- Do not assume anything
- Expect the unexpected
- What we know is not much
- Bioterrorism is, among other things, unnatural
- We do not know what we do not know
- We are not ready

Standard, classical microbiological diagnostic tests would be of limited value in a major bioterrorism event, since they are time consuming and labor intensive; unfortunately, newer, rapid testing methods for these agents, such as antigen detection and DNA amplification, are neither standardized nor widely available. Recommendations for antimicrobial treatment of plague or tularemia patients in a bioterrorist attack have been developed for both the mass- and contained- casualty situations (Inglesby et al., 2000; Dennis et al., 2001). The principal recommended antimicrobials are available through the National Pharmaceutical Stockpile. Two of these, gentamicin and ciprofloxacin, are not FDA-approved for treating plague or tularemia. Post-exposure antimicrobial prophylaxis is recommended to protect certain populations in the event of bioterrorist use of either plague or tularemia agents, but it would be difficult to identify populations at risk and administer drugs to them in a timely fashion. In the case of plague, isolation of cases and their close contacts, and quarantine of exposed populations could be difficult to enforce and would likely create fear and chaos (Inglesby et al., 2001).

Historical vaccines for plague and tularemia, based on killed and live attenuated preparations respectively, are currently unavailable in the United States, and a newer generation of vaccines and immunotherapeutics is greatly needed to address pre- and post-exposure prevention of disease. Recombinant protein subunit vaccines (against F1 and V antigens singly, in combination, and as fusion products) have been developed for plague (Titball and Williamson, 2001). One subunit combination product has recently undergone Phase I clinical testing in the U.K. A microencapsulated formulation shows promise for respiratory tract delivery (Eyles et al., 1998). Further, oral administration of a *Salmonella typhimurium* mutant expressing the F1 antigen of *Y. pestis* protects mice against subcutaneous inoculation of a virulent plague strain (Titball et al., 1997). Intraperitoneal administration of monoclonal antibodies to the F1 antigen protects mice against both parenteral and aerosol challenge with human pathogenic *Y. pestis* strains (Anderson et al., 1998). Similar vaccines and recombinants have not yet been developed for use against tularemia, but recent progress in sequencing of the *F. tularensis* genome may lead to identification of candidate immunoprotective proteins (Karlsson et al., 2000).

Recent advances in *Y. pestis* and *F. tularensis* strain typing, using multiplelocus, variable-number tandem repeat analyses are expected to provide rapid tracking of outbreak strains as well as providing a foundation for deciphering global genetic relationships of these organisms that could be useful in the event of a BT attack (Johansson et al., 2000; Klevytska et al., 2001; Farlow et al., 2001). Personal experience gained by participating in CDC responses to bioterrorist use of *Bacillus anthracis* reinforces the need to think freely about potential misuse of *Y. pestis* or *F. tularensis*, to heed lessons learned, and to ensure that preparedness and response needs are met before a critical event occurs.

Bibliography

Alam, Aftab : *US Policy Towards South Asia: Special Reference to Indo-Pak Relations*, Raj, Delhi, 1998.

Allison, Graham: *Nuclear Terrorism: The Ultimate Preventable Catastrophe*, New York: Times Books, 2004.

Amitabh Sikdar: *India and China : Strategic Energy Management and Security*, Manas, Delhi, 2009.

Anderson, J.: *Transnational Democracy: Political Spaces and Border Crossings*, Routledge: London and New York, 2002.

Bandita Sijapati: *A Kingdom Under Siege : Nepal's Maoist Insurgency, 1996 to 2003*, The Printhouse, Delhi, 2003.

Benjamin, Joseph : *China-Pak Relations : Prospect and Retrospect*, Reference Press, Delhi, 2004.

Cheek, Timothy: *Mao Zedong and China's Revolutions: A Brief History with Documents*. Boston: Bedford/St. Martin's, 2002.

Coakley, J.: *The Territorial Management of Ethnic Conflict*, London: Frank Cass, 2003.

Deepak, B R : *India and China : 1904-2004 : A Century of Peace and Conflict*, Manak, Delhi, 2005.

Dhanalaxmi, Ravuri. *British Attitude to Nepal's Relations with Tibet and China, 1814-1914*. Chandigarh, India: Bahri, 1981.

Dixit, J.N. : *India and Regional Developments : Through the Prism of Indo-Pak Relations*, Gyan, Delhi, 2004.

Gao, Mobo: *The Battle for China's Past: Mao and the Cultural Revolution*, London, Pluto Press, 2008.

Ghosh, Ajoy : *Indo-Pak Conflict : Threat to South Asian Security*, Reference Press, Delhi, 2003.

Gupta, S.: *Disrupted Borders: An Intervention in Definitions of Boundaries*, London: River Oram Press, 1993.

Huntington, S.P.: *The China Defence Modernisation Military and the State*, N.Y., Vintage Books, 1964.

Jagannath P. Panda: *China's Path to Power : Party, Military and the Politics of State Transition*, Pentagon, Delhi, 2010.

Jha, Prem Shankar : *India and China : The Battle Between Soft and Hard Power*, Penguin Books India, Delhi, 2010.

Kant, Adhikari, Krishna. *Nepal under Jang Bahadur, 1846-1877.* Kathmandu: Buku, 1984.

Nair, A. M.: *An Indian Freedom Fighter in Japan*, Bombay, Orient Longman, 1983.

Nayyar, K K : *National Security : Military Aspects*, Rupa, Delhi, 2003.

Pemble, John. *The Invasion of Nepal: John Company at War*. Oxford: Oxford University Press, 1971.

Phuskele, Preeti : *India and China : Emerging Superpowers*, ICFAI University, Delhi, 2009.

Posen, B.R.: *The Sources of Military Doctrine*, Ithaca, 1984, Cornell Univ. Press.

Rhodes, Richard, *The Making of the Atomic Bomb*, New York: Simon and Schuster, 1988.

Rosen, P.: *Societies and Military Power: India and its Armies*, Ithaca, Cornell University Press, 1996.

Schroeer, Dietrich, *Science, Technology, and the Nuclear Arms Race*, Ontario: John Wiley & Sons, 1984.

Schurmann, Franz: *Ideology and Organization in Communist Nepal.* Berkeley: University of California Press, 1971.

Sijapati, Li, : *A Kingdom Under Siege : Nepal's Maoist Insurgency, 1996 to 2003*, The Printhouse, Delhi, 2003.

Spector, Leonard S., *Going Nuclear*, Cambridge, MA: Ballinger Publishing Company, 1987.

Stuart R. Schram: *The Political Thought of Mao Tse-Tung*. New York: Praeger, 1969.

Thampi, Madhavi : *India and China in the Colonial World*, Social Science Press, Delhi, 2010.

Tse-tung Mao: *Mao and the Nepali Revolution*. London: Oxford University Press, 1965.

Index

❑❑❑